BEING BRAVE

By Larry Meyler

This book is dedicated to me ma and da.

Chapter 1

No sooner had I opened my eyes from another restless night before the tears filled them again, blurring the dark grey walls of the small room in a shared southwest London house. I lay in bed, James Dean on a canvas above my head looking down like some sort of rebellious angel unable to offer guidance. I could see my wardrobe in the corner from the light slicing through the break in the curtains, my clothes organised with regimental precision. I stared blankly, memories on repeat, and again unable to scrape myself up for work. In this now more frequent state I questioned where all my fearlessness had gone, where the teenage boy who had arrived in this city all those years ago full of wonder, excitement, determination and an unshakable fake-it-till-you-make-it self-belief had ended up. I had been a little Tasmanian Devil, but was now almost quivering like some bog-eyed Bambi. My head was thumping from the remnants of the previous night's booze; yet another binge-drinking session started in the hope of putting a halt to a racing mind. The morning inevitably summoned more feelings of crippling anxiety and self-loathing, poking my OCD in the eye with a sharp stick. My adamant positivity now seemed blurred by a premonition of ending up in a bedsit, eating my own body weight in ice cream with scraggy cats licking my face.

For so many years London has been my racing lane, the class clown from a small coastal town in Ireland jumping in with the big boys in hope of finding his way and making his dreams a reality, a chance for a better life. Over the years so many surreal events and fun opportunities had appeared, but stalking clouds were never far off in my rear-view mirror, which now seemed to be leaving me in their dust. My once effortless, even robotic daily routines like taking the tube now felt like I was entering an angry and claustrophobic wasps' nest. The traffic and noise of the West End became headache inducing and the thought of work started to bring nothing but a sick feeling in my stomach. So much so that sometimes I would turn around at the office door feeling so low and make my way back home, or into the comforting arms of a friend. London was now, more than ever, the Hyde to my Jekyll.

I thought about the events of the last couple of years which had led me here or, as one counsellor described it, 'a layer cake of loss' which had started when I was a little boy and recently had the final cherry placed neatly on top. Heartache mixed with heartbreak. Now on my own in these, the loneliest of moments, any bravery seemed so far off. Trying as I might to be Jolly Larry and roll with the punches didn't fool anyone now, especially not myself. The house-share I had moved into for a new start, coupled with the step-up in my career as a celebrity picture editor, had both turned out to be big fat shit pies, and I'd had my fill.

Above anything else my mind jumped between the two prominent recent events that had derailed me once and for all; confusing, gut wrenching and all consuming. One would temporarily mask the pain of the other before swapping over again like cartwheeling, crazed clowns in the circus tent that was now my head. The main game-changer and something I was still dealing with and trying to get used to every day, unsuccessfully, is losing my dad - Tommy.

Lying there in the spring of 2015, looking up at the ceiling from my pillow, I saw myself all those months earlier: standing on the ship's deck sailing back to the UK after his funeral, the August sea breeze filling my lungs, watching Ireland disappear into the distance through tear-filled eyes. The memory still so vivid. The holdall of me da's stuff was held tightly in my hands: keepsakes, paperwork, photographs and memories. The only physical things I had left were all there in that cheap sports bag. I remembered how I knew things would never be the same again and I just didn't know what to do with myself.

How different that crossing felt to leaving my hometown of Wexford the first time around, 17 years old, at that very same port of Rosslare on the southeast coast of Ireland. I stood there with me da and his best friend Mick in January 1997, London-bound. He asked me not to go, he said he was sorry for everything, for all the fighting. I was too, but I just couldn't stay; I feared my life would waste away if I did. I had my dreams and a blinkered determination to get out and follow them, to make things better, to go back to the place where, to me, anything was possible, and the place where I'd last held my mam's hand.

I was doing what me da had done many years earlier himself, a fearless and somewhat broken young lad taking himself out of a dead-end situation in search of a happier life. For my dad it was at a time when it was common to see a sign in a guesthouse or pub window reading 'No dogs, No blacks, No Irish'. He'd fought all his life so I hoped he would understand why I had to get out too. Even though he didn't want me to go, I'm sure he knew, deep down, that I had to. If I stayed then I would have fallen into a desperate place, the other paths not even worth thinking about. Wexford's beauty and pride, its history stemming from Viking times to a thriving fishing town. So much creativity harboured in its streets, but where it was easy to be derailed by drugs or end up in prison, and where suicide had started to become commonplace amongst the young, amongst my hometown crowd. The small town mentality of the place could be suffocating so there was really no choice for me. I wouldn't allow that for myself. My friends had been my only salvation; and it tore me apart to leave them behind. How we'd grown together. Their handwritten goodbye letters were kept closely guarded in my pocket, but they knew I needed to go and to this day they have never stopped rooting for me.

So, with £137 savings in my pocket, my grey buckled suitcase in hand complete with my treasured East 17 and Spice Girl posters, I looked my dad right in the eyes. We broke down into floods of tears in each other's arms. I loved him so much, as he did me. We had been through a hell of a lot together; he'd kept me with him always, scrimping and scraping and dodging about. He would've done anything for his little boy and he tried so hard but his own demons never let up making it impossible in so many ways. At that moment my heart broke for him. The two of us were so lost, but we had a love that never waned, even through all the pain and misery; a broken man and now a broken boy. I let him go, and I sailed off across the Irish Sea. On that day in 1997 I left all I knew behind and was unable to stem the flow of tears.

Now so many years later, I had to say goodbye to him again, only this time for ever. I was still a lost little Artful Dodger heading to the same big city but, this time, the bright lights of London had very much lost their glow.

Back in my small room and, just as I'm about to drag myself out of bed, relentlessly on cue, the reality of event number two hits. And so transpires the heartbreak.

We'd met in a drunken haze at a party, a look and a kiss that could've blown the national grid there was so much electricity. Fast forward a few weeks; after a few messages back and forth, our first date. We sat on some benches outside a local bar on a fresh April evening, in person enchanting, charismatic, a bit weird and, above all, hilarious. Not only did I leave that bar thinking what the fuck am *I* gonna bring to this, but also with a smile I hadn't smiled in quite some time. My defensive walls were very much up, but something clicked.

And so our romance started, but at a time when my stress levels were at an all-time high. It was right in the middle of my dad suffering a major stroke. So, just as quickly as it started, this new relationship became a dangerous roller coaster of emotions. It stopped and started, half on, half off the tracks, but continually drawn back to each other over the next year or so.

Then, in the months after me da passed away, the relationship became my sole focus. I wanted it to work more than anything. I wasn't going to lose this person, the one I'd eventually opened myself up to more than anyone else, the one whose presence had an unwavering ability to make me smile, the only one that mattered, who had a heart of gold and kindness, but who could cripple me and shut me down with knee-jerk reactions. Intentional hurt wasn't a factor, we were just in a tornado of frustrating miscommunication and bad timing. Life pressures got in the way on both sides; one falling for the other, the other falling too late. Walls up and walls down, one inevitably not standing a chance.

Our time together taught me that timing itself is a very important part in being able to make a relationship work and that the time just wasn't right. Behaviour and understanding are also pretty damn important but those seemed to get very messed up too.

I've never been a deluded person and always try to see the reality and bigger picture in situations, especially with regard to my own wrongdoings. The emotional state I was in from the get-go of this relationship – trying to deal with Dad's situation and him in the run-up to his death – should have made me question whether a relationship was the right option at the time. Underneath I was crumbling and the unrelenting intensity was at its height when we met. The feelings inside me ranged from guilt to anger to sadness, and memories and fears were overwhelming me on a daily basis. I felt fucked up in the head. But it was too late for any questioning; my heart overruled everything.

Opening up has never been easy for me, but playing an initial role of bravado was a mistake, afraid I wouldn't be accepted as just me. My habit of texting in capital letters like I was constantly shouting didn't help and neither did my moods. If I'd known my stupid actions and words were tainting things with little hope of redemption, I would have done it all so differently. Some desperate days I'd wish we could go back in time, before these new-to-me lines were crossed. Other, draining days I just wished I'd never got involved.

But, still, I wanted this love to grow more than anything. I hoped we could bear with each other and support each other through testing times. So I tried to keep the good times and the fun as the linchpin which could save us, knowing those hard-to-find fundamentals were there. I knew I couldn't let something like this go; that undeniable spark we had together shouldn't be dismissed. As time passed, in my head and heart, I truly believed and hoped that it could be fixed. For me, the adventures and experiences together always outweighed any negatives.

I fought the fight; a crushed lad trying to save the only thing, in my eyes, worth saving. Eventually, however, I started to forsake my self worth in the process. I felt I was getting somewhere at times but by the end I was walking on eggshells just so the boat wouldn't capsize. It was all to show the one I loved that we were worth the chance, worth going out on a limb for. But I banged my head against a brick wall as I carried on hoping it would sink in. Through streaming eyes, I fought on, frustrated in knowing that if simplified it was a fight which never needed to be fought. If that understanding and patience were given a real chance, we could have soared.

And, at times we did. Those looks when you're together and you just know; the belly laughs that exude pure connection, and a support for me through the toughest time, my dad dying.

It was five months after his death and, unsure where the relationship was at, and with the thought of going back to Ireland unbearable, I'd decided to get away and spend Christmas in Benidorm with my relatives, a place me da really loved. So knowing I was going there for my dad made it feel like he was there with us. Being there with my relatives also made me feel less lonely and, miraculously, a breakthrough in my relationship came too. Having seen each other prior to leaving, we kept up communication while I was away, obvious at that point that we both didn't want to give up, so we decided to give it another go. I hoped this was a turning point, that the new year would be the start of the healing. But, after a beautiful, belated Christmas together, it stalled again. At the time I didn't accept that this was it for good; more battles and hurt ensued.

It all became too much, too draining. There were too many misread signals and we both just needed to step out of each other's lives. Eventually it became one-sided, too much expectation fighting against not enough want. I had to decide to let go and so I did. Reluctantly and brokenheartedly, I stepped out and the communication between us eventually stopped.

Having to let go of the person who made me smile and laugh more than any other before, the one whose kiss could lift my feet right off the ground like an Acme cartoon scene, who the sight of, even when it was bad, could turn it all around and, well, the one who I saw my future with; letting go of that was too much to bear.

These two life-changing events – the death of my father and the death of this relationship – would lead to a change in my life's trajectory in a way I would never expect. Here and now though, they crashed back and forth in my head like a ship in a storm, becoming more damaged as time passed, eventually a battered hollow vessel lost in the unforgiving waves.

To make things even worse, my house was plagued with problems. It felt cold and I didn't want to go back most days. All my housemates and I spoke about was what needed fixing or who could be in to meet the latest repair man. It was an environment which had lost any sort of homely feel; not my housemates' fault at all. After all, their worlds were still turning but mine was going into free fall. Even the habit of wanting to call me da most mornings wouldn't shift. I rang his number one morning, maybe just to feel some comfort. The line had been arranged to be cut off, so when it actually rang I was scared to death; what if he answered? I'd be haunted for life. I quickly hung up and sat on a wall to breathe. I never tried again after that, having to come to terms with the fact that another connection was broken. Where was my home now?

My job, which had started off so well, had also become ridiculously stressful. The then editor would pile on pressure to deliver content for her venom-spouting vision of this weekly gossip magazine. My new deputy was a sweet, pretty and very likeable girl. She struggled at first with the career step-up, but I wanted to give her the chance and opportunity. She worked so very hard and gave her all, she just needed patience and guidance in certain areas. The Wicked Witch of the East didn't give her this for too long though. Eventually she was gunning for her. It was done in a smart, underhand way. She had to be careful as not to add to the volume of complaints HR apparently already had on her behaviour towards previous staff. I could see through it and this brought us to loggerheads.

With a few weeks off and back from Ireland after the funeral, the boss's attitude was that I'd now been given enough time to get to grips with the job and enough time to grieve. So I started experiencing her wrath which I had heard about but so far avoided. It was a complete volte-face from the sometimes hilarious and kind woman who had enticed me to work for her and whose achievements I respected. I would never forget how she had handled my dad's death with compassion and initial support, I would always be grateful for that. But I was slipping from grace fast; in the midst of grief and heartbreak the golden boy quickly lost his shine.

Still, I was proud of how my team and I turned the inherited mess of our department around, despite the bitching. Praise came from other departments and outside contributors, so I carried on trying to leave my inner turmoil outside the office door, only confiding in close pals at work when it got too much.

But after ten years in pictures I sank to a low point. The human misery required for the content needed for this publication made me question if this was what I wanted to be doing with my life: 'find a fat picture of this person', 'find a haggard picture of that person' was mostly my remit. Intelligent and funny women, whom I respected, were editorial targets and I could feel the universe and my soul frowning down upon me. Some days, I would leave the office feeling like I was going through the regularly mentioned menopause myself.

Then, out of the blue, redundancies were announced and we were to be bundled together with two other titles. As if a bucket of water had been thrown on her, the editor vanished leaving only the sound of bottles popping from the closed door of her office on her last shift, before she disappeared without a word.

I prayed I would be in line for redundancy, but unfortunately the opposite was offered; promotion. WTF! I had no interest in taking this new role. I was barely getting through the days as it was without that added pressure. That and the thought of a way out was already in my mind. At least the witch was dead (not literally) and the new merger of magazines released the pressure.

My new editor was straight down the line and no bullshit; I also had someone new above me who had taken the promotion and she was now overseeing everything. She was a lovely woman who I could confide in but, as the days passed, things became hopeless. I couldn't make it out of bed some days and, when I was at work, I just stared at the screen in front of me unable to concentrate. I felt guilty about letting the team and myself down, passing on work to try and keep up.

Above any job, status or glitzy party, happiness and love have always been my priority. Now it felt like they would only ever be temporary or fleeting realities, like sand through my fingers. I'd failed at love, the only one I'd wanted had given up on me, on us, and it tore me up.

Life in London became so tainted and my life was now unrecognisable to me. I desperately tried to pick myself up and carry on. As I battled the days my friends were a constant support to help get me through, but I couldn't avoid the obvious any longer. I was living in a limbo, I questioned daily if I'd hit rock bottom; it certainly felt like it.

I dragged my eyes from the ground one day whilst sat in the park and looked up at the sky. I saw myself as a little boy again, lost and lonely. The life and spirit was draining out of me like never before, my fearlessness and positivity dwindling away. Was this it? Is this what I was worth? Pretending to the world that I was OK but dying inside? I was so broken. It was in that moment that I decided I'd had enough and something inside me refused to give up. I decided that before it becomes a life that slips away, I had to make a decision. I decided to give myself a chance. The only thing left to do was to take myself away and out of this dead-end situation. It felt like I had nothing left inside me; some days it felt like I couldn't even breathe.

I'd had enough of living like this. Waking up every morning with my head suffocating in loss, hurt and loneliness, feeling so lost and with such an endless lack of direction or way out that you can't even see straight, to the point where you don't want to wake up at all any more, just so it will all stop. That's a clear smack in the gob that it's time for an epic change.

The more I thought about it, the more I knew that this was the only option left now. To do it, to save myself, I needed to summon that last flame of hope in my belly. It was as if I had just been struck by lightning; suddenly I could see an adventure and hear a backpack screaming my name. It was, after all, a thought which had always been there – to backpack the globe. Me da had wanted me to see it all and that's what I was going to do. Where, I didn't know. I just needed to get out of here, to go and see the world. It became clear that the only way to change things was to give all this up and just go.

With the decision to leave now made, I had something to focus on, but the struggle to carry on didn't disappear. In fact it was the opposite. In the spring of 2015, just a few months before my dad's first anniversary, my relationship was now over for good but the pain in my heart was still alive and kicking and suicidal thoughts were now a daily occurrence. I was at the point where I just didn't want to wake up at all and by what means I could make that happen, the thoughts of ending it all became more persistent. Embarrassed at myself for becoming so pathetic, the weeks rolled by not getting better.

Fed up of feeling so low, I finally visited my doctor. I had been twice before in various hungover states and had been referred to alcohol management sessions and grief counselling. I stuck at them, desperately wanting to break through this, but when the days were brighter it didn't last long. So now, sinking fast and at my lowest, I laid it all bare and she uttered the diagnosis, those words. And, finally, I could see it as something real rather than that I was losing my mind. It was a weight lifted in some ways; the knowing that someone else could recognise it, this suffering state which I had gone through on and off since I was young but which had never been confirmed.

It's a funny old thing depression. When it takes hold, it manifests itself into an all-consuming tunnel vision, like you're not in your own body any more. Like it's a stifling weight holding you back as you try to run from it. Or as if you're being dragged out to sea with no real chance of fighting the current; the only option is to wait and hope you'll be washed back to shore.

I told the doctor that I wasn't there for any quick fixes or medication, that I wasn't there for some time off work. I emphasised that I knew how easily the word is thrown around and I didn't want to be that person: 'Oh I'm so depressed, blah blah blah', but that this was so all-consuming that I just needed someone to tell me I wasn't losing my mind. So, when depression was diagnosed, if nothing else, I could leave her office with a better understanding and an opponent I could now fight in the battle ahead rather than just darkness.

I decided it was now time to let the unknown hold my hand, rather than what I thought I needed or craved. To stop relying on the broken comfort of imaginary scenarios, telling myself these crutch like scenarios just don't exist, but I do. I decided that it was time to focus on the here and now, realising more than ever before, that this chance I was giving myself must go hand in hand with the understanding that my happiness must come from me. No matter how deeply buried it is there, it may be flickering dimly in the darkness, but it's there.

I knew the months ahead would be tough, but at least I could start to clear a path through the debris with a goal and a focus. It was a scary one but I didn't care. I had already handed in my notice both on my tenancy and at work, three long months' notice, but I'd have the summer with the people closest to me, so all I needed now was a plan.

Chapter 2

To this day I still get people in Wexford coming up to me, old family friends who are happy to remind me what I was like when I was a little boy. Apparently I used to throw the most almighty tantrums so, without fail, they always say the same thing to me: 'oh you were a little bastard'. Nice. These unwanted but interesting statements are always met with an awkward and slightly embarrassed laugh, especially when you haven't got a clue who these people are.

I was a kid of the Eighties, obsessed with music and especially TV with all its Golden Girls, Dempsey and Makepeace and Moonlighting splendour. I used to dance around for me gran. I was only tiny but would be popping out Michael Jackson routines like a bad thing, which she used to love. Both my grandads had died before I was born and so I only ever met my grandmas, and I loved them both dearly. It was at this young age when a passion for dancing and performing started; I was fascinated with Hollywood and American glamour. I imagined what Tom Cruise or Jack Nicholson's lives were like and dream that one day I would be able to visit that magical place.

The first memories of my mam, Joan, are of me clinging to her side. I remember her head of raven black curls which she detangled with a brown Afro comb and her glasses with black rims; this was the Eighties after all. She exuded warmth and had a constant glow about her, which enticed you in. I've only ever heard people heap praise upon her; she had an aura which radiated from her soul and a non-complacent attitude. I've seen pictures of her when she was 18 years old and she was so pretty and glamorous, dressed up to the nines in effortless 1950s style.

Being brought up an only child, all I wanted to do was dance about and make people laugh, but I somehow always ended up in trouble; a bad boy with good intentions.

I guess I was, let's just say, quite 'different'. One bleak childhood scenario I remember was when we lived in a council house in one of the many housing estates in Wexford, a two-up two-down plonked in the middle of many other mirror properties. On this twisted occasion I snuck into the kitchen to find a knife, the biggest knife in the drawer, and took some ketchup from the fridge. I then proceeded to lie down on the living room carpet, rip a hole in my small white t-shirt and stick the knife through, just near enough to my armpit so that it would look like it had gone through my heart. I covered the tear with the tomato ketchup and lay there, murdered, until one of my parents came in and discovered the horrific scene. The result and less-than-surprised reaction from me mam didn't go as planned; she screamed about the mess I'd made of my t-shirt and the carpet and where did I get that knife from, much to my Wednesday Addams-esque annoyance.

It highlighted that she kind of expected such shenanigans from her funny little boy. This was either an act to shock or for attention, but I remember thinking it was very normal behaviour.

I also thought ripping the heads off Barbies (never Sindys) to hide behind the sofa so I could brush and plait their hair with a la la la la attitude was standard behaviour for a five year old boy too.

My first-ever memory was of me da. Not him cuddling me in his arms but dropping a lizard into my cot when I was a toddler; not your usual glowing Pampers advert scene, eh?

I remember he had brought the little reptile upstairs to show me, presumably as a prospective new pet, but it somehow leaped out of his hand and into my cot, darting around my blankets and scurrying over my head. I often thought I dreamed this scenario but, years later, he confirmed it happened. It made me laugh and kinda shudder a little too.

He was always coming home with something, whether it be a puppy or a hampster. I believe, once, prior to me being born he tried to bring a monkey back to Ireland from some exotic land he had sailed to, like something you would expect from Mutiny on the Bounty times. That was just my dad; he had a blatant rebellious streak and was very much a chancer too. Once he got something into his mind he didn't care what anyone said and it was very hard to convince him otherwise.

Tommy, me da, was a hugely kind, generous and popular man. He had a very eventful and tough life, and he struggled with an internal anger. He worked hard all his life in whatever he turned his hand to, such as the back-breaking dock work like his dad before him. Wherever he went he left a fond impression on the people he met and was hilariously funny to boot, so he could have a pub full of people in stitches without even trying. When he wasn't getting himself into trouble too, that is.

Travel was huge part of him, it was in his blood. His whole hearted love of the sea took him around the world as part of the Irish Merchant Navy. He told stories of sailing to far-flung places like Mombasa, the Suez Canal and Australia. So I guess my decision to go travelling is partly in honour of his life as a sailor. That and having also inherited the travel bug and some nautical naughtiness too.

A life at sea seemed only right for me da, ever since he was young he found it immensely hard to settle anywhere; we lived in ten different council houses, flats and bedsits in Wexford by the time I was 17. His mates often joked that the council should just offer him a house on wheels. I'm sure they thought we were of gypsy descent, trying to shake off our travelling trailer roots and unsuccessfully settle in bricks and mortar.

But it was in the house where my 'murder' took place that a decision was made that would change things for ever. We'd only been at number 33 for a short while, but the decision was made, nevertheless, that we would be leaving that family nest for pastures new. We were London-bound in search of a new life away from the prying eyes of a small, gossipy town, drink-fuelled arguments and, well, away from any drama.

My mam was the opposite of me da, she was a hometown bird. She also loved her friends and her family very much, but she had a hard time from some of them, especially my grandmother. Mam loved her but I know me grandma relied on her way too much; she was at her beck and call until she met my dad, who could be a handful at times himself.

He had already taken her away from it all once before; they had given life in Wales a try. In fact, that's where I was born. Withybush hospital in Haverfordwest on the 8th September 1979, hello world. They were married in the neighbouring town of Milford Haven. Me da in his grey suit, shirt with big seventies collar and a mauve tie, me mam in her white slim-fitting lace dress, statement glasses and white lace-panelled sun hat, with just two witnesses. But again, it didn't last long there in the land of the dragon and they upped sticks and quickly moved back to Wexford, with the addition of me as a tiny baby. They were both in their forties at this stage. But in the hope that this would be the last move, mam agreed to give London a go and see if we could find some peace there. I think she hoped our peace would be in Wexford but, unfortunately, as my dad just couldn't settle, that family unit stability was still out of reach.

So it was time for a change. We started a new life across the pond in the big smoke, where my dad had previously lived, worked and gallivanted for many years, along with thousands of other Irish men on the building sites of London town and across the UK. But what followed led to the beginning of a downward spiral for me as a kid, where the layer cake of loss would start to rise, and my first real taste of heartache would begin.

My first-ever memory of arriving in London was vomiting all over the back of the black cab taking us from Paddington to my aunt Kathleen's flat in Putney. We had arrived in the city via the boat, from Rosslare to Fishguard in Wales, then the train to London, suitcases in hand and not much else. I can still sense the churning in my stomach as we stopped and started through the busy streets in the very warm cab. I suffered badly as a youngster from motion sickness, which only really stopped in my teenage years. I'd be car sick, boat sick, bus sick – you name it I vomited in it. Almost every mode of transport there was, apart from trains, which I seemed happy enough chugging along in.

After staying with various relatives and in one dodgy basement bedsit where me da had to sleep in the bath, we ended up in a halfway house, or hostel, on Holloway Road, hoping it wouldn't be long until our names reached the top of the council waiting list and we would be offered a house so we could really start our new lives. The Holloway Road residence was a huge building housing all sorts of people from drunks and people who had fallen on hard times to other families also on the housing waiting list. It had massive concrete steps up to the various entrances and a huge grass area at the back where the kids could play. We had to stay in two rooms, me da in one and myself and me ma in the other. Cockroaches took up residence in both, but I felt happy. I didn't exactly love the place, but I loved being in the big city. I loved that there were often parties upstairs so I could sneak up and watch the teenagers breakdancing on lino as eighties hip-hop filled the air. I also loved my school and the little see-through plastic pouches with zip locks which we kept our colourful stationery organised in, and that in London you could strip down to your white pants and vest to run around like nutters in P.E class, although I was always nervous in case anybody saw my willy as I thought it was tiny and hated the thought of anyone catching a glimpse. I also loved that I had black and Asian friends and the fun we had together. I hoped that one day soon we would have our own house and we would be happy.

My only memory of London after that was sitting at my aunt Winnie's table in Essex as the rest of the family on both sides tried to get the money together to have her body returned home to Wexford for burial. I don't remember the funeral and I don't even remember seeing my dad much, but I do remember it was discussed where I should go and who should look after me. They all offered, as did mam's sister Carrie too, but my dad was having none of it. So, rightly or wrongly, it was with him I would stay.

It was just after this that I believe a form of OCD started to develop within me. I would have dark dreams of being at the graveyard and having this enormous black balloon or engulfing cloud which represented a huge debt filling the sky and suffocating me, trapping me beneath. It frightened the life out of me. I guess this came from the fact that all I'd ever known was us being poorer than most in a make ends meet environment, watching me da ducking and diving about, trying to get bits of work here and there or visiting loan sharks or charities with him.

Then the repetitive behaviour started too. For example, we would pass a sign on the road for a guesthouse and I would have to read the entire thing every time, if I didn't something bad would happen. That or I would hear a song, the most memorable one being 'Spirit in the Sky' by Doctor and the Medics, and it would frighten the life out of me so that if I sang the words 'that's where I'm gonna go when I die' I was also going to die so I had to quickly blur that line out of my head before it went past my ears, or again something bad would happen.

These feelings of anxiety and OCD would stay with me for many years to come, taking on different forms but always with the underlying worry that if I don't do this or behave in this way something bad will happen to me or someone close to me. It was a hefty shackle for a little boy and one that I would find hard to break loose from right up to my decision to travel. Especially after my dad's death, I was desperately trying to find something to control, to have some sort of order or comfort in my life just for a moment in an uncontrollable chaotic situation. For me, this trait, condition, or whatever term it goes by, isn't completely debilitating but it's still a daily occurrence: making sure everything is in its place, not touching toilet door handles or standing near anyone coughing or sneezing for fear of catching germs, everything in my wardrobe, cupboards and fridge aligned correctly, TV channels on even numbers and volume, repeating myself or having to be one hundred per cent clear on plans until they stuck in my head. Sometimes it was exhausting, sometimes it affected relationships, but it was mostly annoying to people and it stressed me out. Maybe this went hand in hand or was part of the reason for my sometimes bossy and controlling nature. It was never, ever malice. In my head it was just the need to make something right, usually over excitement to get things done and organised so there could be a happy outcome for all involved. More often though it came across differently and, now, that happiness seemed like a far-off illusion.

After the depression diagnosis, I opted out of any chemical routes, although they may be helpful for many. I knew what was wrong with me and I decided I would tackle it head on at the source rather than numbing it with pills. I also found comfort in knowing how lucky I am to have an amazing group of people around me, both in the UK and Ireland, catching me before I fell too hard, friends providing an endless supply of support and who just listened to me constantly banging on. To me, my friends are my family, the boys my brothers, the girls, including my closest cousins, my sisters. Through all the years of sifting through wrong'uns, or ill matched friendships, I have accumulated a group of people that had become blood, that I would sell my soul for. It was only in the previous few years that I started opening up more.

I always felt that I should be the one they could come to, this figure to offer advice and solve problems; the one who would always remain strong. But, after a previous heartbreak, then the recent break up, mounting stresses with my dad then his subsequent death, I had to let them in more. In turn I was unleashing gushing rapids of built-up emotions; a broken lad beneath the surface gasping for air.

But, boy, did I felt guilty for this, again adding to my continuing stress. I was boring myself with my woes and I didn't want to be like that all the time with my friends too, to the point where I worried they would forget why we were friends in the first place. With me now being in this constant state of whinging for how ever long, it made me wonder how much more they could stand.

It was also fast approaching my dad's first anniversary. Aside from basic travel planning, I was just living for binge-drinking at the weekends, not wanting the party to end and having to go back to an empty room, the thoughts of my ex and the rest. I tried my hardest, I tried desperately to keep on laughing with my friends, but it became increasingly hard, and going out boozing only heightened all the bad. A demon which I never dreamed would take hold of me, especially after my upbringing with my dad. Meaningless one-night stands came into play, void-filling sexual encounters which have never fulfilled me in any way. It was a temporary and dangerous comfort which, when combined with the booze, became the emancipation of my demons, igniting the flames of self-loathing and my OCD tenfold.

The travels and a route still needed to be sorted, and I didn't know where to start. I tried to simplify it. I thought about how in my dad's final years, my choice of birthday or Christmas presents for him had changed. I'd no longer get him jewellery or household stuff. Now it was things that would help in his new state of illness, like foot spas to ease pain, DVDs like Westerns or sea pictures which he could get lost in. For instance, on a road trip with my uncle Jimmy we stopped at a roadside cafe trailer where they had a huge world map on the wall and I watched me da stare up at it for ages in wonder, no doubt re-living the memories of his adventures around the globe. I then bought him a huge map for his bedroom so when he woke up he could be reminded of the good times and escape from his condition for a moment. I decided that's how I would plan my trip; I would just look at a simple map and plan a route, it came with ease. The Caribbean, South America, Australia and New Zealand, the trip snowballed into a much bigger thing pretty quickly but with surprising ease. It felt right to do it this way, to be giving it all up and just going. Considering the hurt consuming me, my determination to go didn't waver in the run up to leaving. But the final destination eluded me; where to end such an epic adventure? I wanted it to be somewhere far, far away, somewhere exotic and raw.

One travel agent told me about her time in Borneo and a guy she met who ran a jungle lodge at the Tip. She talked about it with so much passion and excitement, re-living her own journey in front of me, I decided Borneo would be my aim; a global adventure to the Tip of Borneo. Unfortunately her prices were sky-high and I wasn't on a Bear Grylls budget, so I had to shuffle out of the shop empty-handed but, eventually, I found a great guy who helped and advised me no end. That was it, I was booked, there was no going back.

But then, finally, it hit and everything stalled. It was like nothing I had ever experienced before. It was my dad's first anniversary, July 29th 2015, something I naively thought I could handle, but it unleashed a torrent of grief and, boy, did I crash. Going back one hundred steps in my head, my heart was once again on the floor. I just wanted my dad there, just wanted him to pick me up and tell me it would all be OK. The reality of the relationship with him I yearned for, which never came to be and now never would, brought uncontrollable tears. In those moments I wanted to be that little boy again, clinging to my mam's side. My heart was broken in every way a heart could be broken, from loss, from love, from all that could've been, and I just wanted to die. This was my true rock bottom.

But I didn't die. It was so close to being curtains, but the thought of what the upset would do to those I loved stopped me. With my last bit of fight I pulled myself back from the edge, aware now that I needed support more than ever. So I started seeing a counsellor the doctor had suggested, the second one since my dad had passed away, and it was a relief. I let it all out and she understood. Going to her helped lighten the all-consuming burden and make some sense of this emotional vortex. To also have a professional to offload to in these final few weeks gave me another outlet and, in part, took my mind away from the darker and much more final option. Music can be a powerful mood changer too, so I stopped listening to the heart-wrenching lyrics of Sam Smith and swapped my music for uplifting and positive words. Randomly, or not, it was the opening intro to Cheryl Coles album 'Only Human' which struck a chord. A famous quote by Alan Watts, about finding your true heart's desire and what's important to the individual. I gorged on positive quotes and visuals to help me through.

In the midst of all this there was the little matter of the decision I had made to give up everything and take myself out of this situation; that was also the light that helped keep me going. I told myself through determined vision to get back up and give this a shot. I'm was going on this journey expecting nothing, only time; for the first time since I started working at 15 years old I'd have some space to breathe. I had to keep going and I had give myself this chance.

With the prep under way again, I now spent time with the people I loved and was going to miss so desperately; it also helped me beat myself up a little less each day. Seeing a counsellor at the same time also gave my friends a break. Perhaps one they didn't want or need, but I guess my view had become somewhat skewed. As the weeks rolled on and departure day approached, I knew leaving them would make me so sad but I knew each and every one of them was right behind me with massive encouragement and love. Then and now.

At this point it's safe to say the run up to this trip had been infused with all sorts of emotions and reality had now set in. Not only the nervous feelings of the challenges ahead, but also the fact that it's not just me taking 'time out'. It's actually a massive change of existence encompassing packing up my not-so-ideal but at least familiar life, my job, my tenancy and all that comes with that decision. The packing up part had turned out to be quite cathartic: organising my life into clear plastic boxes, (OCD, check) getting rid of so much stuff; magazines I'd hoarded, bag upon bag of clothes, things I just didn't need, which helped lighten the load.

Like anyone setting off on such an adventure there have been so many moments of FUCK…WHAT AM I DOING?! which still crept in at times. I told myself, like all clouds, they'll pass to let the clarity and excitement of the sun and the ever-changing horizon shine on in. It was time to try and be kind to myself; the point of this whole thing is about being brave. So that would be my motto for the trip, #BEBRAVE, and I needed to keep that in the forefront of my tricky little mind, and I'll repeat one of my favourite lines as I go, 'adventures ahoy'. Like some kind of twitchy Irish pirate.

So, as the day arrived, I pulled on my backpack, my life (neatly) condensed into just two bags, and jumped in the car with one of my best friends, James. As the September wind blew into my face on the way to Gatwick, I looked at him in a tsunami of thoughts and emotions and thought of all those close to me. No matter how alone I felt inside, I knew I had my gang, a diverse group of people with the binding rarity and raw essence of true friendship, all of us together until the end. The kick-ass birthday/bon voyage party I got to send me on my way proved that in abundance. I boarded the plane, eyes red from tears, in that moment all of the fears, the hurt and the heartache was replaced with their faces, and I was full of pride.

Chapter 3

I walked up the aisle of the plane in a world of my own, reiterating my motto so that it lodged in my brain, only to be brought back to reality by a shrieking 'Helloooooooo, welcome aboard' from a deranged looking air steward with blindingly white teeth. He made me cackle, which lightened the heaviness of the moment. I took my seat, next to a frisky posh couple, think Steph and Dom from Gogglebox, both necking wine and petting each other like no one's business. It was kinda cute as they seemed madly in love, but I was less than impressed with 'Dom' for unfolding his oversized Financial Times just before take off, blocking the window and my last view of London for the foreseeable. Not that it made a difference as, like on every plane I board, I seem to always sit above the wing, making any teary movie scene moments of *au revoir* somewhat redundant. There was nothing left to do but follow suit with my snorting neighbours and dive into the complimentary drinks. Oh I do love a free airplane bar, drunkenly sinking into a few movies and the swirling thoughts of my life.

As the plane ascended toward the heavens, I knew I would have my wobbles in the coming months, and I could already very much feel the absence of my regular life and comforts, even if they had been ice thin recently. But a new determination told me that instead of faltering in the dark, I was gonna ride all these emotions like a steel-balled rodeo cowboy and face them head on.

After a one hour stopover in Antigua, again not seeing much tropical beauty through the window, just the tarmac and the old faithful wing, we landed at Robert L. Bradshaw Airport in St Kitts. Stepping off the plane was like stepping into the opening scene of Jurassic Park, a lush green valley and mountainous backdrop unfolded before me. What also greeted me was 85 degree heat, even though the sun was on its descent at 5.50 in the afternoon. I felt like a right soggy old tampon in my great choice of thick jumper and, as would be the case for the rest of my time in the Caribbean, the sweat began to drip. Not an ideal look in a tropical oasis.

Like a dope I'd forgotten to print out the address of where I was staying, but remembered the name, Fern Tree B&B. So, with that sinking 'I'm gonna get ripped off here' feeling, I hailed a dodgy looking taxi to take me to the guest house. The village, Conaree, was a two-minute drive from the airport and thankfully I wasn't ripped off and taken on some mystery ride of the island, nice guy that taxi man.

My first impressions of the area were mixed, lots of chickens running wild, rusty old cars, and some suspicious looks from the local lads drinking beer outside a rickety bar. If I'm honest it made me think 'Fuck, why didn't I book a resort hotel?', but I sucked it up and put the looks down to my bright coral shorts, gleaming Converse and sweaty head!

The owner, Hazel, greeted me at the B&B. It was probably the warmest welcome I've ever received. Within the first half hour I was in a car with Hazel's friends, Moses and his Brummie missus Vanessa, having a free tour of the island so that I could get my bearings. I knew then I'd definitely made the right choice of accommodation, although Moses' eyesight might need retesting as Vanessa had to grab the wheel a few times to avoid some head-on collisions with chicken trucks.

Hazel's cooked breakfast was a sexy little treat each morning, which always came with two big juicy portions of fried plantain, which was like having a dessert. I hoovered it up whilst chatting with the other two guests, a couple of lads from Nigeria working on the island. Steering the conversation away from football, we managed to find common ground in chatting about rugby and our different backgrounds, while munching down the brekkie and enjoying the views from the outdoor porch area. Hazel asked about my family and I told her about my dad passing away. This brought out her motherly nature and she looked out for me during the rest of my time there.

That first evening as we sat together on the porch, a cold beer in my hand which Hazel sold from her huge fridge in the communal area, she asked more about my dad. I told her he was one of the kindest men there was, that he was the type of man who would never see anyone go without, even when we had nothing ourselves. That he loved his brothers and sisters dearly and never forgot anyone's birthday or their Christmas cards, and although he tried that his cooking wasn't a patch on hers.

Me da's disastrous cooking efforts began when we lived in a bedsit back home in Ireland, one big room near the Main Street in Wexford with a separate toilet and little kitchen. We had a gas fire with a cavity behind it where the real fire used to be, so when he wasn't looking I used to quickly scrape the attempted dinners off into the hole and push the fire back in place, hoping he would never notice. I'd hand the plate back with an 'ummmm I'm full' sound. I thought I had found the perfect plan, fill up on crisps and sweets at the pub, or dinner at my friends' houses, and scrape away the burnt or half raw offerings from me da. This lasted for about a week, until one evening when we were sat watching the telly and a roast potato rolled out from behind the fire. We looked at each other and I ran to the corner of the room as me da pulled the fire out and saw piles of uneaten dinners and a big rat munching away. Suffice to say I got a fair few clouts for that one.

Another gourmet offering back in the bedsit came one Pancake Tuesday. As I walked home from school, I felt jealous at how all the kids would be going home to their families and having their lovely dinners, followed by pancakes glistening with sugar and lemon juice. As I opened the door and plonked down to watch cartoons, me da appeared from the kitchen with a ship like structure on a plate. He'd managed to make some dough and then form it into a cruise ship complete with chimneys, browned it in the oven and plonked jam over the decks. It was in moments like this that I forgot about all the bad and just love him for trying, but the excitement didn't last long. As I cut into the vessel crust, raw dough spilled out from inside, I looked up to see him smiling with pride and got a 'sure that won't do ya any harm' line of encouragement to tuck in. He was still a car crash in the kitchen but I was grateful he tried. As not to hurt his feelings I nibbled on the jammy crust then returned to the telly to get lost in animated fantasy for a few hours, sparkling desserts a distant memory. But who else had got a doughy QE2 'pancake'?

As I finished my beer, and with Hazel sat on the little wall beside her kitchen listening intently, that story made us both smile. I looked out at the moonlight on the Caribbean Sea, there was now so much ahead, adventure and the unknown, but I was too shattered to even think, so I headed off to bed.

I'm very glad I got to experience the island from the local's side, and tried to throw myself into their daily life. On the second day I decided to head to the island's capital, Basseterre, and duly walked down to the local bus stop. Well, by bus stop I mean a non-descript part of the road with a pole sticking out of the ground where a van pulled up. I would have never recognised it as a mode of public transport had the door not slid open revealing lots of local guys peering out at me, presumably on their way to work. Thinking this meant 'bus', I jumped in and just went with it. Eventually someone collected my fare of 2.50 Eastern Caribbean dollars – bargain. To say I stood out like a very pale sore thumb would be an understatement, but I got to my destination easy as pie and went on my merry way.

Before taking in the sites of the capital, I decided to take the ferry over to the sister island of Nevis to do some exploring. However the scheduled departure time had been put back by an hour and a half with no explanation and to the annoyance of some American tourists. But I'd already learned in my short time in St Kitts that things go at their own pace. Their slogan, 'we rush slowly', was plastered everywhere for a reason. With time to spare I mooched around Basseterre and purchased my first morning beer of the trip at 9.30am. I sat chatting to the bar lady, who had Adele playing on loop loudly in the background the entire time, which sort of killed the buzz. So before I sank into a lost love lyrics depression, I finished up and went and sat patiently at the ferry terminal, looking out at the endless sea and becoming mesmerised at the enormity of a cruise ship which had just docked, only to be brought back to reality by a fat lad clutching a monkey wearing a nappy, and trying to perch it on my head. Personally, I'd rather have a non-Pampers wearing monkey perched on me over one with a suspicious looking nappy, which screamed diarrhoea or some other manky monkey disease. I shuffled away.

On the small ferry, the captain let me sit up at the front, or in nautical terms the bow, which provided amazing views of both islands on the way over to Nevis. Having this special privilege didn't last long though as I was joined by lots of other passengers, including big boy and his monkey, who he'd stuffed in his backpack. Maybe the monkey suffered from seasickness and the dark of the rucksack helped it. Great I thought, a monkey spewing from both ends in a sweaty bag not three feet away from me, but he did allow the little fella to pop his head out at one point for some sea air, and thankfully not a hint of monkey sea vomit in sight.

I felt a bit bad for the lad though, one of the crew asked him to move to the other side of the boat to balance it out, which he did graciously amid embarrassing shuffles, so I gave him a 'good on ya lad' smile, which he unfortunately took as 'let's be best friends'. I let him down gently and quickly when we reached Nevis though, and rushed off exploring, while he set off in the other direction to peddle some more monkey business.

Nevis is a much smaller island but with great colonial history like St Kitts. It didn't take long to explore the capital Charlestown and I was left wondering what to do. The lady in the tourist office, randomly another Brummie woman, said I should pop along to the beach bars and have some lunch. I decided to walk along the glittering coastline, and eventually reached Summertimes, a famous spot on Nevis, and spent the afternoon listening to reggae, chatting with some locals and getting tipsy on their speciality cocktail, the Killer Bee, before merrily getting the boat back to Basseterre and wandering around the shiny tourist-friendly port area to finish off my day.

I'd said hello to a Hawaiian woman called Bonnie and her husband Harvey on the ferry to Nevis and then met them properly on the trip back. Bonnie was a larger than life lady who almost instantly announced we were friends to the whole boat – cringe – and proceeded to yap at me for the entire return journey. She told me about how she came from money and that they were visiting the island to purchase even more property for their portfolio. Harvey didn't utter a word the whole time and she didn't come up for air. As she rabbited on, I wondered how she would've survived growing up on council estates. I wondered if she even knew what one was. I disembarked with a pain in my ear and arse from not being able to move away, but politely waved goodbye and wished them well. I'd like to think she knew money wasn't everything but we never got that far.

I'd been told another great way to see the island is on the St Kitts scenic train ride, and that its open-air carriages take in amazing views of both the Atlantic and Caribbean Seas, and the remarkable scenery land side. The years of slapping on every moisturiser under the sun must have paid off as I managed to wangle a half-price student discount, thank you L'Oreal! Well I say wangled, but I think the fella just took pity on me and my sweatiness. I hopped aboard to find the bonus that the journey came with a free bar, day three and yet again I was on the breakfast booze, 9am Piña Coladas this time. The other passengers seemed to lap up the free drinks too, making me feel much less like an alcoholic.

As well as the history from the comical local guide and the on-board choir who sang sporadically throughout the ride, I got to experience my first tropical rain en route, getting soaked in the process. The plastic roll-down blinds couldn't see off this bad boy downpour. It came in from all angles and even through the roof, so we all had to huddle in the middle of the carriage, cocktails in hand, laughing as the train chugged along. The rain lasting for the rest of the day was not so much fun though. It puts a bit of a damper on things being a solo traveller on an island full of couples and groups of American and Canadian students – not the easiest groups to approach without looking like a total desperate Norman.

As soon as the rain eased off I went wandering down to 'the strip' in Frigate Bay which was to be my base for the final two days on the island, and as evening descended the clouds disappeared and the sun made a Mariah Carey style comeback, bursting out of the sky like one of Miss Carey's far too tight gowns. Where I'm going with this comparison I don't know. Anyway, with the sun came a shed load of the American and Canadian students from the huge veterinary university – random – to play volleyball tournaments on the beach. I decided to grab some beer and watch the games. The students proved a tough bunch to infiltrate though, so it was just a couple of awkward hellos and off back to Hazel's bosom I went. Bed by 9pm had become a theme, rock n roll eh.

My final two days in this little Caribbean pearl were spent back in Frigate Bay, at the Timothy Beach resort. As much as I loved Hazel's, the humidity in the room was not helping the sweaty mess I'd become. The desk fan that was nailed to the wall worked like a bitch to cool the air down but unsurprisingly fell short, but it didn't matter as Hazel had helped ease me into my travels a treat. I couldn't have been more grateful for the air-con which Timothy Beach provided though, on top of the welcome from the head honcho, Richard. He was a captivating man with a James Bond-esque air about him. He not only let me check into an upgraded room with a sea view six hours early, but also got his delightful staff to sort out my washing for free, chuffed I was. And thinking it couldn't get any better, I opened the door to my room to find an oasis of Golden Girls charm, literally like stepping into the set of the eighties comedy titan. My heart fluttered and my balls were tickled pink with this tropical boudoir. It had charisma and warmth, the only thing missing was some cheesecake!

A relaxing and quiet couple of days lying in the heat and swimming in the turquoise sea followed, well apart from when a huge family popped down to the beach for a day out on what was St Kitts and Nevis' Independence Day. All good fun, I thought, until the matriarch grandma of the clan proceeded to cart her granddaughter, who obviously couldn't swim, out to the rest of the bunch in the sea. What followed was about forty-five minutes of tranquillity shattering screaming from the little one. It reminded me of something me da would have done when I was a nipper, and it did me no harm (coughs).

But alas it failed to cure the screaming kid's fear of the sea, and she ran shrieking up the beach with grandma behind kissing her teeth in disappointment.

My last evening was spent popping in and out of the beach bars for a chat with the bar staff and some locals, while throwing caution to the wind and getting royally pissed on rum punch, a fitting goodbye to this first and short leg of my travels. I even managed to stay up until 10pm, all in all a St Kitts success. I'm glad to have started my travels on this chilled yet striking island, to have had some time, mainly on my own, to take stock of all I had left behind and had still to tackle ahead. Even though a swirling concoction of feelings were still there, having this time to breathe had begun to stake a claim within me too.

And so onward to the next leg of my journey, it was time for the real backpacking and hostel life to begin, and where I planned to spend the next three-ish months. Buckle up South America imma coming to get cha!

Landing in Peru's capital Lima was a culture shock to say the least. The lush tropical environment of the Caribbean seemed a distant memory as I was presented with blanketed grey skies, followed by a taxi ride through a landscape resembling something out of Mad Max. It was blatantly apparent that this part of the city was cast aside for the very poor, with broken down shacks for housing, dusty building sites, stray dogs limping around and people selling anything they could on the streets to earn a living. It was quite a depressing scene, but you have to applaud people who live in these conditions, who make do with what they have to survive. It was something I didn't expect to see so immediately on arrival.

But I kept an upbeat demeanour, and translated the familiar opening beats of George Michaels 'Faith' from the battered old taxi radio as a sign that the universe was sending me a camp thunderbolt of positivity. It still didn't change the scenery outside though. As I gripped the seat we stopped and started through the sprawling city, heading towards the politically prettier and affluent side of town, Miraflores.

Looking out through the dusty taxi window and seeing the little kids playing in the rough streets surrounded by rubbish and fumes, I knew it probably wouldn't be my last experience with real poverty on my travels. But I was glad to see it too, I have so much respect for people who fight on and fend for themselves. We don't choose what we're born into and I've always prodded my own consciousness to recognise the people around the globe, and at home, that are in much worse situations than me. But I guess we can all be blindsided by emotions and only see the world through our own eyes at times.

The outside environment also reminded me that even though we didn't have very much at times, me da would always find ways to make it work. Not often the right ways, but his survival instincts would always override any restrictions. He was always wheeling and dealing, like an Irish Del Boy. After his path as a working sailor ended, he found jobs when he could, from grave digging or labouring to working on removal lorries, but generally we just lived off his dole money left over from the pub, hand outs from St Vincent de Paul or loans from either the credit union or a private lender in town known as Lowney.

Shoplifting, or going on the rob, was the norm for a lot of people in similar circumstances back home. It's just how it was, and I was shown the ropes when I was 7. I picked it up pretty quickly, like the Artful Dodger I could be in and out with various necessities in the blink of an eye. We would go out together but sometimes me da sent me out to pilfer on my own. Inevitably, when something like that is ingrained in you as a kid, I started to steal for myself, toys and sweets mainly. Always from shops and big stores and never ever off a person or from someone's home. Not that that makes it any more right, because it was wrong, but I guess I saw it in a kind of Robin Hood way – rob from the rich to give to the poor. The poor being us and the shoplifting to keep us off the breadline in the early years. But unfortunately this habit became the norm and continued for many years after, a highly addictive habit with a deep-seated rush and very hard to shake off.

I only ever got caught twice, once when I went out without me da's knowledge when I was 12. I knew he had gotten me a truly horrific dark brown itchy jumper to wear for Christmas Day. I was mortified, as Christmas Day in Ireland is the day when everyone gets dressed up, and shows off all their new clothes. If he thought I was wearing that polyester monstrosity he could think again. So I took myself off to Penneys, the department store, but on this occasion and out of character I wasn't very on the ball, shoving a new jumper up my top and trying to leave the store looking like a pregnant midget, only for the store detective, a stern woman with frizzy blonde hair, watching and waiting to grab me by the shoulder as I stepped outside, and ushered me back in to the manager's office flanked by the security guard. The tears came and I explained the situation, but was taken to the Garda station, cautioned and taken home by the Guards. Of course me da couldn't really reprimand me and inside I blamed him anyway.

The other time I was caught was when I was out robbing big bars of chocolate from a supermarket with my friend. We were more messing about for a laugh than any planned Great Train Robbery type haul, so not being cautious enough we were spotted and chased out of the store by the detective, who proceeded to launch himself through the air and land on top of me as if I'd stolen solid gold bars instead of an Aero mint. In the process he crushed the minty goodness which I'd wedged down my trousers and it broke in a million pieces. My friend thankfully got away but I was taken into a store room. Again the waterworks were on cue and eventually they let me leave with a slap on the wrist, and some green-y brown stained underpants.

The same supermarket became a regular robbing paradise. In my teenage years I would walk in as bold as anything with an empty trolley, fill it to the brim with the weekly groceries, the better brands that we couldn't usually afford, and brazenly walk back out and over to the packing area, bag it up and ship it home. We ate like kings for a good few weeks until they clocked on and appointed a member of staff to stand at the packing area checking for receipts. It was back to the normal basic weekly dole shop and Government butter vouchers after that.

Even though money was tight, especially in my younger years, me da did start to give me pocket money, and I would look forward to it every week. He gave me £1, or punt in those days, a week, to buy whatever I liked from the pound shop. I would meet up with my friends and we would scurry down town running around the shop wildly. I absolutely loved toys, so gravitated towards anything that I could bring to life in my head. I had a huge collection of teddy bears back at the bedsit, one of my favourites being my little glow-worm pal. But on one particular pocket money adventure, I had a hard decision to make. Would I buy a tub of slime that made farting noises when you put your hand in, or would I buy the huge poster of Madonna from the squeaky poster rack?

She had just released the video for 'Open Your Heart' and I adored watching it, likening myself to the little lad cast alongside the famous singer. I would imagine I was him trying to get into the peep show. Only problem with the poster was that she was posing provocatively in full on lacy knickers and bra, sprawled on a bed in black and white, all Herb Ritts style photography. My dad was very conservative and prudish when it came to anything related to sex. But with me being the little liberal rebel I was, I abandoned the farty slime and went for the poster. Well of course he came home from the pub and saw it hung with pride over the double bed we had to share and went mad, tore it down and gave me a hiding for buying such filth. But it didn't affect mine and Madge's relationship, I loved that wild American temptress.

The reminiscing was quickly halted at this point when a Peruvian goods truck almost veered into the side of the taxi. The driver yanking the wheel hard to avoid the collision, and my heart almost fell out of my arse. Let me tell you about the traffic in Lima, fucking hell it's some crazy shit! Thousands of cars on the roads combined with the fearless and chilled air of Lima's drivers as they suddenly change direction, pull out in front of each other and avoid head on collisions by mere millimetres. It was like some sort of free-for-all Gumball rally, the type of city you do not want to drive around in a Maserati or Bugatti. Poor Britney would be straight back on the meds with the stress of it all.

Oh and it was here I made my first effort at phrase-book Spanish, asking the driver if the cost was ´cincuenta cinco soles por favor?´, which he understood and I was chuffed. That's about £11, not bad for an hour in a cab.

I arrived at the Pariwana Hostel, a great place to start hostel life with its social scene, amenities, free brekkie and cleanliness. I was greeted by the camp male receptionist, who flirted outrageously and got a little too close for comfort in the baggage room, blocking me in and chatting Spanish at me to test if I'd put the effort in to learn the language. I just laughed awkwardly as I edged past, and gave him a wink to send him on his way.

I was stinking from the almost twenty hour transit via Miami (I promise I rarely ever smell) and my mouth was like a nun's undercrackers at a Dreamboys' show, not a great first impression to chat to new people.

After a quick shower in the surprisingly decent shared bathroom, I wandered up to the rooftop cafe where there was a couple of groups of people, and settled down to what I would come to find is the staple hostel breakfast in Peru, bread and jam. A sudden awkwardness and lack of confidence came over me, but I said to myself no, get up, get over there and chat. I spotted one of the guys was wearing a Bolivian Death Road t-shirt, a trip I wanted to take myself, so I saw my chance for conversation and went over. He was an energetic lad called Sidney and introduced me to what would be my new hostel crew, including among some other cool guys, Ben and Chris from Guernsey, Matt and Alex from the deep south of America, Sam from London and big Robert from the Netherlands. I found a renewed confidence, which created an encouraging start to hostel life.

I spent two days in Lima with the lads, going on a free walking tour of the city to find out the history of the place. 'Free' my arse, same price as a normal tour in 'tips' at the end, but worth it to hear the guide's passion and pride in his country, and a bonus pisco tasting session, the Peruvian national liquor, to finish. A highlight of the afternoon was standing on a bridge overlooking an impoverished part of town. An old lady came up to chat to Robert and me, even though it was ´no comprende´ from me I tried to grasp what she meant. She had no teeth in her head but massive kindness in her eyes, and I got the gist that she was a very proud Lima lady indeed. I'd started to really bond with Robert. We had different backgrounds, fourteen years age gap and about two foot height gap, but it didn't matter, and it was with him I got my first sense of what one of the main things travelling solo was all about: the connections you make with different people.

After walking for hours it was time for a drink so we called in to a one hundred year old bar called Bar Cordano. Anyone who knows me knows I love a historic pub, and this one was oozing with old charm, as well as cold local beers. It had been frequented by some famous faces over the years with photographs displayed proudly on the walls. I could only make out a black and white shot of a younger Mario Testino relaxing there over a drink wearing some eighties white linen, very snazzy.

Back at the hostel it was a combination of ping pong tournaments and drinking games, but my favourite part, and also the campest thing I've ever done with a group of straight lads, was a salsa class. The teacher was a local, a big lad with hips like Jagger and some pretty funky zebra print leggings on, which meant you couldn't help but follow the moves via his arse, like one of those trippy optical illusions.

While in a city I thought I'd take the chance to tidy up my hair, as it was starting to look like a microphone. Now I have a skinhead, but it's no slapdash skinhead. My barber Ben back in London grades it weekly – four grades people – so trusting it with someone else makes me anxious. A grade too short and I look like a BNP member crossed with a tennis ball. Sadly my fears were realised. I mistakenly opted for a backstreet 'hairdressers' as I couldn't find one of the 'Papi' style barbers I'd imagined, like you'd see in the favelas of Rio. After showing her pictures on my phone from Ben of what it should look like, and nods of ´no problemo´ from Ms Scissorhands, I realised two minutes in she hadn't a clue how to use clippers. So forty minutes later there I was with tuffs of hair around my head like Sloth from The Goonies, and ending up taking the clippers off her to just shave it all off myself with a zero! I begrudgingly paid the stupid wench and left, avoiding any mirrors for the next day or so. Never again. Me da would have done a better job and at that moment I wouldn't have minded him slapping lard in my hair, like he used to do to try keep my two cowlicks down.

I felt two days was enough in Lima. I know the weather can't be helped, but I was glad to jump on the bus to my next destination of Ica, waving adiós to the grey skies and car horns of this historic, proud and hard-working city. This was also my first taste of saying goodbye to new chums, a little comfort in a strange land, but which I knew would be a consistent event travelling solo. But after working out Robert was travelling a similar route, we said we would definitely meet up again further along in Cusco.

Ica was just a day stop, where I would dive into sand boarding and rip roar around the desert oasis of Huacachinain in dune buggies. I excitedly got off the bus and hopped in a cab to my hostel base for the afternoon. This one had more of a hedonistic vibe about the place with an in-house club and pool. I decided to grab some quick grub, but my stomach wasn't feeling so great, Peru belly maybe, so I thought it best not to eat it all before getting thrown around huge dunes in what is basically a pimped-up go-cart. After a couple of mouthfuls I offered my mayonnaise laden chicken salad to a girl on the next table, and chatted with her and her friend for a bit while she wolfed down the grub. It turned out they were tour guides on a sort of 18-30's adventure bus and this was one of their stops – rather them than me.

Strapped in to the buggy, we sped off into the sandy horizon. I took my day bag with me as it had everything important in it, so I decided I'd wedge it between my legs. The ride was adrenaline filled, with deafening screams from the two Columbian girls in front and gritted teeth from the rest of us. It was amazing fun, stopping, starting and flying over the grainy desert mountains. Then it was onto the first of five dunes of varying height for the sand boarding part. These boards were not the most modern or slick snowboard type pieces of apparatus which I had envisioned. They were literally like something you'd make as a kid, with Velcro foot grips that had seen better days and waxed with cheap candles by the driver, but it added to the craziness. Only one lad stood up to successfully glide down the sandy pistes, but he was apparently a pro snow boarder. The rest of us either fell off into a face full of sand or lay down on our bellies, gliding down like penguins on ice.

Leaving the desert behind, it was on to my next stop Arequipa. I'm going to try and gloss over my stupidity on this next part, the part where I left my passport and all my bank cards on the bus from Lima. That night, spending twelve anxious hours on an overnight bus to Arequipa, I was thinking fuck, I've either been robbed or else my nerdy bumbag containing the very necessary items had fallen out of my bag in the desert, never to be seen again. But after having time to think and with the morning came a 'let's just get it sorted' calmness. So with the help of a fellow passenger, a gent called Ruben from Amsterdam, and also the bus terminal lady, who both rang around the previous locations for me, they found it, thank the Lord! The honesty of the Peruvian people had prevailed, someone had handed it in at Ica, and the bus company agreed to courier it to me for the next day before my departure. Although little, I felt waking up with a new sense of calm and a 'let's get this problem sorted' attitude may have been my first achievement. A small but important breakthrough putting the anxiety and worry to one side and just riding it out.

As promised, the package arrived at the bus station the next day, and I've never been so happy to see a fanny pack in all my life. I bought the lady some chocolates to say thanks and Ruben some beers. I missed out on a prepaid Colca Canyon tour but didn't care, anything was better than spending days in a consulate and hundreds of pounds calling UK banks. With a massive sigh of relief, I strapped the little fashion killer under my t-shirt wherever I went from there.

Back to Arequipa, and the first time I felt that I was truly in South America. It had great weather, a great vibe and at the centre a bustling main square, with kids happily feeding the pigeons with bags of seed from the old ladies peddling them. A proper old school romantic scene, and the pigeons looked a lot less rabid than the ones back in London too. The inhabitants here were about 99.9% Peruvian, and seemed like a really happy and content bunch, always smiling and happy to help, expecting nothing in return. Even the women in traditional dress and the street sellers didn't hassle you here, and took 'no gracias' with a positive air. Two things that stood out as bringing great pleasure to the city were music and food, both in abundance and adding to the pleasant atmosphere, apart from the pictures of skinned and deep fried guinea pigs sprawled out like those seventies style tiger skin rugs, heads still on, which are advertised on many restaurant menus. I'm all for trying weird and wonderful new foods, especially in the countries I'm visiting, but having had guinea pigs as pets as a kid I just couldn't this time. Plus they just looked like deep fried rats.

My hostel in Arequipa had much more of a hippy vibe, but with friendly people passing through. My roommate for the night, Neil from Bristol, had a wealth of travel knowledge to share, as did a South African girl called Hannah, a double for model royalty Karlie Kloss, who basically provided me with a well travelled and well approved itinerary for my time ahead in both Bolivia and Chile.

My time in Arequipa was short, only two days, one night, so I hung out either on my own or with Ruben, taking in the sights and chatting over pisco sours cocktails. We had eerily similar recent stories too. I guess there's a reason you meet people eh? We chatted about our mums, the hard time he was having with his and, well, just the memories of mine.

As we left a bar on my final evening, we came across a little church yard where we watched some local teens in what seemed like a dance troop taking to the stage for some traditional Spanish style dance, before murdering Beyonce's 'Single Ladies' routine. It didn't matter how uncoordinated they were as they just seemed really happy to be up there enjoying their passion. I know that feeling very well and I commend them for it, out of sync or not. One of my main passions, and I felt only talents, growing up was dancing, from learning routines from the weekly Top of the Pops performances and all the new music videos, to dancing with my crew during our youth club years, breaking many of me da's ornaments along the way with overzealous moves. An unbroken love affair in which I could lose myself and not have to think about all the shit.

Next morning it was time to leave this city, which had added even more spark to the excitement and adventures ahead. I said goodbye to my new pal Ruben and my hostel companions, and shared a cab with a couple of girls also on their way to the next stop, Cusco, the gateway to the mighty Machu Picchu, the pilgrimage for many a South American traveller, including me. To reach the Inca wonder Robert suggested joining him on the jungle Inca trail trek, which includes white water rafting, mountain biking and zip lining. I had not packed for any of these activities, but seeing as I was trying to say yes to everything (apart from cremated guinea pig) it just added to the fun. If you're gonna do it, do it big I say.

Chapter 4

When backpacking, all embarrassment or etiquette when talking about bodily functions goes out the window. So far I've overheard or found myself included in many conversations from both sexes about how many shits they've had that day, and in great detail too. My favourite quote was from a British girl reporting that 'it ran out of her like gravy' – how lovely!

Anyway enough toilet talk and back to the travels. After a twelve hour bus ride, I arrived in Cusco. Note that long-haul buses in South America are like planes, with reclining seats, your own TV, and food and drinks served to your seat. The security is very much like an airport too, bags checked, body scans, and, for good measure, actually being filmed in your seat just in case the passport control wasn't enough.

I'd been warned about altitude sickness prior to my arrival in the Inca capital as it's 3400 meters above sea level, but thankfully I didn't experience that treat, instead just a bad case of cracked and dry lips.

It's a massive city spread out over the surrounding rolling hills with a pretty and historic centre, a lot more touristy than Arequipa. I met up with my Dutch mate Robert at the hostel, and also made some new pals Neil, Charlie, Kira and

Corinna from the UK, as well as the dude himself Bubba, a skydiving instructor from New Zealand, and another merry band of backpacking pals was formed. Together and sporadically, we visited the city's sites and dived into the local dishes, like the Alpaca burritos in a quirky little restaurant called Tabasco. Again I avoided the Guinea pig carcasses staring up at me from the menu.

The local chocolate factory had a free tour, which made us all feel fantastically kid like. Our guide was a sweet and very small Peruvian lady with a big hat, which added to the whole Charlie and the Chocolate Factory fantasy feel. The free samples were in abundance, from 100% cacao, pistachio milk and hot chilli chocolate pieces to chocolate teas and shots of chocolate liquor. We finished up in the cafe with a massive sharing fruit platter and gooey chocolate fondue, as well as brownies and the DIY Willy Wonka hot chocolate cups, before all shuffling outta the place like chocolate obsessed hogs.

To walk off all that extra lard, three of us took a steep hike up through the colourful hillside houses to the great Cristo Blanco statue that watches over the city, although doing it in flip flops wasn't my brainiest moment. When we finally made it to the top the effort was worth it and we had amazing panoramic views of Cusco. We took a tiny cab back down the hill to the main square, Robert's legs squashed up by his chin in the front. As I got out of the taxi there was a local tramp standing there motionless, who then proceeded to flop out his knob and take a piss in the middle of the street, the splashes just missing my battered and exposed feet. Grim.

Cusco has many churches, a stand-out being one just off the main thoroughfare called La Merced, and the most bling place of worship I've ever been in, like something out of Big Fat Gypsy Weddings. Dazzling chandeliers adorned the ceilings, and it had an altar that would put the Harrods' Christmas displays to shame.

The holiness of the afternoon and Peru's obvious Catholicism got me thinking about my own relationship with the Church. Although brought up as a Catholic I certainly don't subscribe to its guilt-ridden 'moral' code, but I can still understand that there is some good intent and appreciate the beauty of their churches. There's a certain peace when sitting in a huge ornate basilica with just your thoughts, and maybe it's that ingrained feeling that draws me to visit from time to time, to either light a candle or to have some silence. Though, I certainly don't feel drawn to listen to any of the self-serving sermons.

I'm all for faith helping people and giving them peace, but cannot bear the all-too-regular ostracising and demonising elements that comes with most religions, that sickening and vilifying 'we'll love and welcome you, but only if you're like us' mantra. Although I believe in my own version of what may come after, my own take on spirituality, it's safe to say I don't see myself as Catholic anymore.

As I stood looking up at the beautiful golden altar, the truthful and exposing lyrics of Hozier's 'Take me to Church' on loop in my head, I could feel my eyes starting to glisten with tears as pictures of me da formed in my mind, and also an anger thinking about what the Catholic institution did to him.

He found it very hard to stay in one place, and maybe this was also part of the reason why I upped and left. His mind would wander and his patience was non-existent. The source of this was his own childhood, not just the hardship he and his nine siblings experienced growing up in poverty in a small two-bedroom house with no bathroom in 1930s and 1940s Ireland, but primarily because of his time incarcerated as a boy in the hell hole that was the Artane Industrial school, run by the Christian Brothers in Artane, Dublin. One of the many institutions dotted around the country and under the heavy-handed rule of the Catholic Church, where boys and girls, either orphans or 'badly behaved' kids, were taken and left without much explanation. Where sadists and paedophiles hid amongst the staff and preyed on the young, knowing the government and outside forces would rarely interfere. And even if they were reported, they would just be moved out of sight or to another facility to start all over again.

The Artane was an infamous boys' school, where the young lads lived in unrelenting fear and would often go hungry and cold. The place was a formidable building with a haunting presence, and for six long years between the age of 10 and 16 me da was locked away behind its secretive and cruel walls. His crime? Bunking off school and stealing an apple. The beatings were brutal and constant, as was the rest of the torture inflicted on those often poverty stricken and defenceless young lads at the hands of the evil men who hid behind the Teflon mask of Catholic Holiness. In those days that mask and position made you God, and seldom did anyone question it. This journey would damage my dad beyond repair, the horrors inflicted on him in those years not only changed him forever but also created an aftermath that was felt by those close to him – especially me.

In my younger years he would never speak of any of it, but as I grew up and when he was emotional after a few jars he would sometimes say "I'll tell you some things when you're a teenager." I never understood what he meant when I was young, but I knew he needed to explain, to make his son understand why he was the way he was.

Years later he handed me a book called Fear of the Collar, written by Patrick Touher, another inmate at the Artane Industrial school, and he asked me to read it. I did, for the most part through blurry red eyes and with tears streaming down my face, having to stop many times before I finished it. I couldn't cope with imagining the scenarios and my dad as a little boy living through that hell at the hands of the very men who were supposed to be on this Earth to be kind and to protect him, to guide a blinkered flock to enlightenment – bullshit. It was only when I closed the book that I finally understood what he had gone through and how things had come to be.

The Irish government eventually opened a huge, controversial and somewhat messy investigation into the crimes of the Christian Brothers that took years to be heard, with many victims coming forward (including my dad) to finally be granted some justice. Although his experiences at the school had broken him in many ways, it hadn't broken his spirit and he found the strength to stand up in court and testify against the organisation, with my two aunts outside for support. Not only did he do this for himself but, like so many victims of the cruelties who came forward, he did it to shine a light on their ordeals, to take a stand and help prevent it ever happening again. In turn he and the other victims that testified helped open Ireland's eyes to the barbarity that their precious Church is capable of, and to expose the cover-up and the shameful attempt to save their own arses. The same Church who used the heavy hand of guilt and scare mongering to remain the primary influence over an entire country, but whose brittle backbone was starting to crumble under the weight of their own guilt.

Surprisingly me da never lost his faith. He regularly attended mass and also had respect for the few good Catholic priests, the ones that took their roles as they were intended to be taken: for selfless reasons and to help others. His long-held faith and loyalty emphasised to me just how much religion was ingrained into the hearts and minds of his generation.

On that afternoon in an amazing church so far from home, I lit a candle for him and all the others that had suffered, and left feeling somewhat angry and confused by it all, but also with a feeling of contentment. I felt him there beside me, if just for that moment.

While in Cusco I also managed to catch the total lunar eclipse, or the Blood Moon as it's also called, a very rare occurrence. We all lay down on beanbags in the hostel courtyard with some beers to take in this astronomical event, pretty cool I must say. And then for the main event: next morning a 4.30am wake up call to begin our jungle trek to Machu Picchu. There were only four of us, myself, Robert, Bubba and a new girl, Marianne from Denmark. After a long bus ride to our starting point, which consisted of a blasting early morning playlist of heavy techno and gangster rap favoured by the Peruvian driver, we arrived 4200 meters high up on top of a mountain for our premier task, the biking. Literally so high we were above the clouds, a shivery exciting feeling came over me as I chose my bike and put on my stunt racer style protective gear. I remembered how I used to love being on, and was rarely off, my neon green and black mountain bike in my early teens, and the freedom that came with that. I never thought one day I'd be speeding down a mountain in the upper Amazon!

All geared up and after a pep talk from the guides, we set off down the winding and steep mountain road. Thankfully we weren't on the cliff side and didn't have to look down at the endless drop below. The feeling of freedom was exhilarating as we zoomed past one another on the roads, only to get back in line when a convoy of American style trucks approached. All the scenery changed as we descended, from the cold cloudy mountain top to the more humid environment of the jungle below.

At one stage I was leading the pack which felt very cool, and picking up speed too, until Robert and Bubba sped past. At this point we'd taken a few wet corners, all fine if a little nerve racking at speed, then came another one. The boys passed through without a hitch. I however had this sinking feeling as I approached, I was going too fast and I knew it. I was too far wide. I tried to break but my front wheel got caught in a ridge. The bike skidded out from under me and threw me clean off into a concrete waterway dyke. I bounced along like a rag doll, my helmet smashing against the wet ground taking most of the impact along with my shoulder and knee. From inside the helmet the experience was like those TV camera views from a Formula One car, the whole world shaking and it left me very dizzy indeed. As I got up, feeling shaken and battered, I checked I was still intact. My shoulder was thumping and one knee pad had slid off so my left knee was pumping blood, but thankfully the helmet, bike and jacket took most of the damage. Apart from a bloody hand and knee I was fine.

The guide mopped me up and told me I needed to get in the van for the rest of the ride. I was like hell no, and eventually persuaded him to let me back on the bike. After a very Driving Miss Daisy cautious start, I got back into the swing of it and finished the ride with the rest of the pack. It was only then that the guides informed me the corner I had bounced around like a ping pong ball was known as 'The Gringo Killer'. They laughed in a 'oh these silly gringos' kind of way, as I rubbed my wonky shoulder and managed a smirk.

From there, there was no time to sit back and take in the adrenaline filled morning, it was straight onto the rafting part of the trek. I was not prepared for this. Still wet and cold from the crash and without any proper swimwear and having not yet applied my bug repellent, we were thrown into a rafting briefing.

This is where the mood changed for me, and I did not like what met me there - the spawn of Satan that are mosquitoes. I fucking hate mosquitoes and there were thousands of them, as well as sand flies, again another of Satan's little minions eager to suck the life out of you, especially juicy white Irish skin. So as well as the cuts on my legs, now bloodsucking bites started appearing all over me. By the end I looked like I'd just stepped out of a scene from the 1600s plague. Applying the 100% Deet repellent wasn't the sanctuary I'd hoped for either, it was like battery acid, tearing colour and paint off anything it touched and it stunk too. My skin was screaming out for some Palmers Cocoa Butter!

Anywho, back to the trek. Apart from the dreaded mossies and their cronies, rafting on the Urubamba river was another round of living by the seat of your panties fun. Six of us were in a raft with the guide at the back, bellowing the instructions and working us hard. I wondered how much I was going to ache the next day after the crash bang wallop, and now this heaving rowing session.

The rapids were rip roaring, and I managed to stay in the boat when a particularly big one hit us, sending one American man flying into the river and me legs akimbo into the lap of the instructor – awkward. We stopped and the instructor asked us if we wanted to jump from a huge rock into the river, just for the fun of it. Another raft had joined us by now, and all apart from two girls put their hands up to take part. There wasn't much prep, it was just kinda suck it and see, jumping off a sharp slicing rock into the fast rapids below. When my turn came, I looked down at how unexpectedly high it was, but just jumped on in with gritted teeth and thankfully popped up with clean underpants after. A brilliant experience and end to what started out as a nightmare bug ridden afternoon.

The whole experience made me feel like I was back in the Scouts. It reminded me how much I loved being part of that club, learning new skills and going on outings and adventures. Once we went to Dublin for a weekend, staying in the Ringsend part of the city right beside the canal, sleeping in huge tents with my pals and playing tricks on each other, like putting toothpaste on sleeping kids' faces. The prank I woke up to wasn't so innocent though, opening my eyes to find one of the lads trying to wipe his arse on my head, nasty.

Although part of the Scouts team, I did stand out. Me da didn't have the money to buy the uniform, so I was the only one not in sync with my band of scouting brothers. This was never more obvious than when we attended mass in the local church, a little green army of coordination apart from me sticking out in my normal clothes, but I did catch the eye of a pretty blonde Dublin girl. Thankfully someone eventually gave me a jumper and toggle. I tried never to get in trouble when I was with the Scouts, and apart from falling head first in the muddy canal I was getting on great on that trip, until one fat lad took the piss out of me not having a mam and I broke a mop over his head.

We left the river wet and with arms aching from all the water work. A very wet van load of adventurers were carted back to the rafting HQ, shivering in towels and still getting bitten by the mosquitoes which were now inside the van. I wanted to cry, but just kept my head down and the towel over me to avoid even more upper body bites.

The van stopped at the bottom of a jungle hillside, and the guide shouted to the four of us 'all out my friends and don't forget nothing'. Looking up at the overgrown hill ahead it dawned on us this wasn't the end of the hard work for the day. Instead of going to the hostel in the nearest town with the rest of the people in the mosquito carriage, we headed up the steep jungle path to Monkey House lodge. After a sweaty and breathy hike, a marvellous sight appeared from the jungle, and the tiredness of the day was forgotten. Monkey House poked out of the hillside, surrounded by banana and papaya trees and with views of the entire valley. It turned out to be a welcome and authentic addition to the trip. After washing up in the outside showers, we had our food lovingly prepared by the lady owner while we sat squashing bugs into our skin and played the Dutch card game of Skip-Bo, and drank beers for the rest of the peaceful evening.

Now this trip really brought out the fearlessness in me early on, because about 3am I needed the loo, so got out from under my mosquito net, my favourite kind of net, and in the pitch black of the jungle night with only a small torch made my way to the outdoor toilet. Normally this kind of environment would have me recreating every horror movie I've ever seen – I was haunted for years after watching Freddie Kruger – and running screaming back to the safety of my bed, but not this time. As I looked up at the star filled sky a real peace came over me. I even sat on the toilet with a huge black spider on the wall beside me, staring right at me, but we both decided to go about our own business and say goodnight.

Waking up in the jungle was beautiful, and even my aching body couldn't dampen this freeing feeling, a favourite moment of the trip so far. Sitting on the hammock looking out over the vast jungle canopy from the wooden walkway outside our rooms, the rising sun cut through the haze of the jungle mist, the air so far removed from any opaque city fumes. I thought about how happy the host family seemed living there: The kids in their battered sandals, and with gappy heartwarming smiles running around below playing with their puppies. It seemed like all they needed was right there on the side of that steep hill in Peru, living each day with fun and gratitude. I thought about how they would probably never leave this place. I thought about all the unsettled feelings I had when I was their age.

After breakfast we were taught all about the local products and way of life. We had our faces painted like warriors and got to dress up in the traditional Peruvian gear. Then some visitors arrived, a dandy little emperor tamarin monkey, with his hipster moustache, and then the Peruvian picuro, which is like a creature from Wind in the Willows, who happily chomped on a banana I bought for him, he was cute beyond. Waving goodbye to Monkey House and all its inhabitants, we set off on a three hour hike to our next stop.

This hike was tough in part, but walking through the jungle past the coca and pineapple fields was very peaceful. It gave me time with my thoughts before we got to the original Inca trail. The trail mainly wrapped around the Puma Chaca mountain, and is basically a ledge the Incas carved out of the steep rock, and varied in width as we walked.

Now I really don't like heights at all, especially while carrying two plastic bags with blue and red ink coming off me due to the toxic bug spray. While manoeuvring my way along these ledges and sharp drops of thousands of meters is a great personal achievement, it taught me that confronting your fears doesn't cure them. Unless you have Paul McKenna yapping in your ear, but what the hell eh, on we go. So I gripped onto the rock for dear life and sweated buckets the whole way. Just to add to the vertigo, we arrived at a viewing point which was a thin ledge protruding high up from the mountain side. We edged out and sat for the next forty minutes having an Inca history lesson from our guide. It was truly breath-taking but I didn't move an inch the whole time, only standing up and braving the all too close drop for some pictures. I couldn't help thinking if only the teachers in school had thought of this scary body-freezing classroom location, I just might have listened more and made it to the end.

I'll skip over the mosquito-ridden lunch that greeted us next, and so back to the trek. We were now off the mountain and down through the valley below walking alongside the river. With parts of my trainers actually falling off at this stage, we crossed a wooden bridge, with quite a few slats missing to reveal the gushing waters below, very Indiana Jones. It was then into a man powered cable car, two at a time, to cross the river and up the final push to our destination, the hot springs of Cocalmayo.

The springs were supposed to be a welcome relaxation after all the walking and sweating, but I couldn't relax, as – yes you guessed it – the place was over run with mosquitoes. People dodged and dived as they left the tranquil waters to apply more chemicals and avoid more bites.

After a night at a crappy hostel with cold water in the town of Santa Teresa, I was happy to get on with day three, zip lining through the nearby valleys, where the skin on my calf was etched away by a scorching wire while trying to master a Spider-Man position. Another jungle war wound. It was then onto our final part of the trek before Machu Picchu the next day, another three hour hike along train tracks in the shadow of the Inca mountains, with the rest of my trainers falling off along the way.

Turning the final corner of the trek, Aguas Calientes, a town carved into the mountainous valley, appeared from nowhere. The town is a testament to human being's ability to forge and build a community in such a remote location – spectacular.

At a stupidly early hour the next morning we bused up the winding Scalextric roads to the mountain, and arrived at the gate, eagerly presenting our passports and tickets to the guards. We entered the city, climbed up some pathways, and finally there it was: Machu Picchu's ancient grounds unfolded before us, and it was a pretty awe-inspiring sight. Somehow we managed to be part of the first group in, meaning we got to experience this special place relatively empty until the gaggle of international tourists descended on the ancient site, which included the stereotypical groups of Asian tours, dripping with every gadget known to man, and selfie sticks galore.

I still couldn't believe I was there, it looked like an artist's impression or postcard dream. We had a short history lesson and tour, only to be interrupted by a hungry llama mother and her offspring looking for some breakfast bananas, which totally upstaged our guide Pedro. After mooching round and exploring the deceptively massive site, I opted for a hike up to the Sun Gate, and boy was it a hike. I was sweating my back off in the midday sun, but with supportive outbursts from passers by on their way down telling me I was nearly there – including some Scouse girls I'd seen passing through the

Monkey Lodge with their fake lashes still in tact – I made it to the top. The views from all over this magical mountain were majestic, a total 360 of the surrounding landscape from such a colossal height.

How an ancient civilisation managed to build this entire city upon an unforgiving mountain is just mind boggling. For all the bad in the world, standing atop that mountain, looking over that ancient city highlighted the resolve and determination human beings have had over the centuries to invent and create.

It had been an unforgettable few days, at times challenging but giving each of us a massive sense of achievement in what we had done, and also in what we were part of. My obsessive compulsive anxieties had started being pushed and unaligned too, using a remote jungle 'cafe' toilet the day before with no toilet seat, no light, minimal toilet paper and a black fragment of soap had made sure of that.

It also emphasised that when it comes to my own emotions, these epics events and reaching these goals were helping lift me bit by bit, further away from the stifling life I was trying to get on top of. But heartache and loneliness still had a way of creeping in, it didn't differentiate between moments or geography. It could hit while laughing at a party full of people or right there on the top of that Inca wonder. But the city before me had been lost then found, it had crumbled but emerged again from the undergrowth. I hoped in that moment my life could do the same.

Chapter 5

Back in Cusco that night we all wanted to let rip, and headed to an infamous place called Wild Rover, an Irish hostel chain in South America. I'd never heard of the place but its reputation had gained speed as I travelled. It didn't disappoint, it was exactly as advertised: WILD! After a night drinking and dancing with some absolutely mental outback Aussies, who were touring the globe through a haze of booze, I woke up for my flight the next morning with a fuzzy head and my first hangover of the trip. A turbulence ridden flight to Bolivia's capital La Paz didn't help things, thank the Lord for airport toilets.

Myself and Dutch Robert had decided to team up and carry on traveling together for a bit. Both of us had minimal Spanish, but thankfully on the plane we met a German guy called Lukas who was fluent. The poor chap suffered from a severe fear of flying, and had asked us to keep chatting during the flight to take his mind of his very visible nerves. He almost crushed my hand he held it so tight. To say thanks for the chit-chat, he got us a cab into the city centre and helped us buy our tickets to Copacabana, which was a Godsend, as it became apparent that barely anyone in La Paz spoke English.

The city was a culture shock to say the least, and for the first time I felt like an alien plonked down in a cultural and communication wilderness. Now I don't expect people in countries where it isn't their first language to speak L'anglais and why should they, I mean I'm in their country right, so I should be making the effort, which I was trying to do. Unfortunately the words and sentences that have stuck in my head thus far were both basic and minimal. By the time I'd thumbed through my pocket phrase book, the person I was trying to speak to had usually walked off. I kept trying but I sensed in Bolivia it would be quite a challenge. My wavy hand gestures were getting better though.

La Paz was a short stop before we jumped on the connecting bus to Copacabana, which is out on the shores of Lake Titicaca, but it was a nerve racking glimpse into this sprawling city and its manic pace. I also realised I can't seem to say 'Titicaca' with a straight face, I kept imagining Sid James or Kenneth Williams blurting it out during an innuendo-laden Carry On sketch!

I'd not met many Bolivian people before, actually I don't think I've ever met any. The women really stood out, a lot of whom were dressed in the traditional clothing of colourful shawls, big skirts and bowler hats, worn at various angles depicting the lady's relationship status. Many had gold teeth, which apparently meant they had a few bob. This was my first glimpse of the famous Cholitas. They all seemed to be dashing about, carrying substantial loads on their backs, on their way somewhere to sell their wares and make some Bolivianos. I even saw one crouching down to take a piss in the street, seemingly too busy to find a toilet – apparently this was the norm. I worried about all the splashes on her underskirt.

Soon we were on our way to Copacabana and gone were the luxury buses we'd travelled on in Peru. The bus was filled with locals, except for two dreadlocked tourists at the back. Advertised as three hours, the bumpy journey took closer to five – mainly down to the potholes in the road which the driver seemed unable to avoid. At one point we took a diversion around some sort of roadblock. It turned out to be the entire population of the village, who had parked their cars and vans on both sides of the road and were sitting on the roofs to watch an unidentifiable sport – the definition of cheap seats!

I was surprised to see so many Cholitas in a city, and the bus continued to pick up more of them on the outskirts of La Paz. For these woman with their rough working hands and weathered faces this was a typical weekly, if not daily, journey. They all carried massive weights of supplies wrapped around their backs in traditional blankets with more heavy goods in their hands, a total contradiction to their size. They seemed superhero like, but with a witchy undertone. Definitely made of strong stuff these women, reminiscent of the older matriarchs you would find back in the day in Ireland, and I tipped my imaginary bowler hat to them.

One Cholita boarded the bus and had no interest in sitting down, instead standing directly above our seats. With packages sprawled around her feet she smiled down at us with a mouth full of gold, and her fragrant armpit in Rob's face. She had a parcel on her back. I thought it must be corn or potatoes to stock up or sell in her village, until suddenly the package started wailing. She didn't even bat an eyelid at the racket, instead called to the driver that her stop had come, jumped down off the bus, and a wide-eyed baby popped its head out. It was screeching and swinging from side to side as she made her way up a hill, the Cholita version of rocking the cradle – a reminder to expect the unexpected in the mischievous South America.

Another woman boarded carrying a big doctor style bag made of carpet. In it for the long haul, she reached inside to put her items up on the shelf as the bag itself wouldn't fit. Then, like a scene from Mary Poppins, a stream of endless products appeared from what seemed like a bottomless black hole. I half expected some tweeting birds and Dick Van Dyke to make an appearance, before she happily sat down. The shelf above packed to the rafters with all sorts.

It was evening before we arrived in Copacabana, and before we did anything else we parked ourselves in a quiet little courtyard bar for a couple of beers, and to tap up the Wi-

Fi as we had forgotten the name of the hotel, again. The bar also had a resident parrot perched across from our table. The lady of the manor popped up to take our order, and then ran out to the shop to buy the beers – they obviously weren't used to such a high alcohol demand! She returned with a smile and cracked open the warm brews, which we were grateful for after the long bus ride. A much older lady stood contently watching over the yard, and she spoke back and forth with the parrot in more Spanish than I could muster, rub it in or what!

After ditching our first choice of hotel when the receptionist, a frightening character who was totally off his tits, presented himself, we found another and headed out to explore. On the Copacabana strip, we were drawn to a restaurant with a huge reclaimed and pimped up Harley Davidson outside. Paintings of retro flamenco dancers adorned the walls, you know like you would see a your nan's house, hung alongside lots of quirky local art work.

As we ate and drank a conveyor belt of cocktail concoctions, we got to speaking about what had taken us on this trip. While he munched down on his second main course – boy that lad can eat – Rob told me more about why he was taking some months out from his studies to become a doctor and all about his family back in the Netherlands. His family seemed like a tight-knit group, and from the off I could tell that my new pal had a lot of love and support behind him. As the drink flowed, the conversations got a little deeper. Having previously skimmed over the reasons behind my trip, he asked about what had actually brought me away and about my family.

Discussing my family always made me feel a bit like Oliver Twist or Orphan Annie, but I decided to try and stop worrying about what people thought, and I felt I could trust Rob. The liquor-oiled emotional gates opened, probably further than I had intended and Rob had expected, but it felt right to talk there in that quirky little spot on the shores of Lake Titicaca. I told him about how the previous few years, especially this last year, had been the worst of my thirty-six on the planet so far. They were just too much to take. Grey hairs had started appearing in my beard. Something had to give before a darker and final decision took everything away instead.

I spoke about my dad passing away and the enormous pressure of the situation. I told him about things going tits up with my ex, the frustration of it all, how we hadn't spoken in four months, and the fact that I still missed that face dreadfully every day, but was trying to remain strong and focus on me now.

Before I drifted too far off into the memories, I snapped back to reality to see Rob in front of me listening intently with his eyes filling up. I felt really bad as the last thing I wanted was to depress this happy chap who was on his adventures too. But he told me not to be silly and that he felt honoured I felt comfortable enough in his presence to share some of my story. I knew there and then I'd made the right choice travelling with this top Dutch dude, and felt the first real backpacking bond of my travels. It was a heart warming feeling, and I started to feel like this trip might just help me to start healing.

We both totally crashed out that night, a tip-top sleep in our hotel away from bunk bed dorms, and the 3am wake up calls of noisy hostel life. Next morning we took a boat trip to Isle Del Sol, an island two hours out into the massive freshwater lake. We were greeted by, well, not much on arrival, apart from a man speaking very quick Spanish and some hairy pigs paddling in the still waters. After a translation from a Catalonian passenger, it turned out we had to pay this guy 10 Bolivians (approx £1) for entry to the island's heritage sites and a guided tour. Not being any the wiser we followed the guide up along the island paths, and didn't understand a word the whole way.

We passed islanders selling souvenirs and reached a gargantuan holy rock with a gentleman sitting opposite, who started, I think, explaining the history of the place using historical looking items on the stone table in from of him, again me not understanding a syllable and at this stage just making it up in my head. The rock was shaped like a puma, if you looked closely enough, a prominent symbolic animal in these parts, and following the guide's movements we all laid our hands on the it to invoke some of its positive energy, which was actually a really lovely and peaceful moment. Then it was onto an ancient stone maze, and the most I got from Speedy Gonzales was that it used to be some sort of fort to protect the island. Finally zoning out of the tour, I took in the islands beauty, with its gleaming seas, the hot sun reflecting off the ripples and with contrasting snow capped mountains as a back drop.

It was then back to the boat, passing a school on the way where the kids were playing basketball in the courtyard and donkeys roamed past the gates, to take a short trip to the south of the island. There seemed to be more life and electricity down south, with beach front hostels and restaurants. We had some lunch while looking out at the mountains and lake, and I tried to soothe my scorched ears from the crossing, before heading back to the mainland.

The boat ride back across the vast lake brought about a feeling of contentment, like I was settling into backpacking life and the realisation that this wasn't a regular holiday and I didn't need to fill every day with activities. That it might be ok to be alone with my thoughts. Backpacking was my new way of living for the foreseeable, so I tried to settle into the freedom, breathe in the air, and lap up the absence of the self-constructed and unnecessary daily pressures. I was even getting used to living out of two bags, although I had packed with coordinated military precision, every colour and garment could make at least two or three 'outfits'. But I now understood that this was enough, and I didn't need the extra three wardrobes I left behind in my friend Ewan's attic. As the days passed I started to feel the hefty chains of the life I left behind losing their grip a tiny bit at a time. I knew there was still so much to sort through and get my head around, but the free time and ever changing environments were helping me understand and dissect some emotional cycles.

The contentment was soon marred by memories creeping up, memories on repeat which as always knocked the wind out of my sails. But there and then I decided to challenge this pattern, and to start the declutter. I had to start with addressing one of the biggest catalysts in deciding to leave. Now a month into my journey, and with the previous evening's open conversations still in my head, it was on this boat ride back where I decided to write to my ex.

It was so frustrating that even here on the other side of the world, the gut wrenching hurt and heartache hadn't budged, so much so that at times I felt impaled by it. What if as the months rolled by I kept on thinking, missing and longing? I hated that these emotions might never leave. At night would that face still pop into my head? Were there even more restless days ahead? On treks through jungles or when swimming in crystal clear waters, would I still drift back, forever reminded? I knew there was no going back to the relationship, my friends would have had me sectioned if I even tried, but the frustration and anger at myself for not doing it all differently from the start, and the love I still felt, blurred that reality with hope.

It's funny, I'm very much a believer in never losing hope, all over the world people say it on a daily basis, but I needed to lose this particular hope, now more than ever.

I needed to breakthrough this blanketed cloud above my head, step off this troubled path, and it felt right to do it now, to say it all with bravery and honesty. This was my time to be honest with myself, and also the person who was still very much on my mind every day. So with my head buried in my phone, forsaking the return journey views and crisping up even more in the blazing sun, I just wrote and wrote and wrote. My fingers ached from tapping the keys but I couldn't stop.

I addressed my part in the relationship failing, my wrongs, my flaws, our good and our bad, my honest view of it all. As I wrote I realised maybe I had been looking for too much, maybe for this person to save me, in a tornado of hurt and my life crumbling around me at the time, and that maybe that wasn't fair. Then my sensible side stepped in, questioning why some ground rules weren't set in place at the start, one grown up chat which I should have insisted on would have helped everything, and which I kicked myself for not doing. Together we weren't sensible though, and I guess that was part of the fun. But on the flip side when it inevitably went wrong, I ended up feeling like the one who constantly wanted to 'talk', like some nagging fishwife. These talks were pained and we threaded lightly, temporary Band-Aids, which never really got us anywhere for long.

The brakes had been slammed on our relationship so quickly at times, worse than anything when it was too late for me to put my walls back up. Dizzying and confusing, every word and action magnified. If only I had seen the obvious signs from the start, that longevity was there within reach. Instead I let my fears of rejection and initial defences blinker me and I sped past them, hoping to wing it like I did most things. I felt angry that I wasn't given some slack, real understanding of who I was, some time to air all my demons and show my flaws and move forward together. That's what couples do, right? Why was I expected to be the perfect package so quickly, at least that's how it felt sometimes. Or maybe the hurt, and the clambering to save the relationship just wouldn't let me see straight at all. All these frustrating instances took us away from why we were together in the first place, and knocked the fun and laughs off course, of which there was lots when it was good. When it was good it was real good; that, I will always be sure of.

Before I placed useless blame on either side, I reiterated the fundamentals, stripped it back to our connection.

Above the miscommunication and silliness, we had something beyond just a sexual bolt. The certainty that neither of us had ever met anyone like the other before. And that I had fallen hard and had just wanted it to work.

But being a relationship moron, I didn't know how to do it right, or even know how to be myself. Summarising these things in your head can drive you crazy, the 'what if's, the 'if only's and the questions. The cringeworthy moments pop in too, like why did I drunkenly piss on the floor in the spare bedroom on our first night together thinking I was in the toilet. Why did I let fun moments become draining and patience testing. I knew it was all out of fear and worry of losing the relationship, my fear of those moments never happening again. Which led to losing it all anyway.

But I was on this new journey, and I had to try and let go, to let the hurt subside, to let the person who had felt like my almost everything move on, and find happiness elsewhere.

Realising that my vision of the fairytale reconciliation was pathetic in their eyes, no doubt replaced with a 'better off without me' stance, now so far removed from what we had, and probably onto a safer bet. Having given up on me. It was a hard pill to swallow, knowing that someone else will probably get the best of that person. Timing and behaviour have never quite been on my side. But the wallowing and any bitterness subsided quickly, a feeling I don't ever entertain or engage with for long anyway, and there it was.

Sharp, to the point, honest and laid bare, written in front of me, forever private words which would hopefully be the start of the healing for us both. Approaching the islands south shore, my finger hovered over the send button, and a sick feeling came into my stomach. Would it even be read, would the reply cause even more hurt and knock me back again? But in order to move forward I had to have courage. Sent.

That evening I wondered about the response, would there even be one, would it be taken wrong, would it make things worse? Why was I putting myself through this, was it best to just say nothing and move forward? No, the impact of this relationship on my life had been too monumental. I decided to tackle any anxiety there and then, and knew that if nothing else I'd been true to me, and realised that unless I addressed these things with truthfulness and honesty I would never start to heal my heart.

To take my mind off it, I contacted a fellow traveller whom I'd met briefly in Cusco and was in town, and that evening met up with Christian from Germany. There really isn't much to do in Copacabana, apart from eating and drinking on the strip, but a drink sounded perfect after all the heavy thoughts and typing. The strip reminded me of being on holiday in Gran Canaria or Ibiza's west end, with PR guys waving menus one after the other trying to get you into their establishments. I did the universal yellow pages walking symbol and the 'we'll be back down in a minute' sign language routine, hoping they would get the gist and piss off. That final night of our short stay we settled on a bar called Nemos, which had some hippies jamming outside. It looked livelier than the rest so we drifted in and watched the local gypsy band, along with their dog, take the stage to play familiar covers in a Gogol Bordello style.

After a crazy dream filled and anxious sleep, I woke up that next morning and hesitantly checked my emails on Rob's computer. The reply was there. I felt sick as I opened it. But as I read, very much to my surprise, it couldn't have been better. Every point from our relationship was addressed with surprising openness, both writing with kindness, our joint desire to stop any more pain and hurt was paramount.

Once I would have seen this as a window, a chance to try and start again, to hold hands and take the leap, to build on and learn from our history. At least it would never be boring. But something stronger stopped me in my tracks: I knew then that it was time for us both to move on and try and be happy in our lives.

A few emails followed back and forth that morning, but the urge to try and rekindle our relationship was nipped in the bud. So as we both signed off, we knew we still had nothing but respect for each other.

I felt so proud reading that reply. I knew it wouldn't have been easy to write, and even though my heart still hurt, I still felt the love, and missed what could've been desperately, it was my time to move forward with some peace too.

As myself and Rob dubiously travelled back to La Paz that afternoon, I knew thoughts of my ex would still creep in over the days, weeks and months ahead, and there would always be a love and kindness between us. I thought about how I would process all this, and although there would still be hard days, just wishing to have that person in your arms, at least now I had a new foundation, and clear air to breath. What a pair eh, such a silly loss, but I guess love doesn't always turn out pretty.

Chapter 6

La Paz would be my base for the next few days. It's hard to know what to make of this sprawling place, and its split personality. The cable cars high above the city transport people up from the centre to the suburb of El Alto and its sprawling market. The city's sheer magnitude is magnificent, thousands of terracotta buildings as far as the eye can see, rising up from and covering an entire valley. Mainly unfinished, with exposed bricks and sections still under construction, but with splashes of colour on their metal roofs. A local guy told me that this incomplete state of the buildings is because the inhabitants pay a lot less tax if they don't paint or plaster their homes and shops, hence the blanketed uniformed colour.

We were in the belly of the beast, its air filled with lead from the exhausts of the non-stop traffic, which didn't help me breathing the already thin air at that altitude. The majority of the central buildings are very run down with messy facades, including the bad choice of hostel I was staying in. Compared to its neighbours, Bolivia isn't a rich country at all, and that's reflected in the cheap prices of food and entertainment, but the people here are a very resourceful and entrepreneurial lot. There seemed to be barely any beggars on the streets, instead an endless stream of stalls and shops. The market up in El Alto embodied this proactive spirit, the stall owners selling everything from puppies and kippers to truck parts and knickers.

Backpackers from all over the world relish in the nightlife here, cheap clubs filled with dodgy characters and tanked up visitors. There was talk in the hostel 'rooftop' bar – more like a decrepit greenhouse – of a cocaine bar, which may be part of the lure too. The hostel came complete with mainly arrogant and idiotic bar staff, who apparently only worked there for their food and lodging, much to the annoyance of the punters who had to deal with them. I bumped into a couple of Welsh girls, Hayley and Sam, there one morning, and even after an eighteen hour journey wild dogs couldn't keep them in this dump. I tried to throw myself into the nightlife, and did have a laugh with Rob and some new people we met, but I couldn't wait to get out of the place. I even thought about shacking up in said illusive cocaine bar just to get out of the chaos, but in my delicate mental state that would've been one trip too far.

I did however take the cable car ride up to El Alto by myself one afternoon and enjoyed wandering around the tourist free open air aisles. Knowing that 'pollo' means chicken, I ordered that and left the rest of my lunch in the hands of the Cholita chef, it turned out to be the best grub I had in ages. On the way back down I glided over the city's cemetery, which blew my mind. Instead of the usual field of graves it looked like a school campus, rows of buildings about six stories high dotted with little windows where the coffins were slotted in, all adorned with flowers and other memorials to lost loved ones. A huge white church towering above. A genius and quirky solution, in this tightly packed metropolis.

It sparked a memory of when I was a kid at the annual patron back home, a day to remember the dead where people would descend on the town's main graveyard to pay their respects. It was always packed with people, especially gypsies. I remember one year when attending with me da I witnessed a harrowing scene, one of the travelling men with a grey beard started having a fit. He fell to the ground in convulsions and turned bright purple. I'm not sure if he survived, but I'd never seen anything like that before.

Talking of the cable cars, a backpacking Dutch girl told me she had taken the same car line a week or so before with three blonde Scandinavians friends. With only them in the car, a creepy man jumped in after them and sat in the corner. They tried to ignore him but he seemed jittery the whole way up. By the time they had reached the summit it transpired that he had been having a tommy tank the entire time as he watched the exotic blondes – the dirty old bastard. One of the girls was only 17 years old and on her first trip away from home, so I think it scarred her. Luckily for them, security had stopped the greasy perv from getting back in before he could have another fiddle on the way down. Thankfully this kind of, let's say, sticky situation, hadn't happened to me on my glide up. Worst I got was a gummy smile from the old guy and his misses sat opposite.

In need of a change of scene, it was time to tackle a bit of dare devil biking. The Death Road challenge. A four hour teeth-gritting ride down one of the worlds most dangerous roads, basically a rocky dirt path descent from 4000 feet, with nothing between you and the vertical drop into the jungle hollow below. We choose a biking company that was half the price of the more established ones, which probably shouldn't be the priority when undertaking such a risky ride, but we were on a budget. On top of a windswept mountain, we donned our gear, a retro black, blue and neon yellow outfit that was almost identical to a shell suit I had back in the Nineties.

The first part of the ride was downhill on a main tarmac road to reach the starting point of the Death Road, and after a team talk we were off. There was definitely no speeding this time round, the road was covered with sharp rocks and gravel, requiring total concentration,. I even had to remind myself to look up and take in the astounding views on the decent. The entire ride felt like sitting on top of a washing machine on spin cycle, with vibrations from the severe track rippling through my body, especially my arms. We heard from the guides on the way down why this infamous track has earned its morbid name. They relayed stories of recent and past tragedies to make the point of just how dangerous taking on this challenge can be. If that wasn't enough, the various crucifixes along the way to mark lives lost were a stark reminder to go steady and concentrate.

At one stop we came across what looked like a photo shoot, but was actually Bolivia's version of The Spice Girls, called Las Luminosas shooting a new music video. We jumped in for some snaps with these girls in all their glitz, a total contradiction to the harsh yet beautiful surrounding landscape. Only one of our group fell off along the way, thankfully only suffering some bruising, and after almost four hours, with the last leg being the hardest and most dodgy, we all crossed the finish line. Still intact and looked after brilliantly by the youngest company on the road. Heavy going but definitely exhilarating.

After the high came the lows, and emotions took over when back in the city. I felt pretty homesick and the bleak surroundings of the accommodation wasn't helping. Friends who have backpacked previously had told me there would be days like this, but with me they became magnified. The smallest triggers would have depression clawing at my back and bring other feelings and thoughts bubbling to the surface. The only thing for it was to message friends back in the UK and Ireland for a release. I was determined not to let these waves of depression blur the days together, or at the very least not allow it to last as long it wanted to anymore. I endeavoured

101

to suck it up, and went to watch a Cholita wrestling match – yes you heard correct – to take my mind off it, and told myself that the day would pass and I could start again tomorrow, that tomorrow would be better. And it was, not only because I was leaving La Paz behind, but because I was setting off on a three day trek to see the place I've been most excited for: The Salt Flats of Bolivia.

A three day and two night tour starting in the Wild West style town of Uyuni and finished by taking us across the boarder into Chile. We rendezvoused at the tour company's office and got divided into two Land Cruisers. Our new pack included the fun loving brothers from Glasgow, Fraser and Gregor, whom I had previously seen on the Machu Picchu trip, along with Jools and Adam, a couple from Sydney, Sofie from The Netherlands, Christian and Kirsten, brother and sister from California, and friends Charlotta and Janna from Germany, aka Hansel and Gretel, as I would come to call them. Packed up and raring to go, we set off with our drivers-cum-guides, both called Luis, and onto our first stop just outside of town, the train graveyard. A young lad's dream, full of old western type trains from as far back as 1886, which had been parked up here and left to a rusty end of the line eternity. I was in my element, climbing and swinging from the carriages and driver's car, re-enacting fight scenes from Bond or Indiana Jones with Rob on the roofs while jumping from carriage to carriage, a dusty adventure paradise.

It was then onto a factory to see how the villagers produce an income from the vast sea of gleaming white salt ahead of us. It was a pretty basic factory where manual labour successfully overpowered any modern machinery. Salt from this and similar refineries is transported all over South America, but surprisingly not exported abroad as it's apparently not worth the minimal profit. I got a perplexed look off another guide who caught me taking selfies with a big pile of the salt, pretending it was another South American white export – so juvenile. Factory ticked of the list, we sped off into the white horizon towards the centre of the flats. First we stopped to visit an old building constructed out of salt which used to be a hotel. There was a gang of bikers out front, parked in the shadows of flags from all around the world which blew manically from metal poles spiked into the salt. A travellers stamping site which sent an adventurous shiver up my spine.

Onward to the flats we chugged, after an hour or so arriving at a solitary spot with nothing around only the mountains far far in the distance. It might sound weird getting so excited about some salt but this place is magical. Nothing but the howling wind interrupted the silence, an expansive white abyss flooded with brightness, pure and simple, with only the salty veins running through the ground below disrupting its perfection.

Because of the landscape and how its vastness alters perspectives, many people create their our own photo shoots here, and for the next two hours, which seemed like only twenty minutes, we did the same and got lost in the fun. There was props galore, toy dinosaurs provided by the guides, and an empty cheese Pringles can provided by me. The altered perspectives made us all look like tiny Borrorwers running scared from the prehistoric giants or as if we were jumping out of the can. I brought along some toys I'd found in the El Alto market too, a fat little baby with a wonky eye, a Spider-Man with huge fists, Leonardo from the Teenage Mutant Turtles, and a camp Princess from The Princess and The Frog, in sort of seductive come to bed pose, but we scrapped her as she kept blowing over. Knowing I would probably never be here again, I thought fuck it. I dropped my kecks and let it all hang out for a bare arse picture, my dangling leprechaun blew freely in the salty breeze, tickled by the winds. It was a liberating feeling indeed, and another thing ticked off the bucket list.

We drove on and came to a site that shows nature knows no limits on this planet of ours and life can truly endure any harsh environment. Cactus Island arose from the horizon, and the reflections on the salt made it look like we were driving on glass or still water as we approached this prickly beast. A mass of rock and earth covered in weird and wonderfully shaped giants. I trekked up to the top of the island and surveyed the surrounding white wilderness. Thankfully none of the inhabitants of tarantulas or scorpions made an appearance. That night we all slept in a hostel with salt walls and salt beds, and I got a nasty taste in my mouth after licking a wall to see if it really was salt. The desert temperature dropped to minus 10 degrees, so my rental sleeping bag was definitely worth the fiver. It was a nice feeling to be tucked up all cosy in such a crazy place, and I felt proud of myself for shaking off the clambering dark mood from a few days before.

With no showers on hand it was a thorough wet wipe wash the next morning before jumping in the 4X4s. Luis' sick playlist accompanied the journey, Mr Probz Waves and Jess Glynne tracks filling the air. Embarking on this, the busiest day of the trek, brought us through so many different landscapes and weather systems I was unsure if we were still even on the same continent. Leaving the salt behind we crossed frozen rivers, grey slate fields and dusty deserts with huge rock formations that could've been from the set of the Flintstones or Star Wars movies. The last inhabited stop of the day was at a small town called Saint Augustine and our last chance to buy booze and use a real toilet. I opted for a whiskey sized bottle of some sort of 27% proof menthol liquor, which cost the equivalent of £1.

Alcohol safely packed, we drove into the valley of the llamas, a lush green blanket against a rocky and unforgiving backdrop, where llama farmers kept their prize stock to frolic about and munch on the moist grass. What else was there to do here apart from, well, chase the funny creatures around the field. I'm not sure the llamas felt the same buzz, but it at least shook up their grass munching existence for a while.

Llama-chasing makes you hungry, so the guides decided we would stop for lunch in the shadow of a huge volcano, as you do. The meals on this trek were turning out to be some of the best I'd eaten in well over a month. This was also the spot where my inner Bear Grylls came out. Thinking I had done well by licking a dirty salt wall and not gagging, and by having a wet wipe bath that morning, was nothing compared to what happened next, which surprised me more than anyone. Nature called, literally, and with no alternative in sight, I climbed up the volcanic rubble, squatted down and shat behind a rock, with nothing between me and the great outdoors except some grass caressing my arse. Real adventure stuff right there, but I was grateful that there was some wet wipes left. I thankfully wasn't pounced on by an angry puma either. It was only after the act that I was told they roam the area freely, sniffing out their next lunch.

Our next mission was to drive up to 5000 meters above sea level to the highest desert in the world, the Atacama. I now understood why the travel company had decided on the name Red Planet as its calling card. Another landscape change, but this time it genuinely looked like we had landed on Mars. Dusty red rocks and soil as far as the eye could see, and freezing pounding winds that made it almost impossible to even open the car door and see the flamingo stomping ground we had stopped at. I love flamingos, there's something very eighties Miami about these splendid birds. I was a little disappointed with this first encounter though, no sea of pink unfolded before me, they just kept flying off further across the lake. But the disappointment was short lived, after another drive we arrived at the Red Lake, and there we were met by ten times more birds who were not at all bothered by humans creeping up to take a selfie. This lake was also blocked off from the high winds, so a much more enjoyable spot for glam bird watching. The rest of the penultimate day consisted of more desert visits, taking in poisonous lakes, geysers bellowing out sulphur and hot steam and reaching the highest point of the tour.

That night we stayed at a basic hostel which even though there was no running water, the electricity cut off at 10pm and the toilet smelled like the end of a week at a festival, I found it fine and dandy. This place had something extra though, open air hot springs. In the pitch dark after our group dinner, with only a small torch for light, myself and the team slipped on our speedos and bikinis. With booze in hand we ran through the freezing night air to spend the next couple of hours in the naturally hot waters. We all raised our bottles and gave a cheers under a blanketed sky full to bursting with twinkling stars. Relative strangers all submerged in a dark pool hiding from the blistering winds, just talking about our lives and journeys so far. The stars danced above us. We had all been getting on really well, especially myself and the two Scottish brothers, and it was here as the hot steam met with the icy cold air and the alcohol took affect that myself and Fraser had a heart to heart. Talking about all sorts from our relationship with the booze, to our parents, our histories and childhoods.

The combination of both discussions about alcohol and our parents brought me back to my saddest place yet. I explained to Fraser that after my mam's funeral the council plonked us into a bedsit in George's Street in Wexford, and it was miserable. My dad was in despair, he had always drank lots, as was the norm with working class and poor Irish men and women. But with me mam gone, the drinking increased to uncontrollable levels and I just wanted to get away from him. I begged him to take me back to London to let me live with my aunts, or with my friend's families in Wexford, or to just put me into a home. I was so afraid of the demon he became when drinking to numb his own pain. To this day I still get nervous when I hear a late night key in the door.

I tried to convince myself it was all a dream. That I would wake up and find mam standing there, and all would return to how it was, or that God would instead take my dad and return her to me. These thoughts crippled me with guilt, thinking such awful things about me da, but I hated who he became in drink and wanted it all to stop.

With his drinking and subsequent outbursts becoming worse, I would do anything to get away from him, trying to get out of the bedsit so he couldn't hit or shout at me. But I wasn't tall enough and could never reach the latch on the heavy main door in the building, and would have to go back inside and sit through the chaos and him lashing out. Until eventually he fell asleep or the guilt would wash over him and he would say sorry through heart wrenching tears.

We were lost far out to sea in a tremendous storm of hurt. Me da was unable to deal with his feelings, especially with his past never far off, haunting him profusely. It was a horrible time for us both, I was so young and I didn't understand it, but underneath it all the love never wavered.

When the drink wasn't involved I loved being with my dad. I had my own little saddle on his pushbike's crossbar and we would go to the seaside, the country or to visit his friends or my aunts, uncles and cousins. I got to be known affectionately as Poor Larry, or Little Larry as I spent so much time in other people's houses like an Oliver Twist character. He took me everywhere and when I wasn't with him I was with my friends or cousins. Their mums and most of the women in my life wanted to look after me, which I embraced wholeheartedly, clinging to any sort of family unit. They would see me, a tiny kid on the bike and me da in his early fifties scooting me around the place. Sometimes he would drop me off with my friend's ma, saying he would be back in a few hours, and not come back for a week. I embraced it when this happened, because I was away from his temper and outbursts. But after a while I would always feel bad for him and the pain he was going through.

My hatred for drinking increased, I would close my eyes daily and wish alcohol and pubs were never invented. It was a contradiction in my life, because in a way I liked being in the pubs with him before he got drunk, as it meant I could be around my friends and their families. There was always an amazing atmosphere, the craic being had and songs filling the smoky air. Me and my little compadres would munch like pigs on packets of Tayto crisps and guzzle red lemonade. I dreaded dinner time ahead though, especially if it was a drunken cooked meal – I didn't think it could get much worse than the sober ones.

As time went on it got harder for my dad to control me. He loved me to absolute pieces and he tried his best, but he didn't know what to do with this kid who could be a massive handful, and who desperately needed a mother figure. We made visits to a family who lived in a detached house on the outer part of town, near the graveyard where my mam was buried. Subsequently the dad of that family visited us in the bedsit. He must have been a social worker, because that's when it was decided. To give both me and me da a break

I would go live in a children's home, on an estate called Walnut Grove.

I was mega-excited by this, mainly thinking of all the lovely dinners, clean living and no more anxiety or being scared to death hearing the latch go at night. I had all my teddy bears lined up and ready to go, and moved into the home the following week. I shared a room with some other kids and had my own bunk bed. It was all new and exciting at first and everyone was super nice. But quickly it felt very alien to me and I missed my dad. Within two weeks I decided I couldn't leave him. I packed up my suitcase early one morning and ran away, back to the bedsit and to open arms and tears from my dad. It was decided there and then that there would be no more homes for me. We had each other and we would make it work somehow.

A holler from one of the guides telling us it was late brought the chatting to an end and back to the intoxicated present. The freshness of the night air sobered us up. That evening was truly remarkable and a humbling end to this once in a lifetime trip across the Salt Flats of Bolivia. For one couple the trip was extra special, as he proposed to his missus quietly away from the rest of us in the springs, and she said yes. On the way out of the pools and shivering like a wet dog, I burst into the changing area as the happy couple were lovingly drying each other off. Breathing heavily, freezing me nips off with a willy like a peanut from the cold, ruining their loving moment – awkward!

And so came the end to the Bolivian leg of my travels, we all hugged and said our goodbyes that next morning before switching jeeps and just four of our group – myself, Rob, Gregor and Fraser – heading to the Chilean boarder, and the rest back to Uyumi. I was really grateful I ended up with such a decent and fun group, and even though most of us might never see each other again, we all knew that these past few days, and that spectacular night under the stars, would be etched in all our minds forever.

Chapter 7

Crossing the border from Bolivia to Chile could not have brought a bigger change. Gone were the howling desert winds and coarse terrain, and before us lay sun-drenched greenery, with smooth motorways slicing through. It's crazy, the complete change of environment an hour's drive can bring.

I had found a hostel with a real hippy vibe just five minutes outside the town of San Pedro de Atacama, with its white washed walls, chilled atmosphere and colourful flowers adorning the main square. Myself, Rob, Fraser and Gregor checked in. There was hammocks in the yard, a mega-cute resident Alsatian puppy sprawled out in the sun and, praise the baby Jesus, hot showers. After scrubbing the desert dust away, we headed back into the main square which was full of backpackers to sit outside a restaurant and bask in the sun. All amazing apart from finding half of someone's weave in my steak – nice. The embarrassed waiter came and apologised, took the hairy rump away and decided to ply me with free beer for the afternoon, which was fine and dandy with me, but through beer vision I somehow still ended up paying for the steak, slippery little fucker that waiter!

Our hostel was throwing a BBQ that evening. Earlier we had bumped into the Scottish lad's previous travel buddies, and the same trio of Scousers from my Sun Gate trek, Natalia, Steve and Jonny, so invited them along. Stocked up on copious amounts of very cheap booze, we all headed back to our free spirited abode in a taxi-cum-pick-up truck. Four lads in the back like redneck honky tonks clutching onto our liquor on the bumpy sun-baked road. We all sat around a bonfire as the sparks drifted up into the fresh night air, eating, drinking and laughing. Myself and the muscular hostel owner bantered back and forth, which somehow ended up with our tops off doing bodybuilding poses, which had most of the guests cracking up and left some not knowing where to look. Casanova Rob managed to pull himself a lil lady too and stumbled off into the hallway with her.

The night was filled with drunken hilarity. Sitting huddled together around the fire watching the sparks shoot off into the desert sky, I felt a real sense of pride because of the brotherly bond I'd formed with Rob, Fraser and Gregor. Even thought I'd only known this group for a short while, especially the Scousers, being part of it made me feel happy.

I was surprised to find I was actually enjoying all the moving around. I thought all I yearned for these days was to be settled after all the upping sticks we did until my teenage years.

As my face got redder from the flames of the fire, or maybe the booze, I thought back to the only time I ever felt settled, and somewhat happy growing up. Moving around with me da had became a natural part of my life back then. We never stayed anywhere for more than a year or so, but then came a Godsend. With the help of me dad's friends who had influence in the council, we finally got a proper house, not just another temporary dwelling, but a permanent place in the housing estate called Maudlintown where my dad grew up. It had two bedrooms upstairs, a parlour downstairs which became my room, a front and back garden and, best of all, a shower which we never had before. The new house was right next door to my auntie, my uncle was just around the corner, and my cousins were over the road. Lots of my best friends lived there too. I truly hoped this might finally be our real home. I was so ecstatic, because apart from London, Maudlintown was the only place I ever felt at home. We had lived there briefly in my nan's house when my mam was alive, and I always longed to go back. My gang were all there, the two Billys, Mur, Stephen, Alan, Tommy, Davey, Fran, Damien, Pigsy, Tricia, June, Shirley, Mary, Sinead, Naidy, Julieanne, Laura, Danielle, Christopher, Rebecca, Lynn, Warren and all the rest of my the Maudlintown massive, too many to list but all part of that amazing place.

To me, this council housing estate was magic, it was tough and raw, but with an enormous sense of community. It had a big green for us to play on, with annual play schemes when all the kids could take part in the fancy dress competitions, games like tug of war, or activities like painting the walls with bright nautical or summer scenes. The estate was right next to the sea too and the train track ran along side it. We got up to all sorts of mischief, playing around the old factories and breaking the windows with catapults, gallivanting down the railway track, know as 'the line', where we'd let the train crush our pennies and skim stones out to sea. We'd built forts anywhere we could or sneak through the farmer's fields, hoping he wouldn't shoot us in the arse with his pellet gun, to go swim in the hidden deep ponds where we could swing off a rope into the water. We played rounders or went on adventures to The Rocks, a rugged countryside area with huge rock formations protruding from the earth. We dared each other to ride the wild horses in the fields bareback or to climb up and sit in the Devil's Chair, which was just a rock that looked like a chair, but the tales that Satan himself had sat in it terrified me. There was always orchards to rob, scrambling over the stone walls to grab as many crab apples or gooseberries as we could before getting caught, but never being able to eat them because they were always too sour and gave me belly ache.

We built go-karts from bits of wood and carpets and raced them down the hill outside my house. The estate had a local shop where we would buy penny sweets from the shopkeeper, who we used to torment until he chased us out or barred us again. We watched the annual boat regatta from the bank side while munching on cola bottles and Refreshers, making dopey faces to each other with the milk teeth sweets. In mass each week, we sat together and ended up laughing to the point where I could barely breathe, amid frowns of disapproval from the older people.

I set up a stall in our front passage and sold my toys to my friends, quite the little entrepreneur. I constantly had clubs going on in our shed in the back yard. Anything from a nature to an adventure club, and I would throw the biggest birthday parties and invite everyone around, giving them goodie bags as they left, like a little social butterfly.

There was two local pubs across the Green, Brady's and The Dolphin, where me da drank and where lots of the kids would go with their parents. He still drank a lot, was still angry and hurting and still lashed out at times. I started to lash out too: fighting or getting into trouble. But whether I misbehaved or not, the booze never seemed to differentiate. If he was drunk and in the wrong mood he would still start arguing with me. Because I had so much else going on around me in our new home I didn't notice his drinking as much, so it was less consuming. But I still feared his temper.

On days out together and if we didn't catch the train, where me da hid in the toilet to avoid the fare, we would walk down along the tracks or cycle down to Rosslare Strand and the surrounding countryside. We'd visit the dump on our walks to see if we could find anything decent in the mounts of scrap. I found a book of cocktail recipes once and decided I was going to be the next Tom Cruise, and open my own exotic cocktail bar in Miami or the Caribbean.

When we moved back to Maudlintown I was determined to take part in the pub's yearly miming competition, begging my dad not to take me off anywhere on the bike that day. I even asked the landlady of the pub to change the day so I could be part of it. Thankfully me da caved in, and I was soon working out choreography with one of my best friend's sisters, Ann, who I had a massive crush on. I performed my version of Bruce Willis' and The Drifters' 'Under the Boardwalk' in the first competition, and Bon Jovi's 'Living on a Prayer' in the following one, only to be beaten by my friend's older brother and his group also taking on the New Jersey Gods with their version of 'You Give Love a Bad Name'. I used to walk past a girl called Kerri, who performed Tiffany's hit 'I Think We're Alone Now', with my jacket hanging off one shoulder and hoping she would notice me. Unsurprisingly she never did.

Maudlintown was an exciting place to be, with a tremendous community spirit, and it let me be a kid again. Living next door to my aunt Lily, the matriarch of the family, was at times challenging. She could be so funny and caring but fierce too, but it didn't matter because she was family and I loved her, and I loved being close to all my cousins and best mates, playing in their houses and gardens. Whilst living there the sadness seemed to ease up for a while, and though I still longed for a family unit, for the first time since my mam died it wasn't so engrossing. I still wondered what life was like across the sea back in London, and would we ever go back? I had been badgering me da to take me back for so long, but being in Maudlintown definitely helped ease that longing.

After mam died, my da had a support network around the town: his friends, relatives and my mam's sisters were always willing to take care of me and help out. Although he would never give me up, he would allow me to stay with other people, which I was more than happy to do.

My mam's sisters were always there, especially Carrie, Breda and Annette. Carrie reminded me of my mam, she had such kindness and never stopped running around the place, even with three boys of her own she did, and still does, love me like her son. I always felt welcomed by my aunt Breda too, a hilariously funny woman with an unbeatable strength.

We were close to the Hendricks family who lived in the Talbot Green part of town, the ones me da had left me with for a few hours, aka a week. Breda, the mum, ate the head off him for that trick, but you couldn't be mad at me da for long. She would always help when she could, and I loved hanging out with the Hendricks clan. Other family friends, Eileen Nolan and her sister Patricia, back in Maudlintown would welcome me as their own too. I was at Eileen's house almost every Saturday for dinner, myself and the Nolan gang would watch Gladiators and Baywatch religiously every week.

Or I would hang out lots at Patricia's with the Kehoe troop. All my best mates. I felt so much part of these families I never wanted to leave. Going to Eileen's only fizzled out when I got older and felt embarrassed turning up on their door step each week like Huckleberry Finn. They might not have been blood, but those ladies and all the families meant the world to me and me da. I developed bonds with them which stay with me to this day, even if I don't see them for long periods.

Sometimes it would hit home that it was just the two of us, like at Christmas when I missed my mam dearly. Especially when all the other mums in Maudlintown would head off to Swansea in Wales to pick up presents from Argos, returning on the coach filled to the rafters with packages and welcomed back by all the kids running along beside the bus. I stayed in the background when the bus returned, tears building in my eyes but not wanting anyone to see. We were still poorer than most back then, and me da was constantly looking for ways to make money, like betting on the horses hoping for a windfall, but he never saw me go without.

On one Christmas Day as kids played on expensive bikes or the newest games consoles, he presented me with a little electric blue tape recorder. I walked around so proudly that Christmas Day with a swagger and my new 'ghetto blaster' placed firmly on my shoulder, my first ever album, the Dirty Dancing soundtrack, or else my other favourites at the time,

Bon Jovi and New Kids on the Block, blaring out. I had an odd fascination with Michael Bolton, so had his albums too.

At Christmas time with me da, even if the turkey came out of the oven undercooked with a green bottom as it did one year – how does that even happen? – without fail he made sure we had enough to eat and a Vienetta ice-cream on the table, which back then was a posh treat.

Those years hold the only contentment I knew growing up. Some days even now I still wish I could go back. When feelings of hopelessness swarm in, I muster up the memory of lying on the Green on a clear sunny day looking up at the drifting clouds, my heart beating softly and the gentle breeze billowing. In those moments the phrase 'don't grow up it's a trap' never ring more true.

The hostel cockerel and my alarm squawked simultaneously the next morning – no rest for the backpacking wicked. With fuzzy heads, Rob and I grabbed some cold pizza. We said goodbye to our pals and hopped onto a bus to the town of Calama to catch a flight to Santiago. What followed in the next fifteen or so hours was a right calamity.

A quick run through: our flight was cancelled, the staff spoke no English, passengers caused havoc both behind the check-in desk and in the restricted security area of the freezing airport – imagine that happening at Heathrow – and our bags were lost. We managed a few hours sleep at a courtesy hotel before going back to the airport again: two free breakfasts, our bags were found (sent ahead on the wrong flight to Santiago the previous evening), checked-in for replacement, but now delayed, flight, and havoc ensues when the other delayed passengers arrived, while myself and Rob mosey on through 'security', Rob with two cans of Coca-Cola in hand.

We got to the gate in time to see the doors about to close on the earlier but 'full' flight. I saw the opportunity and we approached the preoccupied airline girl in a breathy late for a flight manner, and with a look of confusion she tore our ticket stubs and we were through. Both of us ran on to the plane like a scene from Home Alone and nabbed the last two seats. Our heads down, the plane took off and we somehow got away with getting on the wrong flight. We arrived in Santiago with the whole escapade and the rest of the bewildered passengers behind us, result!

Rob and I parted ways in Santiago to check-in to our respective hostels. I had high hopes for my new residence, thinking things could only get better after the airport debacle. My first impressions were not too shabby, until I saw the bed of my new dorm neighbour, the sheets encrusted with a mixture of vomit and take away burgers. Another guy came into the room and saw the disgust on my face, telling me that the skank who inhabits the shit pit hadn't minded sleeping in his own filth for the previous two nights. Not surprisingly, I opted for a different room. I was trying to see the positive in this establishment, putting an extra jumper on from the ice cold air inside and telling myself the bed incident was just part and parcel of backpacking life. Then came the instructions from the owner on how to use the shower, and to coax out even a dribble of hot water you needed a degree in engineering, as well as octopus arms to turn the various knobs and levers simultaneously. After much knob twiddling I thought I'd worked it all out, jumped on in, then straight back out after the icy water hit my legs. After the last twenty-four hours, I though fuck this for a game of soldiers, checked out and turned up at Rob´s hostel. A much nicer place, with the biggest and best shower of the trip so far too, which I stayed under until I resembled one of the pensioners from Cocoon.

Santiago has a touch of Parisian or European influence about it, but mainly a North American feel. The new hostel was in a bohemian area of the city called Bellavista, where the buildings are covered with street art, and the whole place is like a living museum, popping with colour and imagination.

In South America people are always running in and out of busy traffic selling goods like chocolate or tissues, some basing themselves in the fumes all day with their offerings. In downtown Santiago they seemed much more imaginative. Instead of peddling meagre items, they sold their talents. As soon as the lights went red, I saw everything from hip hop dancing to guys juggling kitchen utensils.

At the top of the towering hill that erupts from the centre of the city stands a colossal statue of the Virgin Mary, arms open to embrace the city below. I took an almost vertical tram right to the top. Standing at Mary's feet looking out at the vastness in front of me, I realised just how huge Santiago is, the city spreading as far as the eye could see right back to the snow tipped Andes surrounding it.

At night the Bellavista neighbourhood really comes alive, the long streets packed from side to side with bars and restaurants, and the culture of alfresco dining gives the whole place an exceptional vibe. The speciality dish here is Lomo A Lo Pobre, an enormous mound of chips, meat, and sometimes cheese all topped off with two fried eggs, if that doesn't fill your belly nothing will. On our final night in Santiago, myself, Fraser, Gregor, Rob and Marianne met up for a curry and some very strong cocktails. It felt swell to be with this bunch again before heading off the following day in solo directions.

I made my way down the Chilean coast to the town of Pichilemu, a playground for the world's surfers. On the way from Santiago, I passed vineyards, high trees and lots of forest greenery. At one point the bus came to a halt as some cowboys on horseback roped a couple of stray cattle on the road – you don't get that sight from the Megabus. We stopped at a poorer area just before Pichilemu. A cute little girl and her dad boarded the bus, she bounced into the seat beside me with a cheeky smile and told me her name was Camilla. She must have been about 9 or 10. I could tell she hadn't got much but she seemed like one of the happiest little girls there was. I decided to give her the only toy I had left from the Salt Flats shoot, a Michelangelo Teenage Mutant Turtle action figure, not typically on a little girl's wish list, but she was over the moon. With an enthusiastic wave goodbye and gracias handshake from her dad, she skipped off at the next stop calling back to me 'ciao Larry'. They walked off together hand in hand, and whatever they may have lacked materialistically it was clear they had love in abundance.

Pichilemu isn't a big place, just a sleepy little coastal town with a pleasant seafront, some historical buildings and parks and some colonial style horse drawn carts for the tourists. I was staying in the surfing cove of Punta de Lobos, my hostel for the night was The Sirena Insolente, an ecological and modern surf lodge built of wood and shipping containers. This place had a great feeling and I was welcomed by a group of surfer dudes on their way to catch some waves. After dumping my stuff I took the short stroll down to the beach to watch the lads in action. The day was pretty overcast and cold, and I was told that this part of the Pacific Ocean was even colder due to a swell from the Antarctic. But this didn't stop the thirty or so surfers jumping right in to ride the freezing waves, and you could feel their combined passion, whether novice or pro.

Being near the sea again gave me a warm feeling, and I sat on a rock looking out at the bay remembering when me da took me to Rosslare beach. They had a surf club and I was always fascinated by the boards and exotic Hawaiian feel of it all.

The little girl, Camilla, from the bus popped into my head, how happy and thankful she was for a little plastic toy. I knew that feeling, how simple things like toys could take you away in your mind. In my case it was always a warm little fantasy halting the cold reality. At her age my toys were so important to me, some were presents, most of them were swiped, but all fulfilled a need for escapism. I developed this passion for collecting things too, especially magazines or books series, like The Gnomes or Beatrix Potter. I even collected stamps like a right nerd-a-tron. Even though I had no money, I always loved sending off coupons from newspaper ads so that they would send me back a newsletter or free starter pack about tigers in Africa or stealth bomber airplanes. I was happiest when I had my pets though, especially my puppies, and would shower them with love. My first little rascal was called Lucky, and I adored him. I came home one day to find he had been given away on my aunt's orders, because he barked too much. It broke my heart.

Although me da was always well turned out and smart, his housework skills were on par with his cooking. What he thought was clean or tidy made me shudder. I hated living in such an unordered environment, with things only half done or pushed out of sight. Inside my mind was messy enough so I hated it being like that outside too. I would always have my room immaculate, everything in its place. In Maudlintown, when days were bad and he came in drunk or we had fights and arguments, if I wasn't taking it out by fighting in the streets, I would trash my room, sending toys flying everywhere. I would be so hurt, so angry and frustrated.

In the aftermath, I enjoyed nothing more than tidying it all up again. I guess this explains my fascination with earthquake films. I built houses or shops out of old cardboard boxes and used action figures inside, making furniture and even adding bowls of flour to the kitchen, before creating my very own earthquake and shaking it destructively till the whole construction was in bits. I'd have my collection of Sylvanian Families figures neatly arranged in their tree house, a blissful countryside fantasy scene, but then feel the need to take it out in the back garden and light a fire underneath and watch the rabbits and squirrels scream and jump for their lives. I would constantly rearrange the furniture in my room too and come up with decorating concepts, like painting the walls all black. A child psychologist's dream or what? I also started wetting the bed, having recurring anxiety-ridden dreams about death. I

127

would wake up soaked, and this carried on until I was 11. I hated telling me da in the morning. He would go mad having to wash the sheets again, and tell my aunt next door which made me feel even more embarrassed.

A frustration and darkness was building in me, from the loss I felt after my mam died and all the ongoing aftermath with me da. I tried to ignore it and just embrace the life I had in Maudlintown, but the sadness was sometimes overwhelming and would leave me in tears and afraid. I didn't understand it and didn't want to speak of it. I didn't want anyone thinking I was weird. There always was a massive contradiction within me too. I had this need to always defend the defenceless and the kids I saw as pure. Maybe I wanted to be like them and not the little tearaway I was constantly told I was, or the boy that got in trouble, or had to deal with his dad on his own. I had this nurturing side, like when I would find little bird chicks which had fallen from a nest. I would pop them in my school bag and rush to school to nurse them back to health, only to find them lifeless after being jolted around between my books – another fail.

Then there was another side of me. I was a little hard nut, like a mini-Rottweiler, always ready to fight if need be. Being small, having no mam and because I couldn't control anything at home, I overcompensated and went too far at times, like scraping a lad's face along the concrete, to show people not to mess with me again. At school I was the terror of the playground and for the teachers. The aggression I displayed in self-defence meant most of the lads stayed on side so I wouldn't beat them up. I wasn't a bully though and hated anyone picking on someone weaker than them, which is funny seeing as I was always the smallest.

I moved schools a lot in my primary years, attending most of the ones in the town. I remember the Christian Brothers' school most. If any teacher gave me grief or got too rough with me – hitting kids was just being phased out in schools at that time – me da would be straight there. Once he had a teacher up against the wall in front of the class, warning him never to lay a hand on me again. I know now part of it was a reaction to his own time being beaten to a pulp by the so-called teachers at The Artane.

My two best friends at school were James Doyle and John Hendricks, who I'd known since before we moved to London, and we were tight as could be. In class we spat toilet tissue through a pen at the Virgin Mary statue or up onto the classroom ceiling. We charged through the playground playing pile up, British Bulldog, or, well, just messing about. We yapped in our made up language, 'Iveaguy wivagil kivagick youragore arvagarse' translated as 'I will kick your arse'. Genius.

I watched a lot of TV too and was obsessed with The Golden Girls. When the others lads weren't around, I got

James and John to play the characters with me. I was Blanche because she was the prettiest, James would be Rose because he was ditzy, and poor John, much to his dismay, would join in and be Dorothy, because, well, he was tall. Me da was convinced Bea Arthur was a man, if we ever watched it together he would blurt out 'that's a man'.

I entered myself and James Doyle into a miming competition once, where we wore cycling shorts and cowboy hats and performed to 'Stay' from Dirty Dancing. The poor lad would be sweating in case he got the choreography wrong, and I would belt him.

In the Maudlintown years me and my crew, we seemed untouchable.

Even though I was a tough little bruiser and always busy at this time, it was at about that age, 11 years old, when I also started becoming a bit afraid. The constant unsettling feeling which came into play after my mam died, an anxiety that something bad was going to happen, started getting worse. These thoughts never left, and brought with it dreams, anxiety and the bed wetting. But now fears snuck in too, irrational fears about having a street fight with my best friends. I was scared I would lose them and be ostracised, that the little family we created would be gone. In reality even if we did scrap we always sorted it out as kids do. But the fear of losing what I'd found had me petrified.

These fears started radiating from me, and became worse when I became a target. There was this one lad, who I was friends with for a while, but then started bullying me, and everything changed. It was horrible. I became so aware of everything, even small things like leaving my own house. I avoided going anywhere near his house, but would inevitably bump into him. I don't actually remember him beating me up, but I dreaded the mental torture and intimidation.

To make things worse, me da started getting itchy feet again and was talking about moving. Even though things were shit with that one lad, I begged me da not to leave Maudlintown. But once he had made his mind up there was no talking to him, so my pleas to stay feel on deaf ears. A couple of months later we moved out of our home and off into the unknown to start again. Why was this happening to me? All my fears were coming true. My little world here in Maudlintown, my friends, my adventures, people looking out for me was all coming to an end. I was gutted things had gone so wrong again.

The surfers were on their way up the beach and I could feel my eyes welling up with all the memories. I missed my dad. His death was still so raw. Before I started bawling in front of a group of manly surfers, I decided to head back to the lodge. I enjoyed the peace of the laid-back environment and had a cushy night having some beers with the surfer crowd. Everyone there was really sound, apart from one old

American crank who barely cracked a smile in my direction, and seemed to think he was Jimi Hendrix reincarnated, meh.

Before leaving Chile I spent some time in the port city of Valparaiso, where the creativity of the city's graffiti was inspiring. It danced to life from its building canvasses. It shows that if a city council opens its stuffy top button sometimes its residents can really let their talents shine, improving the generic visuals of a town tenfold.

Then it was up the winding roads high into the snow covered Andes, and on into steak, wine and tango country, Argentina.

Chapter 8

Past wild horses roaming through smooth green fields, spiked with tall thin trees, then on through rippling western rockiness. I arrived at my first Argentinian base, Mendoza. My hopes of a quaint old Spanish town bursting with character were left flopping like a wet fish gasping for air. Culture was almost lost amongst the city's grid system of endless shopping streets and cafes, but I'd been told Mendoza is best viewed as a base to explore the surrounding countryside, so I decided to throw myself into what the following few days would bring. I was staying in a dorm with a much younger crowd this time, a mixture of English, Norwegian and German. I shuffled myself into this new group and we headed out together to change some money. I was getting better at infiltrating groups of strangers now, you have to be somewhat of a chameleon when backpacking as you can meet new groups of people everyday.

Back in 2001 Argentina hit an economic crisis, and has since struggled to recover. The Peso is worth almost nothing and on advice from other travellers I'd got myself some American dollars back in Chile. Dollars are like gold dust in these parts. The guys from the hostel came from completely different backgrounds than me. Despite their admirable university educations, they had no streetwise smarts at all. To change our dollars into pesos we approached the guys in the street shouting 'cambio' 'cambio'. I managed to haggle for the best rate, but the others accepted the first rate offered, which left them with quite a few less pesos than myself. But although we were different, I was loving meeting people from all walks of life and wealth on my travels. As they spoke, I felt so intrigued by their different upbringings and had a lot of respect at how far they went in their educations, even thought they were pretty shit at being street savvy!

My teenage years couldn't have started more differently, and on less of a Brady Bunch note. By then things with my dad had become strained. Not just the usual teenage angst, we had started to see less of each other. I didn't want to be around him when he was drunk anymore. His outbursts were now more physical, and his words more cutting and bitter. I gave it back verbally, so on bad days it was like a war zone, battling against each other.

He tried to be the best version of what he knew a dad to be, I guess what he thought was right. He did what he could and always put food on the table. I took over the cooking as soon as he would let me near the cooker, and subsequently cleaning too, constantly running around tidying up after him, only fanning my obsessive compulsive flames. He took me away when he could afford it, even if it meant borrowing money. We went on my first ever holiday to the Isle of Man when I was 10, we ate hot dogs on the promenade and watched the TT Races. We even saw The Queen who was visiting the island. Breaks to London in the summer or at Christmas to stay with my aunts and uncle, were a Godsend and a breather for us both.

I was still hanging around with my childhood compadres from the estate and other pals which I'd picked up along the way from the various locations we moved to. I would try to lose myself in television and music when me da was out. When he came back I would give him his dinner and go to my room or out with my friends. He noticed I was avoiding him and this would again cause rows. Rowing never did either of us any good. We both knew we only had each other, and it would summon waves of guilt on both sides afterwards. He felt hurt and angry that I didn't want to be around him because of the drink. Gone were the days on the bike, when he would tell me to breathe in the country air and that the smell of cow shit was good for us, and would put hairs on my chest.

It was very hard for us to communicate when I was a teenager. Me da was in his 60's by now. I felt too embarrassed to talk to him about anything. He didn't have a clue how to speak to a teenage boy about life's challenges, and he was the type of man that didn't talk about things anyway, unless he had a drink. Then he would talk about his past life and my mam. Absurdly, our main bonding moments came through the demon that was destroying us. It was those moments where I loved him unconditionally and felt very protective of him. He loved me so so much but didn't know how to be with me. I just wanted him to be my dad. I was changing and growing up. My upbringing, and constantly moving around, turned my head into a melting pot. My dad and I became ships passing, any open father and son relationship, which I craved, never really got off the ground.

Thankfully one of the few lessons me da did instil in me was manners, and I knew right from wrong. Maybe not when it came to sticky fingers in shops, but when it came to being a good person and not intentionally hurting others. He taught me the simple, but massively important, lesson to be appreciative, and how always saying please and thank you was a fundamental and necessary trait in life. This became the basis for the moral code I developed. Wheeling and dealing to get by was just part of our lives and is one thing, but when it came to respect, loyalty and doing the right thing for others, me da never budged. He was still a gentleman.

When it came to the birds and the bees though, well it was like blanketed pesticide with me da, the poor creatures gasping for air in a lesson-less wilderness. He wouldn't even utter the word sex. I wasn't allowed to watch a kissing scene on Home & Away or Neighbours. I realised pretty early on that asking him about it would be like banging my head against a brick wall. The day I was in the swimming pool trying to pull myself up on an inflatable dragon and my willy had started feeling funny left me very confused indeed, so I had to take things into my own hands as it were. As I journeyed further down the teenage path, I only heard stories from mates, their wanking tales or early conquests, as reference. School was useless, we had nothing apart from a childbirth video in science class paired with some 1890s diagrams. So porn became my teacher, which isn't a great visual starting point for a teenage boy's confidence.

To try to understand all these new weird urges and feelings, I stayed up late to try catch anything on S4C, the Welsh version of the boundary-pushing Channel 4, which we got in southern Ireland, to see if I could understand how it all worked. Or I would forge a note, and myself and the lads would go down to the local video shop and hand it over to the cashier. 'Dear Sir/Madame, I give permission for my son Larry to collect 'The Lover's Guide' on my behalf, thank you, Tommy Meyler'. Surprisingly it actually worked. I rented out naff videos so that I wasn't the only boy who had never seen a fanny, and also to deal with this new guilt-fraught compulsion.

All us lads were sitting around in my flat one day watching the random thrustings of a Lover's Guide video, and me da walked in. Well I almost had a heart attack. I yanked the whole video player out of the cabinet, before ushering me da back out of the room pretending something was broken in my room so the boys could remove the tape through convulsions of laughter.

The aftermath of any self-satisfying fiddle was always shame. I'd be rained upon with Catholic guilt at the filth I'd just done, and promise myself never to do it again, until next time. My dad was a worldly man but having spent his teenage years around sexually oppressed and deviant Christian Brothers, he would have smacked the head off me if he caught me taking part in such dirty sinful acts, or renting cheesy porn in his name. He almost fainted once when I had asked him what 'on the horn' meant and told me never to say things like that again.

Like most teenage boys my body confidence wasn't great at this time, constantly picking at myself or comparing myself to pop stars or models. I was frustrated at my freckles, my wonky nose, my gappy teeth, my cowlick ridden hair, and watching porn didn't help. Why wasn't my willy as big as these beefy lads, or why didn't I have those arm and stomach muscles?. But at least my pubes came when they were supposed to – every cloud eh?. Although my voice took a while to break so I would try deepen it myself, but end up sounding like Barry White mixed with a Fraggle.

On trips to London I always felt like a gargoyle next to my cousin's friends. They seemed so beautiful and spoke in such a grown up manner, the boys with Disney style hair and flawless skin. As a teenager I started to feel a bit podgy. I wasn't really, which was a surprise seeing as I used to eat like a horse, even using the butter vouchers we got from the social each week to buy sweets galore like a right gannet. I used to drink so much pop I ended up with heartburn and on medicine at the age of 13. So to combat any bulging waistline I decided I would start holding my stomach in to look slimmer in my clothes and so I wouldn't have a belly. I don't think I've been able to breathe out properly since.

The clinking of glasses back in the hostel and the smell of red wine brought me back to the moment. Argentina was the place where I was going to properly pop my red wine cherry. The only time I had some was just before I left on my travels from a bottle I found in my dad's cupboard while clearing out his flat. I presumed that because it had 2004 on the label that it meant vintage, so raised a glass in honour of my old man. I realised very quickly as the wine started stripping my gums away that he had probably only paid about £2 for it all those years before, meaning it had turned into paint stripper by 2015.

I cleansed my pallet and started with red wine again here in South America, what better place to dive in to the dark grape? My younger pals and me lapped it up on a bike tour of the Maipo vineyard region. Drunkenly biking around the highways and dusty tracks, by the end of the day the group of five became twelve, adding Belgium, Denmark and the Netherlands to the mix.

I finished my time in Mendoza with these new friends, who invited me to a BBQ at their hostel, then on to a drag night. We never saw the drag show, instead we got hammered on enough litres of cerveza to fill a swimming pool. I fell into a cab back to my hostel, and poor Jeppe from Denmark fell into one of the city's open sewers on his way home, which are weirdly placed right alongside the footpaths. The soaked lad scrubbed the stench off for hours. All in all I had met a good bunch here in Mendoza, and would be seeing some of them again in my next stop across the country to the Atlantic coast, and the capital city of Buenos Aires.

Chapter 9

The twelve hour overnight journey flew by on the most comfortable bus ride yet which included a fully flat bed, and a three course meal with champagne. I arrived in Buenos Aires, which is known as the Paris of South America, and a place which to me has always seemed so far away and alluring. I had a good feeling about this city, and the plan was to spend a couple of days exploring, then a week or so volunteering, my main reason for staying so long.

I explored the San Telmo area together with two girls, Malou from the Netherlands and Victoria from Belgium, who came from Mendoza with me, returning to Buenos Aires to continue their Spanish courses. San Telmo hosts a big market every Sunday. Mulling through in the sun only added to the good feeling I had about being in this city. The streets were bustling with stalls, puppeteers and mime artists, with classical and tango music filling the air. We stopped off at a pop-up outdoor BBQ, which had a cowboy cook racking up the meat. This guy was one cool dude. He was in his 50's and had piercing blue eyes like a rougher version of Daniel Craig's Bond. He flipped and sliced through meats like they were butter. If feasts like this continued, it'd be a case of having to pay for two seats on the next bus to contain my fat arse.

My Netherlands bro Rob was also in the city for a couple of nights, so we met up that evening, along with his new hostel buddy, Lisa, a Dutch bombshell with an infectiously dry sense of humour. We descended on a popular meat eatery in the port area called Siga la Vaca, or in English, Follow The Cow, another culinary extravaganza where you can eat as much as you can handle from the endless supply of steaks and other carnivorous calories on offer. I got back on the old faithful white wine, the thought of red now not so appealing.

We got chatting about our school years which weren't so far in the past for these guys, and once again it set me thinking about those years with my dad.

I'd thankfully left primary school behind, most of my last year overshadowed by being bullied by a relentless girl. Think Regina George but with less gloss. The fact it was a girl tormenting me and spreading rumors made it all the more embarrassing. I still had lots of friends though, but that experience just left a black mark on my time there. I'd all but stopped having punch ups by now, a compete turnaround from the fearless little bruiser I had been. I had enough fighting at home, which was continually adding to my anxiety after leaving Maudlintown.

I was glad when secondary school came. Friends from other schools would be going there too, like John and James, and it was a chance at a fresh start. Unfortunately half of the roughest lads in the town would be going to the same school as well, which was generally fine as I knew them, but a handful were relentlessly evil and if they singled you out that was that.

I had somehow managed to get into the top class, which was called Lime, the class groups were named after trees for some bizarre reason. On day one I was drawn straight away to a couple of girls from my new class, Mag and Valerie. We clicked and started hanging out. Kerri, the girl I had a crush on from way back in the miming competitions, had also enrolled. We hung out too, although we would clash lots. I was, and still am, quite gullible, so Kerri got one of the girls to convince me to ask her how her mum was getting on playing the piano, so I did. Next thing she ran off, yelping 'my mum only has one hand'. I apologised profusely and didn't find out for ages that her mum was very much two handed. But I got her back. She was being a real cow once when we were all at the fair, so I pretended to set her hair on fire with a lighter, not realising she had so much hairspray in it, and she went up in a ball of smoke. I ran after her frantically smacking the head off her to put the fire out. But soon we were thick as thieves, and along with three other girls from another school, Eimear, Jennie and Paula, I had my new group of teenage gal pals, and an unbreakable bond naturally followed.

I did have boy mates too, like John, James and a lad called Richie, and got on well with lads outside of school, but in school the worst happened and I was tormented by some groups of boys, just for hanging around with girls. This sort of targeting was designed to instil fear, mental rather than physical. Unbeknown to them, it added to the fears and anxieties that were already building in me, combined with the arguments at home, the black moods came more frequently. Being both popular and bullied at school was a hard and frustrating combination. Everything felt so disjointed.

It got to the point where I didn't want to go in to school at all, or, when I was there, even go down the yard on my own, feeling like a target when those lads were about. I hated it. I felt frustrated, angry and it only added to my dark states of mind. Where had the little bulldog gone who would have punched their heads in? It felt like I had a split personality at times, always joking and having fun, but with a constant underlying worry which gathered pace. I was still always afraid that any good would come to an end or that I would be rejected by the ones closest to me, and they were my only solace. Fear mixed with fearlessness are hard emotions to understand.

But when I was with my friends, away from all the shit, I soared. Thank God for my friends, our laughs and time together both in and out of school were my saviour. I decided pretty early on that I would have to take the shit parts in silence, and stand by me friends no matter what, and I did.

I had a love/hate relationship with secondary school. Academically, I started out with such good intentions, but I couldn't concentrate. My mind drifted to London and to dancing, still my main passion, which was reinforced after I watched the movie Dirty Dancing. I would sit there and day dream. I couldn't focus on words in books, and couldn't really learn by being spoken at by a teacher either. My rebelliousness would amplify my determined thoughts of leaving Wexford and moving to London, which had started to gather pace.

I became disruptive in class, taking on the role of the class clown, always yanking Mag and Val's hair, or putting thread or flour on the teacher's back. I was more interested in covering my books in coordinated wallpaper and what snazzy pencils I could shoplift. I did take the messing too far once and embarrassed a girl by pulling her skirt over her head and everyone saw her knickers. She was in tears and I felt awful. I had to call her house from a payphone that night to check she didn't top herself. She got me back though and stuck a fork in my head in the home economics kitchen. I would do anything for a laugh, farting, pretending to give birth, setting fires at the back of the prefab classrooms or even once pissing underneath the big sewing table onto the girl opposite's legs. Poor girl, she screamed so loud. I tried to shove my knob back in my pants before any one saw. She also got me back, but accidentally, when she hit me in the eye with a brush in metal work class, scraping my eyeball with a piece of metal. I can still see the scratch to this day when the sunlight hits it right.

By the end of my second year I spent more time outside the class than in it, being sent as punishment to pick up chewing gum wrappers in the yard which I would throw up in the air as imaginary snow, and then pirouette past the window. The whole class would be in stitches, with the teacher's face getting redder. Teachers would expect to see me outside the class daily. When I had a pair of LA Gear light-up trainers, they would come up and ask me to move them so the lights would flash – easily distracted those teachers!

Inevitably with all this messing about, I fell behind in my work. I didn't want to be in school and only went to see my friends. I begged me da to take me out, but he said I had to stay until I was 16, but by the time my 15th year had come it was game over. Me da didn't have the money to give me to sit the mock exams prior to the crucial exams that year, which I would have failed anyway if I had lasted that long. Having had minimal education himself, he didn't see the point in exams, so I didn't get any academic encouragement. He wanted me to behave while I was in school and not disrespect the teachers, then get a solid job afterwards.

I was becoming a lost cause and bar a couple of teachers who didn't want to give up on me, the majority couldn't handle me. They wanted me gone and I didn't blame them. They were there to do a job, but a couple of them literally hated me and were gunning for me. It became impossible to reprieve myself at all.

Unfortunately one of the teachers who couldn't bear me was the principle, a big ogre type creature. Another was our snide-looking mechanical drawing teacher. He would send me outside, along with Mag and Val, before class even started. The 'triangle' he called us.

I had been suspended ten times by the time I was 15. Me da used to go nuts if he found out. I pretended to be sick and stayed home to get the suspension letter from the postman while me da was out, then stay off sick for the extra few days so he wouldn't find out I had been suspended at all. My final suspension was mortifying, as me da was called into the school. It was all down to that dickhead mechanical drawing teacher. Ever the organiser, I drew a layout plan for a sleepover we were having at my friend's house. I drew sleeping bags on the floor and pillows on top showing where we would all kip down for the night. He grabbed the paper off me in class and uttered 'oh I've got you now'. I was bewildered as he took the paper straight to the principle's office. I'd actually done nothing wrong this time. The principle sat me da down, held up the piece of paper and they both pointed out to him that I had been drawing penises in class, and it was disgusting behaviour. My face dropped with embarrassment. I pleaded and pleaded that I had drawn sleeping bags with pillows on top, but it was too late. No one believed me and my eleventh suspension came. I was livid. Me da was mortified and after that I didn't care anymore, so once back at school I went full throttle to get expelled, which didn't take long.

We had a subsitiute French teacher for a while, and she would generally seat me at the back of the class looking at the wall when I was disruptive. One day I pulled Mag's hair and the teacher grabbed my desk and pulled it away catching my fingers on the chair. I stood up flicked the teacher's ginger fringe, and said 'you fucking cow' before walking out. She called me back and made me sit in the 'dog house' under a table, and off she went and got the principle and that was it, I was out.

I was ecstatic to finally be free, although me dad was having none of it and managed to get me back in, much to my annoyance. I only agreed to go to see the new school they had moved into while I was off. I was there all of five days and was expelled again. Permanently this time. I can't even remember what it was for.

My school life was finally over. I had no qualifications, virtually no academic praise, but the best friends in the world and a determination to get the hell out of that town and move to London. Thankfully, Mag and Val did pass their exams and with flying colours. How those two girls got through school with me there was a miracle, but they did and that was enough for me.

Back at the table, and with the Argentinian meat feast devoured, the guys were looking at me like I was deranged relaying these tales, but thankfully laughed, a bit too much. It was unanimous all round that school isn't for everyone.

Buenos Aires is a city bursting with culture and life, from the ornate state and government buildings in the centre, with the apparent non-stop protests on their doorsteps, to the hustle and bustle of the cool bars and nightlife district of Palermo. The nation's legendary first lady, Eva Peron, still shone her light over her people, her image immortalised in a monumental neon art work looking over the streets. Florida Street in the centre is brimming with shops and more 'cambio' men and women exchanging dollars for pesos, repeating the word so much that they began to sound like the flock of crazed seagulls from Finding Nemo. Surely doing that as a job day in and day out can't be good for their mental state. I imagined them screaming the instilled phrase during sex – 'cambio, cambio, cammmmmmbioooo!'

The traditional shoe shiners were busy at work everywhere, an almost lost tradition in most big cities these days. It was great to see that this profession of old was still very much alive in Buenos Aires. It was not looked down on as a lower class job either, on the contrary it seemed these mainly older gents were shown much respect from their customers and the public alike.

Another travel buddy, Bubba from Kiwi-land, who I hadn't seen since back in Peru, messaged me to say he was also going to be in town so myself and Rob met up with him for a mini-reunion, or in other words a reason for some more beers. Rob had to leave again the next day, so it was a pretty tame one, but great to catch up with the boys. That was the end of my travelling with Rob, and it had been a great pleasure to get to know this genuine, caring and enthusiastic lad. I was learning that the friendships you build while travelling solo on the backpacking trail are pretty important. It really helps to see a familiar face in a strange city, especially on the lonelier days, which are inevitable on a trip lasting so many months. It also helps break up the repetitive conversation openers with new people – where are you from? where have you been? where are you going? etc etc. Some days it becomes laborious, so it's nice to laugh with people you've already made friends with and have a rapport.

The Estroli hostel is set over six floors in an old building in the centre of the city, which comes with its own roof terrace and attracts an older and less frantic party-oriented crowd. This gives it a more homely feel and made getting some kip much easier. Over breakfast one morning, I met Wan and her husband, a 60-something Malaysian lady who married her American beau forty five years earlier, and they were still off having adventures together. Her personality and passion for living life was quite inspiring, and she was a great addition to the atmosphere each morning. She liked getting to know everybody that she came in contact with. In her sweet Malaysian twang, she would fill in any new kitchen arrivals with her and the husband's back stories, which didn't just break the ice, but smashed any shyness around the tables to smithereens.

I told her I thought it was amazing that they had all those years together and still found the time to wanderlust and have fun as a couple. To which she turned from the sink and said 'Larry, shall I tell you how it's worked? It's about being able to give in and compromise, not giving up on each other, but communicating with each other and having your own time too. Not living in each other's pockets, you know, because if you find that spark with someone and you can still laugh when you're all saggy like he is, then that's what counts.'

As the words came out of her mouth, I felt a lump in my throat because that's exactly how I view love and relationships, sticking together and not giving up when that spark is there. The thought that I'd almost found the one to grow old with flooded my head. But I stopped the pointless tears from building and realised she'd just called her old man saggy, and we both burst out laughing. It was lovely to have Wan there. She made me smile on those early mornings when she frequented the kitchen.

Chapter 10

I finally found the right charity to volunteer with, L.I.F.E. They work with kids living way below the poverty line in a slum area called Ciudad Oculta, located in the Villa Lugano area. It´s also known as the hidden city, as the government once tried to build walls around it to keep the poverty within out of sight from the international visitors when Argentina hosted the World Cup back in 1978.

After an induction, it was off to the slums with the charity director, Lily. She was a fun woman of a certain age, not sure what, who had a great personality, if sometimes a little distracted. She had been running the charity for fifteen years and the entire neighbourhood knew her well. Even though they had run out of the much talked about L.I.F.E. t-shirts, which volunteers must wear so that they residents know you are part of the charity and not just a random outsider, she assured us that they would know that anyone with her was there to help. As we turned into the neighbourhood, I couldn't believe the sudden change of surroundings. Run down is an understatement and I could feel the change of mood in the air too. But I wasn't nervous about being in this kind of environment, I was more nervous about the language barrier and how the kids would take to me. We were based at a soup kitchen that first day. As we pulled up there was a gang taking and dealing drugs on the corner. On the other side of the kitchen was a decrepit building, housing two crack addict parents and their kids, the poor little things running around, filthy dirty in their nappies and bare feet. The mum, with two tears tattooed under her eye, must've been pregnant most of her adult life. We set up some tables outside the soup kitchen and unpacked lots of toys, not all in the best condition.

The kids then started to arrive. Fellow volunteers told me there was one boy who was a nightmare, and always behaved badly taking everything from the other kids. I spotted him straight away as he was much bigger and burlier than the rest. Lo and behold, he ran at the table and tried to take all the colouring sheets and pencils. I grabbed them straight back with a don't take the piss little man look in my eye, and told him with authority 'oi, no amigo, uno'. The girls were taken aback by this, but I thought it best to nip his shenanigans in the arse straight away so that we could spend time with all the kids rather than trying to make one behave. As I used to be quite disruptive myself, I know how that mentality works, and he seemed to respond. For the next hour he sat quietly drawing, and he did some pretty good work. I commended him with 'muy bueno amigo' and he replied with a fist bump. I had earned his respect, and the other volunteers gave me some nice feedback, which was great to hear on my first day.

The kids were really happy to be there, a mixture of ages from about 3 to 12 years old, and they were so affectionate and appreciative of us being there too. We played games, did skipping, football, jigsaws and colouring for the rest of the afternoon. We ignored the fools on the corner arguing with the mum next door, who seemed to get more off her face as the hours went on. One of her kids had learning difficulties, and was covered in dirt. I really felt for him so tried to involve him by giving him piggy backs. He roared with laughter as we ran around the street. But then every other kid, including the big lad, wanted a piggy back too, an endless stream of kids lined up for a go. Myself and the other volunteers were shattered by the end, so after having some cake provided by the charity for the neighbourhood kids celebrating their birthdays that week, it was time to pack up and head back.

I realised quickly that volunteering wasn't about changing these kid's lives, but taking them away from their daily routine and the sights around them which children shouldn't have to witness. It was also about showing them some affection, smiles and fun, especially the ones who came from violence and drugs.

I visited three areas over the following week, the main one being around an old derelict hospital right in the centre of the slum. The hospital was meant to be one former government's pride and joy, and the biggest hospital in the whole of Argentina at one time. But because there was so much corruption, the hospital was never finished and it became part of the slums, casting a bleak towering shadow over the poverty below. It is now home to a few of the poorest families and an abundance of junkies.

This area was by far the most poverty stricken part of the slum. Even so, some of the kids were always turned out nicely, mainly the girls, hair in plaits and wearing their prettiest pink outfits, but the rest had to make do with clothing donations and trainers that in some cases were falling off their feet. Most of the kids had really poor dental hygiene, and what teeth they did have were either yellow or rotting, which was hard to get used to as I just wanted to line them all up and show them how to brush morning and night. But again that wasn't our role, so unfortunately those things have to be left for their parents. I did however wipe some of their snotty konks and ran after a couple of the smaller ones with wet tissues scrubbing at their crusty nostrils.

Volunteering was an important part of my travels. Having grown up myself in a poor environment, I really wanted to be involved with these kids. Don't get me wrong, I wouldn't compare my upbringing to the poverty these little rascals go through at all. But I could definitely relate to aspects of both their environment and behaviour. I didn't come from a silver spoon background and wasn't on a gap year from an academic institution, so felt I could bring a different approach and understanding to the volunteering. But no matter what background everyone there was from, they were there to help.

At the end of my time, it was hard to leave the work. One of the more experienced volunteers told me she found it really hard to leave after building relationships with the kids. They would be upset knowing that yet again someone they had got close to would be leaving and they wouldn't see them again. She had decided not to tell them she was finishing this time to save tears all round, instead she just waved goodbye as normal and hoped the next day's volunteers would distract them from the loss.

My final day was meant to be back at the hospital, but I decided it would be better not to go and let someone else take my place, so that youngsters that I had spent most time with, especially a few of the little rowdier lads, wouldn't get too used to me and miss my presence. I didn't want to be just another person saying goodbye and leaving their lives. It was tough, but the right decision.

Helping and getting to know these kids, their problems, their talents, their hardships and their loving natures was one of the best experiences I've ever been involved in. Unavoidably, the time with the kids brought me back to my turbulent younger years. Particularly when my school journey had come to an end.

Over my teenage years, me da helped sporadically on removal lorries in the UK and Europe with Mick. He could be away for up to a couple of weeks at a time. At the start I would stay with Mick's lovely wife, Mag, who would look after me and treated me with such kindness, her shepherd's pie was the stuff of dreams. Or with my friend Richie's mum, Joany, who again fed and watered me with warmth. As I got older, I sometimes went along on a UK trip too and I loved it. Out on the road and helping load and unload the furniture. A couple of times just me and Mick went. I was allowed into the truckers lounge on the boat, which made me feel very manly and grown up. Once my sea sickness was in check, I always looked forward to the free three course meal.

These trips, along with the summer visits to London, fuelled the fire in me to leave Wexford and follow my dreams. As I got older, I became determined. The idea had been there ever since my mam died, a longing to go back which I would now make a reality.

After I left school I often spent more time with the family next door than in our own flat. Angie, the mam of the family, knew the score with my dad and she again took on a motherly role. She was always cooking me dinners and talking with me. I helped Angie look after her new baby daughter Kelly too. I doted on that girl like she was my own little sister, and thrived on having that purpose within a family, changing her nappies, feeding her – from a bottle not my nipple – and taking her out for walks. I loved the responsibility of it and I just loved Kelly and again being part of Angie's family. Through the years, I would send Kelly birthday presents, and she has now grown up into a beautiful young lady. She looks up to me like a big brother and I'm so very proud of her.

At age 15, I had taken over almost everything at home: cleaning, cooking, shopping, paying bills and collecting me da's dole money. While all the other kids were in school, I was in the launderette washing and drying clothes as we didn't have a washing machine at home. Half of my tops ended up looking like prom dresses when me da got near them, so I took over any Persil tasks. Although I liked the responsibility and organisation of these things, it wasn't really something I wanted to be doing, but it was easier all round if I did it, and me da was happy with that. But the distance between us widened, which added to the sadness.

I would always hope that one day he would have an epiphany and change the path we were on. I never lost hope that he would eventually see I needed him in a different way, not just there physically and stuck in a routine, not being able to talk. But I knew he bore his own scars. The drink numbed it, a chance for him to forget, enjoy himself with his friends. I wanted him to be happy, and outwardly he was a happy man, but I always knew the pain and loss he harboured inside must have been hard to bear.

It's funny, he could have a pub full of people laughing, and I could have a classroom do the same, yet we couldn't make each other smile at this time. Instead we coasted along, but he would protect me no matter what, that I always knew. At times I felt guilty for expecting more.

I would still meet the three girls for lunch at my old school, messing about all the time. I'd set little fires in fast food restaurants when they weren't looking, they would scream and smack it out, or I'd hang clothes on their backs in the department stores so the alarm would go off. We laughed constantly, trying not to get caught, and making memories. I'd wait for Eimear, Paula and Jennie and the rest of the group at the girl's school at the other end of the town. We hung out in cafes on the Main Street or in Caesar's arcade, talking through the latest teenage dramas and planning nights out. Myself and Eimear recreated music videos thinking we were the dog's bollocks, we were! Jennie and I hung out at the railway station talking about life and all sorts, while me and Paula spent hours in her room listening to music. Me and my gaggle of girls, my best friends, causing mayhem, ruling the roost and striding down the town like we were in the movie Clueless. Mag, Val, Eimear, Paula, Jennie and Kerri, my world.

I'd started hanging out more with lads in these days too, other boys who had been kicked out of school or had just left. Being away from the bullying was such a relief. I still got dirty looks off a couple of idiot boys who were livid that the

159

girls would always run over to me instead of them. My old mates John and James as well as my Maudlintown gang, Billy and co, were never far away either. Unbreakable bonds and friendships, no matter the circumstances or distance.

My main aim after 'leaving' school was to get a job and save up some money. Almost straight away, I started working in the town's big fast food restaurant, Burger Mac, my first real job. It was weekend work, clearing tables, mopping the floors and toilets and putting the bins out. I was used to cleaning by now so it didn't bother me, but the shifts were gruelling, working until 2am some weekends when the place would be full of drunken people from the nightclub across the road. Dealing with them and mopping up sick at 15 years old wasn't much fun. The uniform didn't help either: green trousers, a yellow shirt, green hat and a rainbow dicky bow. I looked like I was part of a fucking circus, and the crowd used to love ripping the piss. After a while I had enough and left the job. Plus I was getting fat from the lunch allowances, which I would stock up on and have my mates come in and eat with me.

Behind the busyness, I had periods of overwhelming depression. I tried to tell myself this kind of thing was part of being a teenager, especially the insecurities. I tried to self-diagnose and understand what was happening to me, which ended up intensifying my dark moods. A lot of the time I would go to a place called Ferrybank, across the town's main bridge, for some quiet time and sit in solitude. I'd cry to myself sometimes as I looked out at the sea thinking about everything and imagine what could be past the horizon, feeling free away from it all for just a minute. Having my friends, especially my core group of girls, around me was so important to get me through these periods. Generally I tried to keep all this to myself as I wanted to be the strong one for my friends to come to. But whether they realised it or not, they were my lifeline.

We were part of a youth club and my passion for dancing turned into an obsession. Dancing became such an important part of my teenage years, it helped save me and was my release. We danced for hours, getting our routines right for competitions or the end of year shows. I never wanted our practice sessions to end. It was the one thing I loved and felt good at. Me da didn't ask about it much or come to watch, but he also never judged me for wanting to dance, although when he would come in from the pub and tut and critique the whole way through Top of the Pops it would piss me right off!

I would have danced every minute of every day if I could have. Music was also so important. We were fanatical about East 17. My room was fully wallpapered with their posters, and we queued up from the early hours to be first in line to get tickets to their concerts in Dublin. We'd get a mini-bus up to the concerts. Some of the lads would dress like Brian Harvey, and we'd all sing the songs and be determined to get to the front of the stage. On trips to London, my mate would show me where they lived around East London and Essex. I would take pictures of generic apartment buildings to show my friends back home. Once I even climbed up Tony Mortimer's fence and snapped a picture of his back garden and inside his car – stalker alert. When the Smash Hits tour came to Dublin, I jumped on to the moving tour bus at The Point theatre hoping to see the boys or any of the other groups from our favourite magazine. We must have looked like a scene from a crazed zombie movie, clambering up the moving bus, almost knocking one the members from the girlband Shampoo out in the process.

I might have had loads of friends who were girls, but was pretty shit when it came to dating. I shifted a couple of girls a few times, but it never went anywhere. I never actually had a proper girlfriend. I think I tried it on with most of my besties, but was totally pied each time. We went to the local discos together every week, getting drunk on vodka we'd bought with fake IDs, necking it in an alleyway off the Main Street, then dancing the night away routine after routine at the disco, commanding the dance floor. The slow dances at the end always made me cringe though, so I would shy away or jokingly dance with my gal pals.

I remember when I was about 10 years old going to the bingo with a mate and his nan. On the bus on the way back, I imagined one day meeting a girl and having my arm around her in the seat beside me, imagining that we would be so much in love, but hopefully not off to the bingo. If I wasn't dreaming of a family unit, it was for finding love of my own, a hopeless romantic in the making.

I still had a laddy side, so was very conscious not to be seen as too girly. But when I was with the girls another side came out in me. I'd always had an interest in style and looking good, whether it was wearing my jeans backwards like Kriss Kross in primary school, or putting Mercedes badges on chains and wearing them to the disco.

I was very particular about what I wore or how I put things together, and always tried to wear something different and not like everyone else. It was confusing, like there was tug-o-war inside me. I didn't want to be picked on but I would still wear stuff none of the other lads would dream of putting on, unable to fight the rebellious fashion fire inside me. Velvet trousers or snake print shirts, you name it, I would wear it. If I saw it on a pop star, like Mark Owen's crop top in the video for Take That's 'Relight My Fire', I wanted it. But that kind of thing was a step too far in Wexford.

My interest in fashion continued to grow through my teenage years. When I was there I was usually the first to school every morning, cycling along the quay to watch the sun over the horizon and have a quiet moment, before hot footing it along the town so I could nab a copy of Vogue from outside the bookshop before they opened. I would flick through the pages of the magazine at school, mesmerised by all the models and designer campaigns, doodling outfits instead of maths diagrams. I was always telling the girls what to wear or, how to do their hair and make up. Although they loved it, this also drove them crazy sometimes. Of course the fact that I never got my vision across right didn't help either, and wasn't great for their own insecurities at times.

I always tried to be good with my money, excitedly opening my first bank account as soon as I was old enough. On trips to London I took what I had saved with me. I was determined to go shopping on Sloane Street one day and buy something designer. The feelings I got from different places always affected me, especially in London, and could bring on anxiety, but Sloane Street and its wealth fascinated me. Eventually I had enough to go shopping there,. There I was, this pasty white Irish teenager, blagging confidence from God knows where and rocking up to the high-end stores like I had money to burn. Gucci, Dolce & Gabbana, Versace, YSL, the lot, thinking I was in a movie. I finally spent all the £65 of my hard earned dosh on a Dolce & Gabbana t-shirt from Harvey Nichols. Skin tight with the logo plastered all over it, I thought I was the bomb when I got home.

Next I got a job in Wexford's poshest restaurant, Something From The Cellar. I was again a floor attendant, and went around clearing ashtrays through the smoke filled air, watching rich Wexford folk sipping wine at the candlelit tables.

I was also a pot washer in the kitchen and man was this tough work, but thankfully I got on really well with the other staff and the head chef, Dave. One day he asked me what I wanted to do with myself and I told him how I wanted to move to London and become a dancer. He asked if I would like to become an apprentice chef first and see where that might lead. He offered to train me himself and said it would be a chance of a career. I couldn't and didn't want to ignore my passion, which lay elsewhere, but I jumped at the offer as Dave really seemed to believe in me. Off the pots I came and me da was delighted. All the waitresses were really rooting for me too, especially as the staff meals doubled in size when I took them over. It was like a new lease of life but my mind was still on dancing and moving to the big city.

Apart from eating the ice cream from the freezer and bringing me da home bacon from the store, I behaved while working in the kitchen and really threw myself into learning the craft. It was great for a few months, but then Dave decided to leave and open his own restaurant. He asked me to go with him to be his apprentice, which I was so delighted about as he seemed to have a real faith in me, but he also had a very fiery temper in the kitchen, like all talented chefs do I guess. His new place opened and I worked there for a couple of weeks, but I couldn't hack this new pressurised atmosphere. It was too volatile and I had enough of that at home.

I spoke to Dave, who was really understanding. He knew I wanted to leave the town. He said he would speak to a contact he had in Claridge's in Mayfair to see if I could transfer my apprenticeship there. He stuck to his word and an interview was arranged. I couldn't believe it. I told me da and didn't give him the option to stop me. I packed my stuff and left the next evening on the boat.

Arriving at Paddington shattered from the overnight journey, I felt very much alone, but my fearless side came out and I pushed away any nerves or worry of being mugged or stabbed and just got on with it. I kind of knew how the tube system worked, and made my way to Oxford Circus. Standing there in my suede trousers and Dolce and Gabbana top like a stylish hillbilly had just rolled into town. I eventually found the hotel. The interview was scary, the head chef shouted at me to take my earring out before it even began, not the best start, but I think he sensed I really wanted the job, and after a brief chat he offered me a role. Unfortunately they had no accommodation to offer with it, so I would have to find my own. I told him I couldn't afford that, and at 15 I doubt any landlords would take me on. I didn't want to put myself on my aunts or uncle, as it wasn't fair to get them involved. This was my thing after all. He suggested going back to Ireland and waiting a while until either some accommodation came up for an apprenticeship, or I could sort somewhere else to stay. So that was that and back home I went, but with an even stronger determination to leave. I didn't look at it as a disappointment for too long, instead I threw myself into finding more work, saving and finding somewhere to live in London.

In my 16th year things were worse than ever with my dad. We clashed all the time and I had had enough of his drinking. He couldn't catch me anymore to hit me for playing up or answering him back. Now I would lock myself in the bathroom and scream and curse back at him through the door until he either went out or I could get out and run. It came to blows some months earlier when he came in one night shouting and bawling about this and that. He sat on the end of my bed spurting crap about my mam and his woes. I lay there looking at the wall and scraping my nails down the paint until I couldn't take any more. I sat up and hit him an almighty kick. He flew off the end of my bed and onto the floor. I was shocked and so was he. He got up and looked at me, unsure what to do, then drunkenly mumbled something and went to bed. After that he never tried to reprimand me with a smack again.

Anytime we argued, I felt massively guilty afterwards, and so would he. He was such a kind and good man, but that cursed drink ruined everything. He was a hero in the pub, and everyone loved him, but none of them had to live with him. I hoped one day he might meet someone else and that would help, but in the same breath I didn't want anyone else taking my mam's place beside him. He tried to find happiness again and saw a couple of other women over the years, but they fell by the wayside. He never got over losing the love of his live.

I finally made firm plans to leave. I arranged with my cousins in Essex to live with them until I found a job. I decided that being a chef wasn't for me. So I left in January 1997, helping the girls with the prep for the All Ireland dance finals first. I opted out of the competition knowing I was leaving. I was determined to follow my dreams and become a professional dancer, aiming to appear in music videos or on tour with Janet Jackson. I saved as much money as possible in those last few months, and spent as much time with my best friends as I could. The Spice Girls had just burst onto the scene with a determination that was infectious. I lapped it up and the timing couldn't have been better. We couldn't get enough of them and I fully embraced their 'you can be anything you want to be' ethos. It made me want to be in the big city more than ever.

January came, and as the boat set sail I looked back at the port in Rosslare, my dad's face and all that had been raced through my mind, the loss of my mam and the hurt crippling us both brought a lump to my throat. There was a knot in my stomach. I was fighting the inner demons and anxiety while trying to keep courage at the forefront. The upset I had seen in me da's eyes as I walked away moments earlier brought tears to my eyes. But there was no turning back now, this was my journey and a chance to make it all better.

After the volunteering ended in Buenos Aires, I wanted to visit another neighbourhood before I moved on, La Boca. It's next to the port and home to the Boca Juniors' football stadium. All I knew was that it had lots of history and colourful buildings, which I'd seen in a brochure somewhere, but besides that I didn't have a scooby. A couple of backpackers had mentioned it also had a notorious reputation.

Its reputation was highlighted with a gasping 'no, no, no' reaction from the ticket woman at the closest metro stop when Bubba and I asked which direction to walk. As she couldn't understand us, and vice versa, we followed a map from the hostel instead, and took a safe looking main road to the tourist friendly part, cautiously looking around as we went.

We walked for ages and were feeling a bit lost, so we asked a señora if we were going in the right direction, and with another frantic hand gestures and a worried look she told us to stay on the left and not to have any cameras on show. With our nerves a little jittery we carried on, hoping the tourist friendly cafe and bar area would be around the next corner. It wasn't. Spotting a man in some sort of uniform I asked one final time where the 'tourista' part was. He pointed down the street while giving me a 'what are you doing here' look.

Another ill advised turn brought us down a street where some groups of lads were hanging out. They had their tops off, showing off their tattooed torsos and were shouting at each other. We walked on quick smart, crossing over and eventually found the colourful streets within the 'safe zone' for the many visitors who bring the pesos to the area. The penny finally dropped and we realised we had been walking in the rough part of the neighbourhood all along!

Even though the place was heavily geared towards tourists, with souvenir shops and the Latin version of those comedy seaside boards you stick your head through for pictures all around, you could still feel the old days in the air.

I imagined all the sailors coming ashore here back in the thirties and forties, tanked up on rum, eyes blurry from the smoky bars, hoping to find themselves some Latin fire in the local señoritas with their tight dresses, red lips and endless legs. I liked that thought. It didn't take long to explore the small historical area of colour bursts, and all that ghetto walking had made us hungry, so we had some alfresco lunch sat next to an uncanny Maradona look-a-like. He was thriving on the comparison, especially when striking a pose for a gaggle of Japanese women sat on the next table who started calling at him and flashing their cameras.

On the walk back to the city centre along the port and river, we came to a bridge and a couple of the dock workers shouted to us to go back. To be fair the desolation which lay ahead didn't look too appealing, so we took the nearest street back up towards our entry point. I had been on the look out for a barbers to get the head tidied up, and what do you know there was a neighbourhood barber shop right in front of us. Before Bubba had time to object I ushered us in and took a seat.

The place was pretty big for a barber shop, and there was only one guy doing the cutting. A few minutes later four more guys appeared from the back, one older fella whose nose looked liked it had done a lifetime in the ring, then three other heavily tattooed lads. Myself and Bubba exchanged looks, no words were necessary.

The youngest lad beckoned me to the chair, where I proceeded to show him pictures on my iPhone of what I wanted, while trying to utter some Spanish words like I knew what I was saying. It was probably not the smartest move to be flashing my phone around and I could see Bubba's expression in the mirror saying 'What the hell are you doing?'. But the lad got the gist and I quickly stuffed my phone back in my pocket. He started asking me questions in Portuguese, which I hadn't even clocked wasn't Spanish at all. With a no comprende and gormless look in response he pointed to his cap which had 'Favela' written across the front and he repeated, Rio. Braaaaa-zil. Finally I got that he was telling me he was from the favelas in Rio, doh!

He handed me his phone with a smashed screen to show me some pictures of haircuts. All the pictures had either a Nike tick or some crazy tram lines shaved in, he obviously hadn't got the gist then. I replied 'por favor' and quickly swapped to Goggle Translate to type in some words to move the conversation along, before I ended up looking like a member of Blazin Squad. His mates came over to see what was happening. The dodgiest looking one took the phone and typed in what translated to, 'this is La Boca, there is no jurisdiction here' while giving me a grimacing stare in the mirror. With sweat now gathering on my forehead and a forced smile, I ignored his glare and took it as a mistake, deciding what he really meant was 'welcome, you are in the area of La Boca'!

With my pupils now dilated and three tattooed lads from the Favelas of Rio standing over me, while I tried to type through a broken phone screen into another language, my smile was becoming quite hard to maintain. Bubba was standing outside the shop after having enough of talking to the menacing older one, and I genuinely thought 'Fuck, this could end badly here'.

But I put that aside and said to myself, no I can't judge these boys so quickly, it's a public barber shop after all and I'm well able for this. So I kept on communicating as best I could, the other lads eventually and thankfully dispersed. My guy got out his blade (gulps) and started on my cranium. The conversation stalled while he was concentrating, but the other guy was still staring at me in the mirror – how relaxing.

My barber then typed into translator asking what music I like, so I said rap and R'n'B, and with an excited smile he brought up YouTube and searched for 50 Cent. He hooked it up to some massive old school speakers and 'Candy Shop' blasted out. We both nodded our heads to the beats, but I quickly stopped seeing as he had a blade in his hand. He then passed me the phone to choose some music, I put on Chris Brown's 'Loyal', which they all seemed to like, and cranked the volume right up. Automatically the atmosphere changed for the better.

The rest of my time there we swapped through some tunes and exchanged fist bumps. I thought it wise not to get carried away and switch over to a bit of J.Lo or Whitney. But it just goes to show music really does transcend any language or culture, and being in that barber shop turned out to be one of my favourite experiences. Plus I got a sick blading and fading job from El Barbero. I happily paid the equivalent of £4, said goodbye to my new mates and left unscathed. Even Bubba said he might go back for a trim!

Now you can't come to Argentina without partaking in a little tango, and I'd booked a lesson with Lisa and Bubba. It was straight after my last day of volunteering. I turned up wearing sweaty denim shorts, dusty Converse and with kid's paw prints all over me, which probably wasn't the most alluring sight for the women in the room. But there was no time for changing, our instructor was waiting. He was a dancer who was well versed in communicating the ardor, command and intensity demanded for this dance.

We all got to dance with each other's partners and even a reluctant Bubba let his Maui manliness go and threw himself right in. We finished with the instructor choosing two couples to take on the steps into the famous tango pose for some photos, and along with another couple Lisa and I were chosen. I brushed off my shoulders with the chuffedness!

After the class, there was dinner and a tango show, called Complejo Tango. It was immense, oozing with Latino heat and fight from every step, the dancers' feet as fast as whippets across the stage. As well as the show, a live band and singer accompanied the dinner and unlimited drinks. The room filled with rhythm, and by the end we were all up dancing (drunkenly) with the professionals who came down into the crowd. Trying to sneak the excess bottles of wine out of the place and back to the hostel was a fruitless task though, the hawk eyes of the moody old doorman not missing a trick. We'd drank enough anyway, and I predicted a big wine headache in the morning as it was.

Feeling a little restless on a free Sunday in the big city, I decided to get out and see some countryside. What better way than to spend an afternoon than on a ranch with some cowboys, or gauchos as they are known in Argentina. There was only four other people on the tour, all South American, and only the guide spoke English. We were welcomed at the gates of Estancia Santa Susana, by a strapping gaucho offering us wine and empanadas, and it was straight off for a horse ride around the huge ranch. The gauchos choose the horse for us, and as always when it comes to me and horses, mine was a little loco. He finally calmed down and we bonded – well he responded to my rein yanking skills at least.

An older lady called Betty from my group was taking a look around the grounds, and I joined her for a little walk. She hadn't a word of English and by the time the bell rang for lunch she was flapping her arms like a chicken in fits of laughter at my Spanish, telling the others how I´d mixed up pollo (Spanish for chicken) and polo (the sport). I couldn't stop laughing at her doing the chicken routine, the two of us not understanding a word but creasing up anyway. I think she actually pissed herself a bit. Anyway it was time to eat, cowboy style, and the lunch was something else, all sorts of steaks and meats brought to your table by the gauchos, and as much wine or beer as you liked, while some traditional dancing was performed on the stage next to us. The others in the group were a delightful young Ecuadorian duo, Jennifer and Mauricio, and by the end the three of us, and the rest of the international crowd, were up dancing, and I couldn't have asked for a better yee-haa Sunday.

Back in the city I caught up with my Dutch friend Leonie from back in Mendoza. We blagged our way into one of the city's fanciest hotels to take in the views from the top floor swimming pool reserved for guests only. We ended up getting more of a view than we had bargained for when the women across from us dropped her robe and dried herself off butt naked, we giggled and ran out before security caught us – so immature. That night there was a Halloween party at Leonie's hostel. I crashed it and had to pretend I was staying there to nab a free horror makeover from the face painter. The artist really knew her stuff with some pretty impressive and scary work on others, but she must have gotten tired or bored by the time we got to her. Instead of looking like Mr and Mrs Corpse Bride, we looked like two Smurfs on acid, with bright blue faces and yellow eye patches, scary alright.

And so came time to move on from Buenos Aires, to Brazil, a country I was pretty excited to experience. I hoped it was ready for a good ol' slap on its big tanned bubble butt!

Chapter 11

Before skipping over the divide into the mammoth Brazil, it was another overnight cama (fully flat bed) bus, taking me to Puerto Iguazu on the Argentinian border, a small but developing town thriving from the consistent tourism which the natural wonder of the world on its doorstep, Iguazu Falls, brings in.

A shudder ran through me when I saw the only room available at the hostel was in a 16-bed dorm. I'd been trying to stick to smaller rooms to decrease the chances of subjecting myself to the pig in labour snoring and bodily functions of bigger rooms. But the dorm actually turned out fine, except for the one Korean girl who was up before the crack of dawn, all the lights on, to trowel on her make-up, only to then cover her whole face with a visor so big it looked like she'd raided Lady Gaga's wardrobe.

I bumped into Dame Dutch Lisa, my tango partner from Buenos Aires, and her crazy Aussie mate Emma, who was sporting a black eye from drunkenly falling up some stairs. I was booked onto a day trip the following morning to the Argentinian side of the falls, so decided to spend that evening with the two girls at an all you can eat and drink BBQ hosted by the sister hostel just up the road.

Plied with wine, I decided to take up male model scouting, something I had a little experience with in London. I told a waiter with amazing facial structure, eyes and the height that he should try out with an agency. A bottle and a half later I proceeded to take Polaroid pictures of the lad which I said I would take back to London with me, which doesn't sound creepy at all!

Very early the next morning, after getting confused with the time difference, I set out to see the Falls. A high powered speed boat met us at the river's edge. With everyone gripping on tightly the boat sped off, zigzagging us up the river and bouncing off the rapids, then turning a corner to unveil our first epic glimpse at the roaring mouth of these gigantic beasts.

We stopped in the calm just at the edge of the spraying mist to take in the tremendous sight, before being instructed to put everything we didn't want soaked into the watertight bags provided. It was time to get wet 'n' wild. The boat surged forward into the mist with screams and whoops from myself and the other adrenaline hungry passengers, all trying to cover our eyes from the non-stop spray. Then, before I knew it and with a split second of clear vision of what was above, one of the giant waterfalls engulfed the boat and all of us ant-like specs inside. The skipper then darted back out of the danger zone before the boat, and all who sailed in her, sank like a bath toy, but once was not enough for this downpour delight, so we heckled the poor man in unison forcing him to take us back in for a second soaking. This was some crazy shit and I absolutely loved it. To have an actual waterfall beat down on your head doesn't happen everyday!

Disembarking from the speedboat, the rest of the day was spent exploring in the sun and taking in the surrounding nature with a sweet Kiwi girl from the hostel. I spent about nine hours in the park, trekking around to view and get sprayed by the impressive and numerous waterfalls, including the aptly named Devil's Throat. A gaping void in the landscape with raging waters enveloping every part of the circumference, the bottom invisible due to the thick rising spray from the impact below, which the playful resident birds seemed to love as they dived in and out of the foliage to cool off. Sadly none of the park's famous monkeys or toucans made an appearance that afternoon, but a circling kaleidoscope of butterflies did, as well as lizards, vultures and the park's resident pests, although I quite liked them, the coatis. We were warned not to feed these aardvark like creatures as they can slice your arm to shreds in order to scavenge your lunch. And when one unsuspecting girl left her sandwich on show, a multiplying pack of them pounced on it. The girl ran off screaming and the coatis shrieked and fought each other for the ham and cheese prize.

The next day, I made my way to the connecting bus to transit over into Brazil to take in the Brazilian perspective of the Falls. I met an Irish guy called David before boarding the bus who gave me some documents advice, and we bumped into each other again at the gates of the park, randomly amidst a bunch of excited nuns on an outing, so we buddied up for the day. The Brazilian side of the Falls is all about the panoramic views, and they don't come much better, showcasing many more cascading waters which you don't even realise are there on the opposite side. They also have their own smaller selection to view from various protruding platforms, and the mist on this side was much heavier, which was fun to run through and dodge unsuccessfully. With an early finish, I had booked a hostel in the centre of the neighbouring city, Foz do Iguazu, but ditched this and joined David on a fifteen hour overnight bus ride to Florianopolis on the Atlantic coast.

It was here at the bus station where my love/hate affair with the Portuguese language began. Not only does it sound nothing like Spanish, which by now I could at least pick up some phrases and get the gist of things, but this was like Spanish's loud drunken friend, bellowing at me with a Russian or French or sometimes Chinese sounding twang, aggressive in part, but also a mesmerising exoticism about it. I decided there and then to just forget it, there was no way I was picking this up, so would spend my remaining time in South America pointing, miming, smiling and awkwardly nodding in response, or at least finding people to hang out with who could utter more than 'obligado' (meaning thank you) like me.

As we were buying the bus tickets, I prayed they had a couple of cama seats left but when I tried to ask, using my arm as some sort of seat elevation demonstration device, it seemed they were sold out. But it amused one sales girl no end and I think she took pity on us, and in return for the laughs she gave us two semi-cama seats for the price of normal ones. What a lovely lass, mucho obligado!

Myself and David picked up a new crew in Florianopolis pretty quickly, and we were all the best of backpacking buddies by the end of the stay. There was Tom, a guitar strumming gem of a man from New Zealand, travelling with seasoned adventurer Naomi from Wales, two German guys called Tony and Florian, Paul, or as I called him Pauly D, from Manhattan, and the two hilarious northern English crumpets, Matt and Mark. We all had some comical times together during our stay, whether it be on the beach trying to surf, playing in the waves, or telling stories over some grub and the lethal caipirinhas on offer, while Tom had an impromptu jam with the bar men.

Caipirinhas, oh now let me tell you about these little monsters, a cocktail embedded in Brazilian culture, pure alcohol in the form of cachaca, and so much sugar you can feel diabetes breathing down the back of your neck after each one. Three or four of these bad boys is enough to send you wild, and give you a fierce hangover the next day. Since being introduced to this tropical typhoon of a drink, I've ended up in the wrong bed in the wrong dorm twice, and God only knows why I thought it was a good idea to book a flight intoxicated on them. Thankfully, with the help of a lovely receptionist and her non-blurry vision, we got it sorted, and I didn't end up with a one-way flight to Bangkok.

Although my down days, when I would feel depressed, kept making an appearance, they were becoming less frequent and less suffocating. I was able to sit back at Barra da Lagoa and think about the previous months and how I got there. It had been fast and exciting, nerve wracking and full of self-delving, but I was learning to dissect my depression with a little more clarity and knowledge, maybe even inching towards its core.

Hearing about my new friend's lives and their stories enhanced the breaking free feeling, as did their positivity towards me. I was starting to feel a bit of a breather from anxiety, and was understanding it was ok to just be me and felt less embarrassed and went a little less red-faced when talking about myself and my past. Conversations about my early life in London seemed to occur naturally. I told the guys to ask anything they liked and I relayed my memories bare.

Back in January of '97, I arrived at my cousin's door in Waltham Abbey, Essex but was greeted with, well, no answer. My heart sank. But before I wandered off, thankfully Michelle answered the door. She was blurry eyed and rushing to get ready for work at her salon in the West End. Myself and Michelle weren't very close, we didn't really know each other that well. It was always her sister Jackie who I'd spend time with on visits in Ireland or London. I thought she was the best thing since sliced bread, and that Michelle didn't like me too much. But she welcomed me with open arms and told me to drop my stuff and come with her to the salon and look around the West End. By the time I had moved over to Waltham Abbey, Jackie was living not too far away with her son and then boyfriend, and the girl's mum, Winnie, lived across the road above the pub she ran with her then boyfriend, a miserable old crank who I didn't have much time for. Over the next couple of months, Michelle and I spent lots of time together.

Most days we headed to the West End, and I explored the crazy place, got used to the transport and looked for work. I memorised the tube map with precision and thought I could go on a quiz show and name any station and line. I was getting used to being a London boy.

At this time I didn't even know what a CV was. The internet was just taking off and a smart phone was a jazzy looking mobile. Some days Michelle would lend me her phone for a couple of hours whilst I spent ages traipsing in and out of shops asking about jobs or absorbing new music in the aisles of HMV before she would call to see if I was ok. I held the Nokia banana phone up with pride, thinking I was some sort of superstar on Rodeo Drive. I picked up application forms for jobs in the West End stores, but hated filling them out. I could never concentrate long enough and the mundane 'give an example of' questions did my brain in, but I was determined to work in the midst of it all.

Michelle and I quickly became like brother and sister, probably to both of our surprise. She looked out for me so much, and with my money dwindling away she lent me what I needed to go out and about looking for work. I didn't feel lost when I had Michelle with me, we clicked. I loved Jackie too, but we annoyed each other at times and I guess we drifted, but no matter what she too had my back and we saw each other when we could.

When I wasn't asking Michelle to drive me to Victoria Beckham's house or stalking East 17, I still dreamed of dancing. With Michelle's help, I found out about colleges or stage schools that might offer scholarships, again clueless of how the college system worked. But a job was the first thing to get sorted as Michelle couldn't keep me forever, and I definitely wasn't going back to Wexford. I would prove the ones who said I would only last a month wrong.

In those first couple of months, my cousin-in-law, Sandra, said she might be able to get me work at her office near Liverpool Street and asked for my CV. Trying to save some money, I decided to draw one up using a pen and highlighters. That was ok for the world of insurance, right? I didn't have a clue what to put on it so I just put everything down on the double sided paper, including my height, eye colour and 'hobbies'. I handed it over with pride, along with the fake exam results paper I had knocked up before I left Ireland using my friend's results and some tip-ex. I almost got arrested after leaving the originals on the photocopier back in the stationery shop.

Sandra re-did the play-school version of my CV, but I never got the job. So it was more trips up west to solider on, making the most of the daily travel card.

Michelle bought me The Stage newspaper every week. A wannabe's bible, the back section was packed with various ads and open auditions, and was the very publication where the Spice Girls had answered an ad for a new girlband. I knew my singing was on-par with Quasimodo's, so I stuck to the dance ads, and started taking classes at the world famous Pineapple studios. I remember wondering after my first ever class why the warm ups took so long. I was always eager to get to the routine. I didn't understand that the warm ups were a very important part and the dancer's conditioning exercises. The day after my first class, I felt aches and pains in places I didn't know muscles existed, but being part of Pineapple and around professional dancers inspired me no end. Even though I was a bag of nerves and felt like the odd one out every time I entered the building, I was steadfast that I wouldn't let it show. My 'fake it till you make it' attitude, which I carried with me to every class and audition thereafter.

After responding to lots of ads, an invite for my first ever audition came. It was to be a prestigious redcoat at Butlin's, just outside of Brighton. I was so excited and nervous, it entailed singing and dancing and I tried to develop some notes, squaking along to pop songs in Winnie's kitchen, while practising various music video dance routines like Peter Andre's 'Flava'. The day arrived, and with heaps of good lucks from Michelle, off to Brighton I went.

The dance part was first, and what luck it was East 17's 'Let it Rain' routine, which I knew in part. There in a big hall, I stood in a line with the other hopefuls and learned the routine, and I busted it out as best I could for the panel. I hadn't really mastered anything technical from the sporadic Pineapple classes yet, and had to improvise. Improvisation would become a constant for me during the audition process. I never got asked back to the singing round for that audition, a blessing for the judging panel's ears, but a resolve to not give up was ignited inside me. On the bus back to the station, although disappointed, I knew more than ever I had to make this London life work.

Then came a break on the job front. Still just 17, I managed to find the store where the Spice Girls got their famous platform trainers from, Buffalo Boots on trendy Neal Street in Covent Garden. I was chuffed and said to myself, right, ok, now let's see if I can nab a job here. The staff were lugging boxes from the old store to the new one across the road, which distracted me as I walked in. As I looked forward again I couldn't believe my eyes: there, right in front of me, trying on some height-defying footwear, was Baby Spice, Emma Bunton. It was as if she was surrounded by an angelic glow.

I almost fainted, and my heart was racing like mad. I froze with an 'OH MY GOD' cod fish open gob until she looked up and smiled. It felt like I wasn't in control of my body and glided towards her as I brazenly said hello and sat beside her. One fifth of the biggest pop group on the planet and me, side by side. I produced a small magazine cut out of her which I had carried around just in case I bumped into her and asked for her autograph. She scribbled, 'To Larry you sexy spicy boy, lots of love Emma XX' and after a few 'I'm from Wexford the same as your mum's family' exchanges and a hug she was gone. I sat there and the staff and manager smiled at me like I was a little puppy who had just chewed on his first toy. I bolted right up to the manager and declared I wanted, no, I needed to work in that store.

She said she didn't have anything right now as they were moving premises but to come back in a few weeks. I wasn't having any of that and told her to just let me try. I told her that I would come and work for free that following Saturday. If I was of no use or crap then we would both say no more about it and she got some free labour. I pleaded and eventually she agreed. I returned that following week in my best gear and lugged boxes across the street all day. I got offered a part-time job and was proud as punch to be accepted into the eclectic Buffalo family. It was the start of many a celebrity encounter and set me on a path which would be dotted with a plethora of career changes and blagging.

Now earning money I paid Michelle back, and with my Buffalo job becoming full time I could move closer to the city. Michelle's mum had moved back in too. Winnie drank too much at times, so once again I had to deal with drunken behaviour, the one thing I wouldn't be surrounding myself with in my new life. I loved Winnie, but it was time for me to go. Michelle was as supportive as always and knew I had to go too. I knew I would miss her loads. I would never really be able to pay her back for all she had done for me, the immeasurable and much coveted love and support.

My flat search began, and after seeing quite a few dumps and getting sick of searching, I moved into a council high-rise block in Battersea out of desperation. I shared it with the owner, a much older man who was a cross between Albert

Einstein and Dot Cotton, and had a grey beard and long moustache curled up at the ends. He chain smoked and most mornings would tell me stories of his previous night's conquests on the cruising grounds of Hampstead Heath, with his dressing robe half opened – shudder. The relatively small flat was adorned with chintzy furniture and tacky China plates with various old fashioned scenes painted on them. My room was extortionately priced at £90 per week. I lasted all of a month before finding somewhere else. I managed to break both the washing machine and CD player during my time there and left with a meagre percentage of my deposit after paying for the repairs. My decision to leave was confirmed when my old roomie said I could take a call from my dad on the landline in his bedroom. So there I am telling me da all was ok, with a huge bag of condoms beside my foot and a freaky painting of a huge penis with a baby's head coming out of the end on the wall opposite. I moved out the following day.

At Buffalo they welcomed me with open arms, and although nerve racking I pushed myself and started to make friends with the team. There was Neil, a true gem of an Irish lad who took me under his wing; Adam from Birmingham who was just as, if not more, lost than me, in London trying to make something of himself; Rafit, an Israeli Goddess with tattoos and plastic hair; Dario, a pretty Italian blonde bombshell of coolness; James, the boy next door and a stunner of a lad from a well-to-do Hertfordshire suburb, whose mum thought I was the devil sent to corrupt him; Maria, a ball of Swedish energy and warmth; Dirk the German ex-military lad, who could flip from a serious stance to smiling with kindness within seconds; and Tonya, model, actress, all round crazy girl who became my dancing partner. We were all under the watchful and caring eye of Ian, the well spoken dad of the store, along with eccentric German bosses Hans, a suave Deutschland dude, and Caroline, who was a total one woman show and had given me the job. At the start I felt stupid whenever I spoke, and was too nervous to join in on conversations. They were all club kids and models, quirky and crazy with their unique styles and attitudes. What did a boy from the council estate of a small town have to talk about with this cool bunch?

Even though I thought my accent sounded awful compared to everyone else and that I was a right munter next to them, I pushed myself and became part of this dysfunctional and wonderfully weird family.

Thankfully Michelle is a very talented hairdresser who regularly cut my hair into crazy spikes, new dos and colours. I would also 'borrow' some of her more out there clothes and wear them to work, matching them with the platform trainers we were allowed to wear in the store to promote sales. I remember bagging my first pair of white trainer boots, the same ones Baby and Ginger Spice wore. I was mega-proud and rushed up Oxford Street to show Michelle, until I stepped in a massive dog turd on the way, which went right up the side of the platform. I don't think I've ever met anyone else who's been unlucky enough to find dog shit on Oxford Street to trod in.

A couple of the boys from work asked me to go out with them to a Sunday afternoon club near Embankment station. I was so excited but so nervous. What if I didn't have anything to say and just stood there like a clown? Or worse it was a joke and they weren't there at all. I asked Michelle if I could borrow some of her clothes, so she helped me get ready, trying all sorts of bright clubby garments which worked on a boy too. I finally settled on a see-through brown shirt made out of stocking material – so very manly – the buttons ready to burst when I closed it, even though I was mega-skinny. This was matched with black suede pinstriped trousers – remember this was the Nineties! So with my hair spiked high, I trotted off to my first real London club, looking like the love child of Worzel Gummidge and a crack head.

Unfortunately I had let Michelle go crazy at my eyebrows, and for weeks afterwards I looked permanently shocked with two rainbows above my eyes, but we laughed through it all and I loved experimenting with all these new fashions and styles. I need not have worried about my new friends hearing my try hard conversations when I got to the club, as I walked in to pounding house music and everyone was smashed. I was a nervous wreck but tried to play it cool like this was a breeze and a regular weekend outing. Eventually I got separated from the guys and kept being approached by crazy eyed freaks. It was time to leave, but still I'd been clubbing in London and on a Sunday too, oh the Catholic guilt of it all.

After that I threw myself into London life. I was making new friends and going out more and more. I moved to the up and coming Old Street area and lived in the same street as Jarvis Cocker, with a guy called Mark who would become my best mate. We were as thick as thieves for a time, out and about all over the place. I went on my first ever foreign holiday with Mark to Miami, a Golden Girl dream come true.

At this time, I was still very much a lost, excitable, annoying and erratic ball of insecurities and contradictions, never knowing when to stop, which would cause arguments between me and Mark, especially on our holiday. The friendship eventually ended after a few years. Mark never really got the explanation he deserved and still to this day it saddens me.

I was hoping to finally find love and affection in the big city. Sometimes I felt crippled by loneliness and hurt from the past, but scrambled forward to follow my dreams. I fell for someone I met in the store once, who was a lot older and my first real experience of romance, but that puppy love didn't last long.

I was still going out and trying to meet people, I was drinking more than I ever had before too. On my 18th birthday I drunkenly called my dad from a West End phone box. We were still estranged to a certain degree, but I used the alcohol-fuelled courage to tell him I loved him so much and that we would be ok, and that I was having the best birthday ever. I wasn't, and he was worried about me, but he had no clue of how I was feeling inside. I cried as I hung up and wished things were different between us, before stumbling back out into the night to party away the memories with these new temporary solutions. The feelings of loneliness started to intensify. I longed for a stable relationship, but little did I know I was nowhere near ready for one. I spent as much time as possible going out to shift this loneliness.

As time went on, London felt like my new home. I'd been back to Wexford a few times, showing off my trendy new look and 'oh my God' outfits, relaying tales of celebrity encounters like when I was pissed and met Jean Paul Gaultier in a pub and got him to sign my belly. Or stories about Buffalo, where a conveyor belt of pop stars like Cher, Seal, The Pet Shop Boys, All Saints and any up and coming bands came, it was the place to shop. I finally met some of the East 17 boys too, and even became pally with Terry which felt so surreal.

We were like stars ourselves, dancing around the store or in the massive window displays to pumped up music, passing boxes of the crazy footwear to the punters. I could turn around and have Hollywood stars like Bill Murray or royalty like the Prince of Brunei asking for their sizes. And when the Spice Girls came in, which was a regular occurrence, it was mayhem. We had to close the doors as hundreds of people and fans outside blocked the street, hoping for a glimpse of this unstoppable pop juggernaut. I was on first name terms with Emma and Geri, and met both Mels too. Victoria stuck to her Gucci heels, so I never met her.

So sought after were the shoes that we always had counterfeiters from around the world coming in and trying to steal ideas, but they always stood out. Older greasy fat men in groups talking about girl's shoes and trying to take pictures inside the store. We would all stand around them or chase them out, shouting at them from the door, 'no photo no photo'!

I was so excited when my friends visited from Wexford. I showed them the sights and glamour both day and night in a packed itinerary. Making memories together in the big city. We all went on our first holiday together to Ibiza and it was incredible. I'd made so many contacts that I managed to blag us all in to the VIP area of Cream at Amnesia through a DJ friend. To this day it's still the best night of clubbing I've ever had. My Irish gang there together, dancing our arses off and raising a glass to a moment which we all knew may never happen again. These unique experiences temporarily helped put the hurt and anger of the past to the back of my mind.

I saw my dad at Christmas or when he came to visit. His son probably looked like an alien to him but he never judged me. He would proudly tell all his mates back home how well I was doing and all the stars I was meeting. He told everyone, and I think he convinced himself, that I was going to marry Emma Bunton as I had sent a picture home to him of me, Emma and Geri. I should have known better, because he and his niece Mag stumbled up to the local paper from the pub one day and it appeared the following week with the caption above reading 'Now it's Wexford Spice' – cringe! But it was all done in love and pride, and even though we still didn't really know how to be with each other, and it was still strained, he loved me no matter what. When he did visit London he stayed with my aunts, as it felt like a familiar and safe ground for us both, plus I was always flat sharing and it didn't feel comfortable to have him there. When my friends would visit it was different, we understood each other. But myself and me da were still on a rocky journey to what still seemed like a frighteningly unobtainable place.

Chapter 12

Life at Barra Beach was like a little bubble away from the rest of the world, and I loved the beach life, waking up in the mornings and bypassing the shower to dive straight into the ocean after breakfast. This was what backpacking was about, getting away from it all and shaking of the shackles of what you think you should be doing each day.

On a moped excursion – with me on a bright orange boy racer bike – we found little fishing villages which freckled the surrounding area. On one beach we saw three dolphins playing off the shore, soaring in and out of the crashing waves. On another, a wooden restaurant was adorned with letters left by its passing clientele covering the walls and ceilings in their entirety, the romantic sentiment and snippets of people's lives brimming from its natural structure.

As I watched the hand written words, thousands of them flittering in the breeze, I thought back to the bingo bus in Wexford, dreaming of having someone to put my arm around and hoping to meet someone to fill the seat beside me. I thought of the failed attempts so far and if I would ever find love again. I knew I would never lose faith, that's for sure, no matter how many knocks I took. I thought of my ex, and how big those shoes would be to fill, and who I missed so much right in that moment. It still hurt when I would see a reminder of our relationship or a couple sitting together, just them and the world of adventures around them. In quiet moments I thought back and smiled, the love still there, but I started to tell myself that was ok now because I was learning to let go. Another little step forward, bit by bit.

I spent the rest of the time in this little diamond of a pit stop hanging around the beaches on the hostel's doorstep, where I was introduced to Brazilian beach wear, or the lack of it. Now I'm partial to a pair of Speedos or Aussiebums myself, but Jaysus it's just obscene in that part of the world. People of all shapes and sizes oiled up and bursting out of sun-glistened lycra like a packet of Richmond sausages on high heat. Some of the girls might as well have a bit of tobacco rolling paper covering their fannies – you can't help but stare. I loved the 'don't give a shit' attitude. They were doing what they wanted and were proud to do so.

As I sat on the beach the unashamed and free spirited nature took me back to when I didn't give a shit either.

By the age of 21 my determination to achieve my dreams became an obsession. I auditioned for anything and everything, and the fame bug had well and truly bitten, infecting my very being. When auditioning I left my immense insecurities at the door. I bagged a job dancing with a new singer called Marc. I'd met his flatmate Kevin out and about and we become great friends. Marc gave me and Tonya the job as backing dancers to join him on his tour around the clubs of the UK for his band, Massive Ego. We even signed autographs ourselves at times. I'd also been spotted gyrating away in the window in Buffalo once and got a part in a Hanson video which was being filmed around the corner. TV promos and more club gigs followed. I travelled all over the country to audition, every no I got making me more determined to do better next time. By this stage I was going for boyband deals too, hoping my voice, which had got a little better, wouldn't let me down. I could bust out a decent version of Westlife's 'Swear It Again' or the classic 'Walking in Memphis', but always prayed the dance audition was first as I generally got through to the next round if it was. I still took class at Pineapple or other dance studios and had professional dancer friends, but life and supporting myself was in full flow, so when it came to going to college to study and train as a dancer, an uncertainty lingered. I applied for the prospectus of the London Studio Centre, a renowned college in King's Cross that had limited scholarships each term. But my lack of understanding of the education system set in, and the fear of not knowing how I would support myself brought on compounding anxiety. Looking back it was so silly, but my head wasn't in the right place, so I decided to go it alone and keep auditioning for whatever I could. A decision that felt right at the time and one I still stick by, whether right or wrong.

Then a break came. I had two auditions lined up in one week, one for a three piece scally boyband based in

Manchester who were looking to fill the third space. The other was a brand new boy and girl project by a management company in London. The routine for the boyband was hard and included a backflip, but I put the effort in and did the whole thing to step apart from the backflip, which I knew I couldn't pull off, so improvised instead and added in my own moves. Some of the other boys from the whittled down group of fifty or so who attempted the flip fell over, so I was glad I didn't. I sang as best I could, luckily a few lines was enough for them.

In the other audition, held by an independent manager, I had to come up with a fully prepared singing and dancing piece which would be filmed. I'd not done one like this before and was bricking it. How was I going to pull it off? I was aiming for a place in a pop band not a solo gig as the new Michael Jackson or Prince. I wracked my brains and a pop eureka hit me. I would go with the number one Adam Rickett, former soap star turned six-packed pop star, track called 'I Breathe Again'. With my kinked curtains flopping into my face, I danced and sang the best I could, hoping the choreography, performance and determination would shine through over the lack of Christina Aguilera notes.

And what do you know, it did, finally. Not only once, but I got both offers!

I ran up on to the roof of the building I worked in when I got the news and jumped around like a maniac with excitement. All those close to me were over the moon. Me da didn't understand the whole thing, but he knew I was delighted. Then I had to make a decision, which to choose. The boyband were ready to record and the management sent me some samples of their sound, as well as prospective merchandise examples. The other London based mixed group was brand new and I was requested to get together with the other four chosen members to meet each other and discuss plans. As tempting as the boyband sounded, my heart was telling me to go with this new project, so I called the boyband manager and let him know I had another offer. After years of trying I couldn't believe I was now calling to turn down an offer rather than plead for a chance. I was so grateful for their belief in me but I had to be honest with the manager. He wasn't happy at all but he knew the business and would have a back-up from the auditions to take my place.

I went along to a dance studio to meet my new group and for our vocal range to be tested. We all stood in the room with the manager who had auditioned us, a fiercely quiet ginger man with a babyish head. His lack of communication skills worried me instantly, but the excitement overrode that. The new group was made up of two blonde girls, Jaime and Eve, a brunette called Sasha, and a bleached blonde guy named Spencer. The manager played notes on the piano and we sang in unison and then separately, doing scales to warm up. Sweat started to drip down my back when it came to my solo as I had never understood scales and so I croaked and found it hard to follow. The girl's vocals were on point, especially Jaime who sang like Whitney Houston. I realised there and then my singing would probably be kept to a minimum. Luckily the manager wanted the girls to take leads.

Next was some practice sessions. Pretty soon we all noticed that the manager couldn't communicate or direct us properly. But a studio session was booked and we recorded some tracks that he had written. By this stage Eve had decided she didn't want to go through with it and had another offer, so we went as a four piece, and a new person would be sorted at a later date. As the guys sailed through their vocals in the studio, I struggled with my harmonies. Everyone had been helping me with my singing and I was getting better, just not that great on the recording day. I stood it the studio thinking I was Mariah Carey, all hand gestures and finger on my ear trying to reach this one note. 'Thanks Larry we'll come back to it later' came through the headphones. I felt deflated and embarrassed. I was trying so hard but obviously still had a way to go before I sounded in sync with the others, but I wouldn't let it beat me and was adamant my singing would improve.

After our studio session, Sasha decided she was going to leave too. We were all getting on so well, but she wasn't feeling that it could go anywhere with this manager at the helm. We were becoming frustrated. In practice sessions he would be mute and we started taking charge. I was worried that the manager was going to fuck this up for us all. I started to speak up, telling him we needed someone else involved to give us direction and take over our development. He eventually agreed and brought in a co-manager who worked more in the rock genre, but we were delighted to have him. Then it was time to find the two new members. An ad went out and we auditioned the hopefuls at Three Mills Studios in East London, it was so weird being on the panel for once, but exciting too. Straight away one girl called Erica stood out and we were all in agreement, but the other girl wasn't so straightforward. The guys wanted another blonde called Laura but I wasn't too keen, favouring a quirky short haired brunette instead, but the majority spoke and Laura got the role.

What followed for the rest of that year was a whirlwind, all of us desperate for this to work. Myself and Jaime were the oldest and took things into our own hands, very Geri and Mel B. We wanted to sack the main manager. He had presented each of us with a contract, which we all found difficult to understand. Thankfully Jaime's mum had a music lawyer friend who agreed to have a meeting with us, and with the manager pressuring us to sign, we went along to his offices in Camden hoping he could help. Straight away he told us under no circumstances to sign those contracts. He said we would be basically signing our lives away including a percentage of any future earnings if we left the manager. We told him about our frustrations with the manager and that we knew we wouldn't go anywhere with him. He wanted us performing gigs before we were ready or had ample or decent material. We didn't even have a name. The lawyer told us if we wanted to leave the management he would continue to help us, and would set us up meetings with industry people, and all for free as a favour to Jaime's mum.

So with that the manager was gone, and Fifth Element was born. He didn't like the name but we felt it was a marketing dream. He dissed my idea for each of us being an element in our first video too, only for the Spice Girls to release 'Holler' a few months later with the exact same idea – dumbass.

The co-manager said he would be our manager for a bit but that fizzled out, and we were on our own. Tensions between myself and Laura started to grow too and it became quite stressful. With the lawyer's help, I was determined we would succeed and didn't want to waste any time. I'd turned down a boyband offer for this and there was no way I would let this slip away. I put my London social life on hold and we practised as much as we could. I wrote letters to managers like Simon Fuller, and would try to get contacts from record labels to come see us. Once and full of flu, I doorstepped the offices of boyband 5ive's management, and the man who had initially put the Spice Girls together, Chris Herbert. I sat there in his office with MTV awards adorning the shelves, and explained our story, pleading with him to take us on and give us a chance.

But none of this really paid off, and my single-minded determination caused arguments, especially with Erica, whom I always felt bad about arguing with. I wanted this to work so bad and for everyone to be with me 100%, and not take no for an answer until we made it. Almost a year in and with tensions high, no money in the pot, a stroke of luck came. The lawyer had spoken to Stock and Aitken, and the famous producers were looking for a new group and we bagged a showcase. They had massive connections at various record labels so a chance of a deal was within reach.

We practised and practised, but we didn't think Laura was giving her all. She moaned, we all argued, and it was too much. We then found out she had auditioned for another group while we were putting our showcase together. I was livid at the disloyalty and that was it. I had enough and we decided to go forward as a four piece. We had an awkward meeting with Laura and told her it wasn't working out. We had two days to reshuffle everything, but together we were stronger than ever, no more tensions, just focus, and the day arrived. We turned up to the studios and met the producers. We sang 'Ain't No Stopping Us Now' and danced in formation, just slightly messing the routine up, but the vocal was on point. Then the girls showcased their singing with 'I Know Him So Well' from the musical Chess. We chatted with the producers but weren't sure what they thought. They said they would discuss it and speak to a label. We knew this was our last chance and we wanted it so very bad. This was our dream, for me it was everything, a chance to succeed in life doing the only thing I believed I could do.

We heard back from the lawyer, and it was felt the boy and girl band market was now saturated with Hear'say and Steps ruling the roost, and it would soon burst its bubble, plus the producers already had a boy girl group called Scooch on their books. It was a massive blow and after much deliberation we decided to call it a day, but remain friends. I needed to do something else with my life. I couldn't carry on dragging myself around the audition circuit, especially with minimal vocals skills. After that whirlwind of a year, I didn't have it in me. That was my one real shot. I only auditioned once again after that. I was more unsure than ever what to do with myself and my life, and felt lost in London.

Chapter 13

Coming to the end of my time in Florianopolis, I wondered where to head next, and Rio had been on my mind. What would it be like there? Could I bring any sort of valuables out and about with me? Would I be kidnapped and become some drug lord's bitch? I mean it's Rio De Janeiro after all, its reputation precedes it like a Rottweiler with a thorn in his balls.

I knew Fraser and Gregor, my travelling Scottish pals, would be there around this time so I dropped them a message, and yes indeed they had been in the city a few days already. The two Welsh girls I'd last seen in the hostel in La Paz were joining them there too. So instead of waiting until the end of my South American travels, I would change my plans and dip my toe into Rio life much sooner while there was some people there I knew. With a very sad goodbye to the beach life crew, I hopped on a plane and stuck two fingers up at any underlying anxiety of what might greet me in Rio, a place many people only fantasise about one day visiting.

Landing in Rio, I was full of excitement and nerves. There's so many stories and scaremongering about this city that it gets your mind racing, plus the fact that the plane looked like it was about to land in the sea didn't help either. With my nails embedded in the seat, I looked pensively at the guy next to me, who just smiled back! Er, hello, I thought, but at the very last second and literally feet away from a watery end the runway appeared. My neighbour found my gritted facial expression quite amusing.

I caught the bus into Copacabana and I could feel a distinct change of atmosphere in the air compared to the chilled out nature of Florianopolis, which was to be expected in a crazy busy city like Rio. I booked into the same hostel as the Scottish boys and Welsh girls and was quite chuffed that I didn't get lost on the way. But as I turned the corner up the hilly street to the address provided, I gulped. The hostel was located right at the entrance to a fucking favela, and there's me with a backpack on looking as touristy as you like.

I carried on, passing some lads on motorbikes who eyeballed me the whole way, but, I wasn't going to be scared here in Rio, no way. I was going to take the city as I found it and try to not let the reputation overshadow that. The hostel on the other hand I didn't take in so openly, and thankfully I had only booked one night. It was a right shit tip, with staff who couldn't be less bothered to help. I bumped into the girls straight away and it was nice to see some familiar faces. The boys were down on Ipanema beach, so I made my way over to meet them. It's pretty easy to get around Rio and the famous beach skyline reminded me of – and this might sound like an odd one – Benidorm. There were a lot less tinsel-covered mobility scooters here though.

The two main beaches, Copacabana and Ipanema, are also easily navigated as they are numbered from one to twelve. I found the boys soaking up the last of the day's sun down at number seven, and it was so good to catch up with them again. We all ate a big Brazilian dinner that night along with Jonny from Liverpool, another travel mate from back in Chile, who was finishing his travels and heading home the next morning. Gregor was also departing on his next leg, so we decided a few drinks and a movie back at the hostel would be the order of the evening.

After a rank breakfast, Frosties with powdered milk, the next morning, I departed Chez Dump and checked into a hostel in Ipanema called The Lighthouse, which was a much brighter establishment altogether.

This day brought my first proper taste of Rio beach life, and thankfully it was clear skies and scorchio. The weather thus far on my travels in South America has been as unpredictable as Ashley Cole's chlamydia results. The whole of the continent had been in the midst of an El Niño weather system. Although constantly hot on this coast line, rain and cloud can pop up at any minute. It was so nice to sit back and take in the vibe on the beach, it felt quite surreal looking around and thinking to myself 'fuck I'm actually here in Rio de Janeiro!'.

You don't really need to move from the beach all day either as there's a constant flow of people offering everything from food and drinks to towels, massages and fake sunnies. We ordered some caipirinhas from a cool cocktail dude, who made them fresh in front of us. Now you don't get that on the wonky stones of Brighton beach.

The hot afternoon was a right laugh, three of us at a time splashing about and getting pelted by the heavy ocean waves, always leaving someone on bag watch, as beach goer's valuables are targeted and can be snatched within the blink of an eye by the little runts on constant look out for unaware tourists. We met a British girl who had her necklace taken right off her neck by one young crook on a bike.

Beach time in Rio also made me think that the cockring market must be a booming industry. I've never seen so many unnatural oversized bulges or full on pulsating outlines in a pair of Speedos as I did here. It's almost pornographic and you can't help but gawk.

As well as lounging in the sun, I noticed lots of people exercising at the free mini-gyms dotted along the promenade, a great addition to any city in my book. By the look of the guys especially, they are in frequent use. It's hard to maintain any sort of healthy lifestyle while backpacking. I grabbed the odd gym session when I could and even though I'd managed to kick the sugar addiction I picked up in Bolivia, bread and beer were still very much a staple part of daily life, more so than ever here in Brazil. With my expanding gut I definitely wasn't feeling very beach ready. But I didn't care too much, which was surprising seeing as quite a lot of the girls and guys here are powerhouses of body sculpting, with abs, fake titties and the Brazilian butt being very much on show. The fellas are just tanks in Lycra.

These days I would rather not stress too much about not achieving an eight-pack, and prefer having fun and adventures with the people in my life. There was a time when I did care though, when I was plagued with insecurities, especially living in a city like London. Instead of feeling miserable, I sought help. My nose was half-inherited, half-battered from scraps and falls, and with suffering from asthma since I was little I couldn't really breathe out of one nostril. I visited the ear, nose and throat hospital in King's Cross to be assessed, and I was a candidate for rhinoplasty. After a year on the waiting list a date was set for the operation to open up my breathing and shave off a protruding bump. Thinking it was like Argos for noses, I brought the 'Men of Boss Models' book with me on the day of surgery. I had all the noses I liked bookmarked for the surgeon to choose from, as I went under I pulled the nurse close and uttered the words 'make me pretty'.

It hurt a lot for the following couple of weeks, especially when having all the inner scaffolding removed. I had to sleep with a bandage resembling a huge tampon under my nose at night, which wasn't so much fun, but I got through it. Then on a night out, I said something to my mate who was bending down, he flew up and head-butted me right in my pretty new konk, and to my horror a little kink returned. It doesn't bother me anymore though, faces are meant to be full of character, right?

One thing that did bother me more than anything though was my underbite. It plagued me. I hated seeing pictures of myself from any angle but the front. On dates I dreaded going for dinner, feeling I looked like a pelican trying to swallow a fish whole rather than chew in front of someone. I think I hid it well most of the time, until one calamity of a date decided to tell me I had teeth like a shark. I would desperately train my top teeth to go in front of the bottom ones, but they never moved a millimetre.

Then on a routine visit to a new dentist, she told me how she used to work in the orthodontics department of the Royal London hospital in Whitechapel, and could refer me. I almost cried with delight and wondered why I hadn't sought this route before. I was accepted by the surgeons and consultant, and a date was set for a new type of brace to be attached and align my teeth before any surgery. I was 26 at this time but I didn't mind walking around like Jaws from Bond, anything to get my gammy jaw fixed. After a year, the operation day arrived. I had opted for just the top teeth to be moved forward as I didn't want to wake up to an inverted chin and no jaw line. They sliced my skull and moved it forward. I woke up to my friends around my bed and four titanium plates in my face, swollen and looking like a chipmunk.

When the braces finally came off, I had to wear a plastic retainer which I sometimes forgot to put back in after eating. I left them on the tray in the canteen at work four times. Having to go back to search through the bins with the kitchen staff, foraging through fish heads and egg shells to find them. But it was all worth it, it completely changed my life and gave me a new confidence. Once I'd learned how to smile again without looking deranged, I knew it was one of the best decisions I had ever made. I was so grateful to all involved for my new gnashers.

As the afternoon came to a close on Copacabana beach, we finished up sunning ourselves, and myself and my three amigos decided to take in the sunset from Sugarloaf Mountain, or Pao de Acucar to give it its proper title. We took the cable cars up to the first smaller elevation, and we were met with one holy vision indeed. Christ the Redeemer, probably Rio's most famous monument, which stands tall spreading blessings over the city, was directly opposite us in the distance. The clouds positioned themselves at his feet, the sun was beaming behind, and it point-blank looked like he was descending from the heavens above. There was gasps all round, with some of the older Catholic contingent blessing themselves and kissing their crucifixes in shock at the almost miraculous sight.

The second car took us up to the summit which was crawling with tourists, but the view was absolutely awesome, all of Rio lay before us with the sun disappearing behind its mountain range. We grabbed a beer and sat with our legs dangling over a quiet viewing point. It was my dad's birthday that day. He would have been 82 years old and where best to toast him than in this spectacular setting. Myself and Fraser quietly clinked cans and I felt some comfort knowing me old da wasn't too far above, probably just across the city in clouds behind Christ himself, asking the big man if he fancied going for a pint.

As darkness fell, the city and beaches below became a twinkling sea of lights, and for the first time I got to see just how many favelas cascade down through the city's hills and valleys. We were really lucky to have that evening and get to experience a beautiful sunset like that, because the next two days brought cloud and rain. So before my first short but sweet Rio pit-stop was over and I said goodbye to the guys, we did the only thing that makes sense with weather like that, got drunk. We had one mammoth night out which took the four of us all over the city, and ended up with myself and Fraser nursing one bastard of a hangover. Mine lasted two days, which isn't ideal as hangovers and travelling really don't mix well.

Truth is they don't mix with me at the best of times, but this one was particularly bad and brought with it an overwhelming sadness. With the guys not around and having moved to a new and unfriendly hostel, I felt quite alone and isolated. Lots of crap anxieties came bubbling right back to the surface and it dawned on me that there was still a way to go before I'd have any grip on my depression. I contacted my friends back home for some pep talks and eventually some positivity and a non-defeatist attitude broke through my clouds. At the same time the rain broke through the clouds in the sky outside, so I took myself out of the hostel environment and went out to explore the city. I walked and walked and eventually came to the botanical gardens. I thought this would be as good a place as any for some time to think. Amid all the adventures and fun, my mood that day was a crashing reminder of the important reason I was doing this trip. It was to give myself a chance and the time to delve, to understand and dissect all that had come to a head and why at this point in my life I was here.

Thoughts washed through my mind and I tried to deal with them as they came. I thought back to when those feelings of loneliness began. They had been there since my mam died when I was a little boy. I questioned if my dad had leaned on me too much afterwards unable to see beyond his own pain. I was so young and confused, just 6 years old. Was that when the scars of the loss and the hurt were inflicted on me? Had the fears that started brewing been a way to play it safe so I could avoid getting hurt anymore? I've always been aware of the good in my life, but no matter how many friends or people were around me, as the years rolled by loneliness and a feeling of loss always seemed to be there, leaving me feeling empty at times. Depression, loneliness and anxiety, three human emotions which had united into a monstrous force and now led me here, all fighting against a rebellious fearlessness that although crumbled at times under their weight, never went away. With these three dark stooges as constant companions, who needs enemies eh!

But I realised that the little gutsy lad in me may have gotten lost or become afraid, but he still had some fight left, and was determined not to be a punching bag for those emotions anymore.

As I walked around the gardens, a sea of wet dark greens with raindrops dripping to the ground, I thought about the years in London. How the big city mentality could be so hard to deal with at times, sometimes suffocating like the city's smog on a blazing summer's day. And yet it was the only place I knew where to be, far from the ghosts of the past and an ever looming awkwardness at home. Now with my dad gone, and having had to take myself out of that environment too, I wondered if I would ever feel home anywhere again.

A natural clarity was now forming in my head away from anger-inducing stresses of London. It was important in these moments to be alone, not to mask it with company in hostel bars, but to look inside myself, to be brave and try to clear a pathway through the shit.

I thought of the good London brought, God knows I'd had to sift through the shit there to finally amass the irreplaceable group of friends I'd found. I thought of the sad losses of the ones who didn't make it along the way, family and friends which this world became too much for and who couldn't find a way back themselves. Why had I escaped a similar fate? What stopped me from ending it all? I thought of the failed friendships too, and the short-lived relationships which fizzled out, sometimes dramatically, sometimes before they even began. A blessing in disguise maybe, too young, too messed up, too much expectation and yearning. I thought of all the people around me now who had so much belief in me, there was so much support. I thought about how in more recent years I'd resigned myself to the fact that I needed that support more than ever, that it was ok to ask for help. The fighting Irish boy had well and truly been around the ring, rolling with the punches enough, and had to fight back now.

As I continued through the ornate gardens and vegetation, I thought of what I would do once this was all over. How would I be in the coming months? Where would it take me? Would I return to London full time? What job would I do? Would I ever return at all? I thought about the bad timing of an email I'd received a couple of weeks after leaving, from a fashion company keen to see me for a job and the anxiety that followed. I realised I didn't want that job, I was feeling anxious because I thought I should be doing it. I felt that I would only be taking the job because it was the 'right' career step, not because I wanted to do it, so I put it out of my mind.

I thought of my working life, how I hadn't stopped since I was 15, how it had become a source of stability and now that was gone. I'd always blagged my way along, ignoring any academic disadvantages. Seeing a chance and going for it. I'd been lucky enough to have people believe in me and I'd built a diverse CV – thankfully not in marker pen anymore – by taking chances and by people who had come into my life and rooted for me. So I would be ok going forward, I'd end up in the right place after this as long as I was being true to myself.

I thought back to the Buffalo gang, how meeting them was such an important part of my journey, lifelong friends and experiences made. Or to a kind Irish man called Patrick who offered me the job at Virgin after I'd walked in off the street, bold as you like, how he saw something in me. Then another turn of events, meeting Neil in a pub, a fun loving, talented and kind guy who took a chance on me and gave me my start as a fashion stylist, sharing his wealth of knowledge with me and entrusting me with the cover of a magazine. An industry in which I loved the beauty of creativity, but hated the fakeness and kiss-arse mentality, so I was again at a crossroads.

Then another pal, Joe a DJ and master hairdresser I'd met in my dancing days, stepped in and offered me role in his Soho salon, changing my path for the umpteenth time.

I learned quickly in London that for someone like me who didn't know what to do with himself, I would have to not only blag and hustle to get places but also take every chance that came my way.

When I became that hairdressing apprentice, I was determined to get what would be my first qualification. The money was so shit that I took an extra job at an Irish pub to help pay the rent. A year in and three salons later, I knew hairdressing wasn't for me. I didn't have the passion, but was adamant I would finish the two years training and get that qualification, and I did.

All these experiences gave me both new skills and new friends, and I'd met my rock and someone who is now family to me along the way, Kara. A Marilyn Monroe blonde Scouse bombshell, like myself and Michelle she too had a hard past and we bonded straight away. All three of us decided to fight on and not become a product of the bad in our pasts. I thought back to how I didn't know it then, but the biggest career chance was yet to come and in the most random and inane of circumstances.

Sam was a regular in the salon, I washed his hair and chatted with him at the basins. He was a top notch guy and a picture editor at a men's magazine. When I told him I would be leaving the hair game, he asked what I wanted to do. I told him that as always I couldn't make up my mind but it would be great to work in media in some capacity. He said there and then 'well would you like to come work with me, I can only give you expenses and the odd fashion styling gig, but you can learn the ropes of picture editing'. Fast-forward a few weeks and there I am at a lad's magazine fresh from a camp hair salon into the manly environment of tits and ass. It was a shock to the system to say the least, but such a surreal opportunity and I ran with it. I kept my head down, made friends with the core guys, and absorbed what I could.

The job was only temporary and as much as he wanted to Sam couldn't offer me a role. Then another chance meeting with a guy called Chris, a gentle giant with a hilariously dry sense of humour. He had just taken on a part-time role in the online department at a newspaper and told me they needed someone else full time. Chris said he could get me a trial day but I needed to brush up on Photoshop, my skills back then were minimal at best. I spent that weekend learning as much as possible and somehow blagged it through my trial day. At the newspaper, John the online picture boss was an older gent with years of experience in that hardcore world of Fleet Street, and had unshakeable union beliefs. He was always fighting for justice amongst the employees, including me, and he offered me a six-month contract.

I'd noticed things weren't so organised in the new online department and the lads hated doing fashion and showbiz requests. I saw a chance and put my hand up for every one. I worked hard, continued to learn the ropes and made myself indispensable to the showbiz and fashion departments. Within a year and a half I became the online Showbiz Picture Editor, complete with embossed business cards, and a very unexpected new career was born. I mean me with a business card and part of an amazing showbiz team. I moved away from the picture desk and its unnecessary stresses and got to sit within the showbiz glass bubble. The walls were adorned with celebrities and the office was always full of life and banter. I'd never forget John for taking that chance on me, or Chris getting me in there in the first place, or Sam for taking me away from the salon sinks, and the showbiz team for believing in me too. This job brought with it some of the most glamorous, champagne-fuelled, and kidney stone-inducing moments yet.

Above all the shite I seemed destined to meet and gather selfless and inspiring individuals in my life, or maybe I'm lucky in that sense, but whatever the case that's the part in life that matters, when you find your true friends. The ones who you're stood shoulder to shoulder with at the end and can never be replaced.

I was standing amongst the giant bamboos and orchids of the Rio Botanical Gardens, feeling depressed and low, but trying to let this new clarity, these highlighted realisations and this journey fight those feelings, feelings which have for too long entangled me.

Then, just as I felt I was getting somewhere, more thoughts of London mixed with the hangover messed with my mind once again, these memories and thoughts created a story book in front of me, painting one of the saddest pictures yet.

Alongside the twists and turn of my working life, a demon was gathering pace in me. I had started going out and drinking more almost immediately after I got to London. The only real let up was my time in the band. Drinking began back in Wexford when I was 14. When I was younger I'd been so adamant that I would never drink, seeing what it did to me da and living with the aftermath made me hate it. But yet there I was as a teenager, down the railway tracks with the lads, necking flagons of cider until we could barely stand.

The years in London had brought out an anger in me too, an anger which felt like it had been brewing forever. And it intensified as I got older, anger at my mam for leaving me, at me da for letting his own demons stifle any open father and son relationship, which I craved so badly.

To battle the loneliness and anxieties, I allowed the booze in, the one thing which caused so much destruction but that I thought I could control. And with it came the inevitable darkness, feeding my depression and anxieties and worst of all, the start of me really beating myself up, through the guilt of drunken behaviour.

On nights out I'd feel so alone and didn't want to go home on my own, for fear that alcohol induced dark thoughts would lead to dark actions. When dating wasn't going well, I settled for one night stands and sex became meaningless and soul destroying. When sober, I've never really been a sexually led person, but in drink I changed. Ashamed to dent the image of myself I wanted to portray by admitting going to bars alone, I kept it to myself. I'd stand there hoping to find something special but the more drink that passed my lips the more I would resign myself to the fact that lust would once again have to do, and I would go with it like a tanked up porn star.

Afterwards I'd panic and worry about STDs, as well as dealing with the hard to shake off Irish Catholic guilt and shame. I would need reassurance from who ever was involved that I hadn't been a total mess the night before, and that they didn't have a disease, my OCD would be in complete meltdown with the worry.

The drink would summon the anger too. I'd be paranoid that someone was looking at me in the wrong way or taking the piss out of my looks. I couldn't handle all eyes on me, especially in those drunken states. Funny seeing as I chased fame, but with hidden insecurities already heightened, it would turn into drunken fights. Contradictions plagued me. I was determined never to feel the lesser again, never to put anyone on a pedestal. I could hold my own and mask any insecuritiues, but too much drink would cripple that stance with paranoia, and I'd lash out. I'd throw fists through bloodshot eyes, the anger of my past and frustrating present hardening my knuckles. One night I ended up getting jumped by a gang of six lads, but the anger was so ferocious I held my own and refused to fall to the ground, landing as many punches as I could, determined not to be seen as a victim or weak. Some poor chap eventually jumped in to help me and came off worse than anyone.

Anger issues became bigger than I'd ever expected, with everything bubbling to the surface once I started drinking.

There had been failed attempts at love, being so unsure of myself I'd ruin things by not knowing how to handle it, or I'd become Billy Big Balls and push people away, good people, who wanted to come in but my walls were too high.

I could sleep with someone in an instant, but it would take someone with something very special for me to go out with them. I wasn't chasing anything unobtainable, just that smile and that spark, those laughs and adventures, a normality which was hard to find in London. I'd see people around me going from one relationship to the next to the next and I'd wonder how they could love so many people or do that to their heart.

Beating myself up became worse, by the end of my 20s the fact that I couldn't find anybody to settle down with intensified my feeling that maybe I wasn't capable of being loved. I was hurting my body and, more detrimentally, my mind. I was so afraid of getting hurt that I settled for temporary affection.

Maybe I was too messed up, too damaged. I'd remember seeing the good kids growing up, the ones with both parents, nice houses and wish that was me. I met people and they talked of their university educations and I'd compare myself. But I wouldn't allow the woe is me to last long, I was determined not to become a victim. I tried to tell myself that I was good too. I knew I was a kind and loving person, the bad boy with good intentions, trying to make the best of the environments around me, but becoming more and more lost in the dangerous world of getting shit-faced. The post alcohol binges of self-loathing continued.

Me da had no idea of how bad things were for me at times. On trips home, family saw the shiny version of me that I presented, but not being able to talk to me da was killing me. He worried about me all the time though. Sometimes I felt he would die from fretting, if only we knew how to talk to each other, if only I could get all this out to him.

My friends were there, they knew and they always tried to help. Though underneath I felt like I was swimming against a shit bag of a current, but even though it might sound like Debbie Downer had locked me away in her cupboard under the stairs, outwardly I always retained a positive outlook and would try to instil that in others around me. I tried to avoid finding comfort in pain, even if my messy little head was hard to deal with, I would still try and enjoy life as much as possible.

I got to be part of so many weird, wonderful and money can't-buy-experiences, albeit booze-fuelled – mainly copious amounts of champagne, the best sort, free champagne. Right from the Buffalo days I'd managed to work with and meet oodles of famous faces in different ways, whether washing their hair in a salon, serving them in a shop, working on shoots or just sitting together at club launches, it had been an exciting constant.

But it went stratospheric when I worked at the newspaper. Through contacts, friends and actually working too, I would blag myself and my non-media friends into every party I could. We would literally attend the opening of an envelope. Eventually it became rare that I would even have to blag and would be invited. Which was hilarious really. I worked hard on the picture side but I wasn't an actual journalist. I kept an eye out for stories but generally was too pissed to remember, but not wanting to disappointed those who had been generous enough to put me on their list, in return I provided picture-led coverage and that generally kept the publicists hosting the events happy.

I always knew celebrity was a superficial and sometimes bullshit world, a vacuous bubble. I learned pretty quickly it was always the ones clambering to the top who fed on the hype that were the worst, so I avoided them like the plague. You could meet an A-list star who would be so welcoming and endearing, then the same night meet some jumped up TV girl who would be so up her own arse and just vile. But I ran with it and was having the time of my life. It was beyond exciting and I embraced it all, knowing that these opportunities might never come along again. It was so much better being able to take a mate to a party who wouldn't normally get to see that world. The nights I had with the showbiz team were pretty epic too, they were a marvellous bunch. And bar a couple, I loved working with them, we had a real bond together.

On any given evening, London Town hosts an array of soirées, from the elegant to the wild to the downright bizarre. Film premieres, product launches, awards dos, theatre previews and dinners. It presented a kaleidoscope of personalities and cocktails, from the decadence of the west to the rawness of the east. In one night I could attend up to four or five dos, the key was to go steady with the free booze, but I never really got the hang of that. The hangovers were unbearable, but the showbiz desk were like rock stars, so alcohol-breath filling the air in the morning was the norm.

For the first two years, I was consistently drunk almost every night, to the point where I ended up in hospital with kidney stones from drinking, something I wouldn't wish on anybody. 'It's the male equivalent of child birth' said the nurse as he shoved a morphine suppository up my arse to relive the excruciating pain. But even then I was on the ward looking at my party list for the following week.

I was lapping up this faux party boy life, and my editor, who always rooted for me, even asked me to write a 'boy about town' column. This wasn't for me though, as I didn't want to be a journo. Plus I could barely remember the nights themselves, let alone quotes. I did start writing online reviews for concerts and theatre shows though.

I hadn't written anything before apart from letters and postcards but I loved it. I was able to be expressive about the arts and pop culture. My reviews would be published online, but I almost got sacked once for attending a show I wasn't supposed to be at. It was Legally Blonde, the musical in the West End starring a lovely girl I had gotten drunk with at a festival, Sheridan Smith. It blew me away, in fact I used the line, 'blows all other musicals out of the water'. I got the review published quietly and thought no more of it, but the PR company spotted it, loved the quote, and subsequently started using it and my name all over the place. Like wildfire it was in newspapers, on the side of London buses, and even on the front of the theatre itself.

So much for flying under the radar, the editor of the entire newspaper spotted it too and went straight to the showbiz guys. I received a bollocking including a warning letter from an odious boss who was outside the showbiz bubble, reminding me of my place and role. The review was taken down, and the whole thing blew over quickly. Having had it displayed everywhere, especially seeing it on the sides of buses, was nuts and after the initial drama died down I was mega-proud. Me, a lad who was kicked out of school with no exams, had my name and a review I'd written up there with the big boys of journalism.

I also met some wonderful new mates through these crazy years, including James who dropped me to the airport at the beginning of this adventure and is now one of my best friends, and like my big brother. When James started out he was my plus one to events and now I'm happily his, which I wouldn't have any other way. He has gone on to become one of the biggest showbiz journalists in the business. Funnily enough, it started out with me thinking he was a bit of a dick. I would see him out and about wearing boxing boots and vests to parties and roll my eyes. When we eventually talked, we got on great, and within no time we were going to all the parties together. Our first was a Mariah Carey signing and a true friendship was born. We both failed to get a picture with Miss Carey herself, but I settled for mouthing the words 'I love you' at her while doing a home boy fist to chest pump, to which she mouthed back 'I love you too' – swoon!

The hazards of free bars and drunken antics continued. We ended up everywhere and anywhere. I lost count of how many times I fell asleep on the night bus and ended up somewhere between London and Essex. Myself and Kara caused lots of mayhem. We attended events two common folk like us had no business being at, like the posh gallery launch in Mayfair where we mixed with the arty elite. After too much fizz Kara stumbled backwards into a painting worth hundreds of thousands of pounds which nearly fell off the wall, and on our way out we drunkenly drew a big penis in the comments book, then hid to watch the snotty organiser's face when she saw it, before we ran off into the night cackling and onto the next bash.

Me and my friends could be found running wild at fashion shows, backstage at festivals and concerts, dolled up at awards dos, mingling at cocktail parties. We learned that you always stand near the kitchen entrance for the best chance of being fed canapés and that waiters can be your best friends, a little politeness will make sure the Veuve is kept topped up and your belly full. It was a merry-go-round of 'is this actually happening' moments and VIP fun at the fair. It can get exhausting, but it was wonderful to chat to all sorts of icons, creatives and people we would never normally meet in day to day life.

Everyone is there for their own reason, whether it be to peddle their business cards of just for the freebies, but we were there for the fun. I mean when else could you neck a cocktail worth £25,000 in a posh hotel, or be so close to Miss Carey (again) that she stood on my mate Ed's foot while on her way to chat to Naomi Campbell at a fashion launch? The elusive photo with her has still to materialise though.

For all the shit going on internally, I'll never regret this period of my life. It entailed far too much booze, but it also brought with it moments and meetings which are priceless, a snapshot of those went a little something like this:

When I danced shoulder to shoulder with Prince Harry while watching the Black Eyed Peas perform.

Sang along as Kate Moss belted out some tunes in a private karaoke room alongside Simon Cowell.

Interviewed Cheryl Cole on the press run at an awards show.

Ended up on a table sandwiched between Take That and Girls Aloud, and later at the same awards show drunkenly walked up on stage with Dirty Pretty Things as they collected their award live on Channel 4.

Had the opportunity to meet the then civilian Kate Middleton at a Nelson Mandela concert in Hyde Park.

Had Lady Gaga whisper in my ear that I was 'sexy' as we had our picture taken together.

Been too drunk and missed out on after parties with Liam Gallagher, Jonny Borell and at the late great Amy Winehouse' house (twice).

Pretended to play guitar on a rowing oar at a festival with Liam from One Direction.

Posed for a picture with a moody Louie from One Direction while having high tea on the posh British Pullman train.

Chatted with Rihanna, Colin Farrell and Daniel Radcliffe all at once in the smoking area of a TV studio – while James and I looked at each other like WTF!

Met Katy Perry, Miley Cyrus, Cheryl Cole (again…whoop) at the same TV show.

Got up close and personal with Tom Jones and the Stereophonics at intimate studio recordings.

Told Lindsay Lohan I preferred her hair red as we sat with Donna Karen at her Bond Street store party.

Chatted with legend that is The Hoff, at a London triathlon, what a dude.

Danced in a festival field beside Nicole Scherzinger and Jourdan Dunne in the London sunshine.

Walked the red carpet next to Beyoncé for the Dreamgirls premiere.

Sat behind Madonna at The Spiderwick Chronicles premiere.

Had selfies with Patsy, Eddy and Kylie Minogue at the Absolutely Fabulous premiere.

Swigged champagne in VIP areas beside the likes of Robbie Williams, David Gandy, Minnie Driver, Matt Goss and Paris Hilton, and on one night almost got into a fight with some Arabian Prince who started getting bitchy.

Stood at Alicia Keys piano during an intimate gig where she told the audience they were all beautiful before singling me out with 'especially you' – I was both mortified and thrilled.

Failed to get a picture with Britney at her tour launch, but settled for her mouthing 'hi' from across a room.

Sat and chatted with Christina Aguilera and her crew in her VIP section at a Vivienne Westwood Valentines party.

Blagged £1000 ringside seats to watch cage fighting with my great pals Plum and Gavin as a half-naked waitress served us unlimited drinks.

Got to see most of my idols on stage including Eminem, Tina Turner, Jennifer Lopez and Guns & Roses for free.

And well just generally appreciated and made the most of these rare and insane experiences, grabbing autographs or messages for my friends and relatives along the way, and hoping the next mornings fry-up would soak up all the booze.

I was so caught up in my thoughts that I barely noticed leaving the botanical gardens behind as I made my way to Ipanema beach. I sat there for a while looking out at the ocean, memories still flashing past but now with a little more understanding and a calmness from a day of dissecting. My relationship with alcohol and the darkest part of the picture appeared in my head.

In general I functioned and always tried to look forward, but with too much booze I would explode. I wasn't near alcoholism, I didn't crave booze, and it would never consume me no matter what. But unwittingly it became a crutch, a release and confidence builder to become the funny confident Larry. Another binge, not knowing when to stop, inside I was trying to deal with so much confusion and trying my hardest to forget everything.

It all came to a head one night, after being out all evening I returned home and sat slumped and crying my heart out on the floor in my room in a shared East London ex-council flat. Only the moon through the window for light and all the painkillers I could find laying around me.

I scribbled on some pages, words saying goodbye to everyone and that I was sorry. So lost and low and with a dangerous alcohol-heightened confidence to end it all. I finished the notes, and gathered the boxes of pills. I wanted all the hurt to stop. I didn't want this anymore, it was all so messed up. My mind raced and I hated that life was getting harder, I hated myself. Then I envisioned their faces, me da and those close to me and thankfully somehow I stopped myself. No matter what despair I felt I couldn't do this to the people who loved me. I was so deeply sad inside. Crippled with depression, anxiety and loss, yearning for my dad to become what I knew he couldn't. How had it all got so messed up? But in that moment it was their faces that stopped me. I dragged myself up on the bed and went to sleep.

I kept the letters I wrote that night for years as a reminder of that desperate and lonely moment, until finally destroying them just before my travels.

I sought help for my drinking after that, attending regular meetings with a counsellor focusing on the mechanics of what I drank, how I drank and touching on what was bubbling underneath, which helped for a time. I didn't stop drinking, that wasn't the aim, but I understood and learned little by little that bingeing on alcohol didn't need to be the way to tackle things. I was worth more than that.

Periods of good and bad followed and the underlying and undiagnosed depression was still there, but I was determined that one day things would get better.

Sat there in Rio, I realised that geography doesn't make any dent in depression. It comes in waves, lasting days or hours. I was learning to deal with it by finding more patience and love for myself. I didn't know what the months ahead would bring, peace was all I could hope for. I had taken myself away from London, an incredible city but one that can eat you up and spit you out if you let it. I knew there would be many more battles ahead, but here and now I was doing something I'd never been able to do before: looking past my memories and moving forward, to see them for what they are – the past. Taking strength from them instead of sadness. Tomorrow will be a brand new day and a better one, I'll wake up and make sure of it.

Chapter 14

I left Rio and travelled down the coast to another backpacker haunt, the coastal town of Paraty.

I spent a couple of days in this charming fishing port, with its very wobbly cobbled streets and nautical blue and white painted buildings decorated from wall to wall with lots of little flags flapping in the breeze. I was meeting up with Matthew here, my northern monkey mate from back in Florianopolis, who was chilling out in this sleepy little town before he flew back home. We stayed in a little back street hostel with a roof top pool called Leo's Clan, run by Leo, a big Brazilian guy with a helpful and friendly nature. Matthew had already made friends with a Swedish girl named Raquel, who was on a journey of her own to sort out all the shit life can throw at you, and the three of us were now roomies.

Partaking in the bucket-sized caipirinha atomic bombs on my arrival night left Matthew hanging out of his arse the next morning. So it was just Raquel and myself taking a 4X4 day trip to the jungle waterfalls and a local cachaca distillery, picking up a few other passengers on the way. These weren't the stand back in wonder type of waterfalls, more the get your skimpies on and jump in. The first was on the edge of a restaurant called 'Tarzan', what better motivation to get our jungle adventure juices flowing? There was a twelve metre rock standing above the waterfalls and pool below. Our guide, Leonardo, asked if we wanted to climb up to jump off. I was well up for this but seemed to be the only one. I climbed up the ladder behind Leonardo, then pulled myself up to the top using a rope. I looked down at the unexpectedly high plunge below, with a crowd gathering to watch the jump and me in all my skimpy Aussiebum glory. Leonardo told me how important it is to jump in a certain way and in to a certain point of the pool because there are rocks on either side. He said if I was to jump wrong then I could break my arm or something worse on impact. With that bombshell, off he jumped, and made it look easy, with an almighty splash into the narrow landing point below.

My legs started to shake and vertigo took over. Even with Leonardo climbing back up to spur me on and take the jump again himself, I had to swallow my pride and embarrassingly climb back down the wet rock as the crowd looked on.

The fact I hadn't done the Jackass style rock jump was playing on my mind. Leonardo had said there was another opportunity at the final stop of the day. Again we climbed up to the summit this time through lots of jungle foliage, and once there my legs started to go as it seemed just as high as the first one. To add to my nerves we had to jump out and over the massive leaves blocking the view of where we would land. Leonardo, aka Geronimo, went first, and I stood there trying with all my might to summon the courage to blindly jump outward. Just as I thought I couldn't do it, I pulled the fearlessness from deep in my gut and went for it. I rocketed in position through the air and bombed into the waters below. I was intact and it was an indescribable feeling.

The following and final day it was more water based fun, this time on the high seas. The three of us took a boat trip to various beaches around the Paraty coastline.

At one beach stop I really needed the loo, number one mind, so popped over near a big rock where no one was watching. There was some pools by the rocks providing a natural urinal. My toilet break was problem free and I didn't flash any unsuspecting passers by. Until about ten minutes later I saw a fella and his girlfriend exploring around the same rock pools, and before I could shout anything the guy puts both hands into my pissy pool and scoops up the contents to cool himself off, throwing the now yellow water over his head several times and washing his face with it.

I stood mouth open for a second but not speaking any Portuguese I couldn't really say anything, and it was too late anyway. Matthew had also spotted the guy having a golden shower and we couldn't help but, no pun intended, piss ourselves laughing. We avoided our dripping boat buddy for the rest of the day.

Back in port and after a crap nights sleep due to some know-it-all English bloke with his guitar and off key singing until 4am, I carried on to the island of Ilha Grande, where I encountered a few days of rain and an electricity blackout. But where I also did my first ever deep sea dive with Alex, a larger than life Brazilian pro. We came face to face with so much marine life, even an inflated puffer fish and got lost in the glory of its peaceful world. That was until I blew a huge snot bubble which filled up my mask for most of the dive, then ran out of air underwater.

The rain didn't dampen the craic I had with the Irish contingent staying in our hostel, which included David from back in Iguazu, joined by his four Celtic compadres, Stephen, John, Jamie and Sean. Add four wisecracking guys from Dublin and the west of Ireland, Fergus, Trevor, Manny and John, to the mix along with Big Will from Essex, or Prince Charming as we nicknamed him due to his flawless blonde Essex locks and chiselled good looks, plus Daisy, Hayley and Ellie, three up for any adventure girls from the UK, and together we created some raucous backpacker nights.

I had a one night stopover back in Rio with Fraser. Scrubbing up as best backpackers can, we pushed the boat out that evening and sipped on a couple of cocktails. Now when in Rio where else would you do this but at the hottest spot north of Havana, the poolside piano bar in The Copacabana Palace – Barry Manilowtastic! To sit in these glamorous surroundings with my new pal was a welcome break from hauling a backpack everywhere. I could talk to Fraser, it felt comfortable and he was such a good lad. My head felt in a better place after getting through those previous couple of days in Rio. The blue lit waters of the pool, palm trees decorated in fairy lights and tactile couples intoxicated by liquor underneath the Rio night sky got us into the subject of relationships. He told me about his ex-girlfriends back in Scotland, how his brother had been in one long term relationship, but it had eluded him so far, and how he needed to get out into the world instead. We spoke about one night stands and how they can be the only form of intimacy for stages of your life, for far too long in my case, but still a necessity. How loneliness and booze could be a toxic mix, which Fraser understood, but thankfully he didn't have a messed up past so it hadn't become detrimental to his being.

The two of us headed to the Lapa district with its lively Samba scene. It's a free spirited neighbourhood with a non-judgemental atmosphere. The more places I saw in Rio the more I felt confident about being part of this city for a moment in its history. Lapa was one more thing to scratch off my Rio wish list, before I'd return to the city again for the final leg of my South American journey.

Having travelled across Peru, Bolivia, Chile and Argentina quicker than expected I found myself with more time to explore the daddy of South America that is Brazil. It was an early start to my next stop, I headed north to chase some sunshine in the tropics of Salvador and the Bahia region, and hopefully get away from the schizophrenic El Niño weather current. I had been warned the place had more of a fearsome reputation than Rio. I heard stories of people being robbed on the beach by a gang of youths, but I'd braved Rio now so felt I could handle it – hopefully!

The plane descended over the golden coastline and neighbouring greenery into Salvador, and a neat and pretty city presented itself. The landscape below was stacked with lots of pristine Lego-like tower blocks in various pastel colours. From the airport I took a local bus into the city centre, which only cost three reals, about 70p, but took over two hours. Between the high 30 degree heat outside and fully plastic interior, I was literally sliding off the seat like a sweaty beast by the end. En route we travelled through a less pristine area and then onto the long costal highway passing many of Salvador's scenic beaches, which made up for the sweat box conditions.

Unfortunately we arrived not at a bustling central station but at a small stop in the historical centre of Pelourinho. I stood there with my backpack totally clueless. Two very sweet sisters from the bus took pity on me and walked me all the way to my hostel, which was quite a trek, especially in flip flops on the old cobbled hills.

The first sight that met me as we walked through the main square was a group of transsexual and transgender girls sashaying along in all their colourful glory, and no one seemed to bat an eyelid, a refreshing attitude. I'd noticed this already in Brazil, that people are more accepting and seemingly couldn't care less if boys kiss boys, girls kiss girls, and all in between. Salvador especially has a very progressive view and most of its citizens couldn't give two big homo hoots about it. I'm told this perspective has been the case for decades. If only some other locations on our planet could take a leaf, a pretty pink one at that, out of this city's book, it would be a much kinder world indeed.

I thanked my chaperones and checked into the hostel. I liked Salvador a lot already.

It has a rawness to it and an extensive history, but there is also a facade created for visitors, centring around the 'safe zone', or tourist friendly areas in and around the main squares. There's a constant gaggle of police on show, their job to reassure jittery tourists that the city is very safe despite any stories they may have heard, and to keep them penned in around the many shops and restaurants, hiding any unsightly poor areas from their gaze. But their mass presence gave me the sense that there might be a violent undertone lurking here. That they actually need to be around in case anything erupts, quickly tackling situations that could cause any bad press or dent the tourist influx.

I took the Rebel Walking Tour to find out more about the real Salvador, which takes you to the bits of the historical city which tourists are advised against visiting. It sounded right up my street and a good alternative to walking around looking at statues and churches all day.

A group assembled on some steps at the top of the steep Largo do Pelourinho square for the tour. A cardboard cutout of Michael Jackson overlooks the square: The pop legend had once visited the city to film part of the video for 'They Don't Really Care About Us', but this place had a far more bleak and disturbing past.

Our guide Pedro arrived, a local whippet of a lad with a hugely vocal and political personality. Straight away he dived into the dark past and the events that used to transpire right there in front of the pleasantly colourful buildings that now housed souvenir shops.

Salvador was once the main port in all of the Americas for the African slave trade, and this very square was where any slaves who tried to make a bid for freedom were hauled, then tied to a wooden post and whipped repeatedly. Making an example of them to deter any of their fellow unfortunate souls from trying to do the same. There was a sickening feeling in the air as he spoke about this subject, knowing this type of brutality had gone on right where we were standing, and not too far back in our history either.

He also informed us that Mr Jackson only spent around thirty minutes shooting here, before flying to Rio to finish the rest of his video. Pedro didn't seem too impressed by this, but I personally think the tourism impact of those thirty minutes has probably contributed many economic advantages to the city.

As the group walked en masse down the hill, Pedro informed us how the local slaves of times gone by weren't allowed in any churches in the city, but still wholeheartedly believed in God. Then, after a life of knowing nothing else and being worked like dogs until the average age of 55, they were set free. But even as free men and women they still couldn't frequent the city's places of worship. So a group of freed slaves built their own church with their bare hands, using what ever materials they could find. The fruits of their labour still stands today in all its glory at the bottom of the square, just a few metres from the once mounted whipping post.

Pedro steered the tour off the beaten track and into a part of town where tourists are 'advised' not to go wandering. I felt quite embarrassed by this, walking down the middle of the street through this working neighbourhood in this group with about thirty other gringos. People going about their daily business and us lot gawping at them like in some sort of zoo, but our guide seemed to know everyone and I'm sure it was a usual occurrence. He then led us up a dark concrete stairway to show us the reality of a poor life behind the veneer of yet another colourful building. What emerged was a little community of families living just minutes from the touristy part of town, having no other choice but to squat for years in these derelict buildings. The reason he showed us this is because the Brazilian law says after a certain number of years and with no one coming forward to claim the properties they should then be legally handed over to the families. But this wasn't happening here, as apparently the law doesn't take much notice of this hidden world. Pedro and his partner were in the process of setting up a funding site to get lawyers involved and represent this forgotten part of the population, hopefully one day handing them over the legal keys to their doors.

Then it was down to the lower city and to the old financial district, an area brimming with colourful historical buildings which most modern cities around the globe would be embracing and trying to preserve. Unfortunately not in Salvador. What should be this city's pride and joy was being battered and bruised by a government who seem to think flashy and shiny is best. Many beautiful Portuguese colonial and neo-classical buildings had been left to rot, or worse sold off and turned into car parks. This enraged Pedro and the rest of us, because if this was in London, New York or Paris the whole area would have life pumped back into its once beating heart. Hipsters would be sitting outside cafes stroking their beards and tweeting about how retro it is.

Sadly most of the business owners have moved out, favouring the newer financial areas too, but not all, one in particular quietly remained. A barber shop without a name which opened way back in 1922. It now had a soulless car park as its main neighbour, but the original and defiant old bladesmen opted to stay loyal to the area and use only their traditional methods, working with scissors and blades to this very day.

There was a rusty old elevator shaft built to transport the slave masters and their families between the lower and upper parts of the city. But this towering elevator also came with a demeaning story. Once the gentry were helped in by their servants and the gates closed, the clock would start to tick and the male slave would have less than a minute to run like the wind up the long and zigzagging streets of the city to the disembarking point high above before the master got there. The slave would then open the gate and resume his duties. If he failed to reach the top in time, he would be punished.

Our walking tour culminated in a visit through a backstreet farmer's market selling all sorts of bright and exotic fruits, before taking a stroll up an unassuming alleyway where groups of dapperly dressed older gents sat around some tables. Gambling is illegal in Brazil, but for this one small street in Salvador they ignored any such laws and the mainly male denizen indulged in dominos, cards, hidden slot machines and whatever else they fancied to try win a few extra real, and good on them I say.

Back at my hostel I met a new gang, Rubin, Marco and Alex from Germany plus Johannas and Philip from Sweden. We made our way to the Santo Antonio area for a big samba party which happens on the last Friday of every month. The samba had more of a jazz feel but still attracted a massive crowd. Both tourists and locals alike evoked their inner Latin fire and drank until the early hours. We bumped into a guy called Diago, who was brought up in the favelas here but who had worked hard and now ran a hostel. After a dance lesson for Philip from Sweden, who by his own admission has about as much rhythm as a cat trapped in a washing machine, we all broke from the crowd and chilled at an outdoor bar over some freshly made cocktails and a few smokes, listening to the beats drift across the night sky.

I'd noticed in Brazil, more than most places in South America, that public displays of affection are very much the norm. On one boat transit I sat in the middle of three couples eating the faces off each other for the whole journey, and again on a metro ride a couple opposite me were tonguing like their lives depended on it. In all sorts of environments people display their love or lust for each other for all to witness. On a night out in Salvador I'd noticed it was more in your face than ever, especially when standing next to an older couple who were getting more than a little fruity. The woman was almost on her knees and I had to move away before what was protruding from the guy's shorts took my eye out. But this is Latin American, it's hot, it's sexual, so why not? Maybe I'm the one who should shake off my European inhibitions, or maybe I should've thrown a bucket of water over the randy beasts and told them to get a room.

Morro de São Paulo, was the next port of call, sailing out past the impressive Salvadorian coastline, the old town and the prominent monochrome lighthouse.

I sat on the side of the catamaran in the sun listening to some music with the choppy cooling sea spray splashing up now and again. Gliding alongside us were little rebellious flying fish breaking free from their heavy ocean environment to soar above the waves for what seemed like minutes, the sun reflecting off their silvery scales. If you can't forget about the rat race in this setting you never will.

The island's main town was absolutely pristine, so much so it didn't look real at all and reminded me of Noddy town or the set from Hook. Although very lovely, it was totally geared towards tourists, and even had an entry fee, which was apt for this theme park like oasis. It had the most beautiful blue and white painted church, with colourful fairy lights twinkling on its front lawn, one of the few reminders in the 40 degree heat that Christmas was not far off.

I decided to have some time on my own and visit the island's dazzling beaches to chill out. I found one palm-fringed stretch of sand which was like my own golden hideaway, almost fully deserted apart from a lady selling coconuts and some passing tourists on horse and cart rides. The island's hidden gem was an Ibiza-style restaurant bar called Toca, which sat amid the trees on a cliff top overlooking the sea and sunset, with DJs pumping out familiar tunes and singers intermediately softening the atmosphere with some chilled out vocals. After a day of trekking up the island's lighthouse, then kayaking (badly) out to a small island to snorkel in the shallow warm waters with the various shoals of multi-coloured fish, myself and Alex along with his new mate Matheos from Brazil took in one last sunset before I hit the road again the following day.

In Imbassai, I didn't get to see the famous sight of baby turtles hatching and finding their way to the sea in the moonlight but did add 'frango' (meaning chicken) to my minimal Portuguese vocabulary. After that, I went south again and joined Ruben and the Swedish boys for my final few days in Bahia in the surfing town of Itacare.

I really needed a beer after the long journey, so I jumped straight into a taxi to take me to my hostel on the outskirts of town. Five minutes in and we were pulled over by armed police on a house raid. There I am, fourteen hours after I set off, with a group of cops standing around the car wielding guns and flashing a torch in my face. My unflinching tired response was to give a gormless wave and say 'hello' in a very

Irish tone. The taxi driver explained I was just a gringo and we were allowed to drive on. The area I had picked to stay in had a turf war going on – great!

I finally met the lads for a few bevies and we laughed about it. Later that night there were no taxis available to take me back to the hostel. Luckily I met British Peter and Irish Dicky who let me crash with them in the hostel they ran called Bananas, which I then moved to for the rest of my stay away from the drug war.

Itacare turned out to be a right little jewel of a destination, with a laid back surfer mentality and, as with most places I'd visited in Brazil, a strong waft of weed filled the air. The hostel had a great vibe about it too, everyone chatting over breakfast with surfing invitations aplenty. At night the bar area provided fire shows from the resident hippies camping at the bottom of the garden. The beaches in the area were some of my favourite too, all that you can imagine from a tropical day dream. One beach favoured by the more elite surfers was stunning, reached via bus then a twenty minute trek under jungle cover to unveil its palm laden gleaming sands.

Back in the UK or Ireland, the run up to Christmas would be hectic by now, shoppers trampling each other to panic buy turkeys and the latest computer games. I didn't miss that at all, but I really did miss the magical feeling that comes with the cold, the festive films, open fires and millions of twinkling lights. In this part of the world, you're lucky to sniff out a bauble, so when Leona Lewis' Christmas album came on my iPod when I was sunbathing in the heat it made me smile a festive smile.

With my short visit to this Brazilian oasis coming to an end, I was back in Salvador for one night before an early flight to Rio. I was fortunate with my choice of hostel as my second choice just a few metres up the hill had been robbed the previous evening. According to Mark, a traveller from the UK who had been staying there, an armed gang got in through the roof and rounded everybody up in the main bathroom. They made them hand over all their possessions one by one. A harrowing experience, but thankfully no one was hurt. It was a reminder of the undercurrent of crime in Salvador which can turn into a tidal wave at any moment.

There was a fun bunch staying at my hostel that night, within a couple of hours of meeting we were all finishing up the free cocktails provided and were off dancing behind a samba drum band as we followed them through the streets. A fitting Latin way to wave goodbye to this melting pot of a city.

I was back to the diamond in the rough that is Rio, which would sadly be my final few days on this continent. It was a chance to tick off my shamelessly touristy list of sight seeing to-dos. Luckily a few of my fellow backpacking compadres were in Rio too. Fraser was finishing up a volunteering stint, and Charlie from way back in Peru, as well as the two Welsh tornados, Dave and Ben, whom I'd last seen in Chile, were all there to greet me. I was due to meet Charlie and his gaggle of Aussie and Canadian mates to take in the Rio sunset over a few beers at the Arpoador rocks over looking Ipanema beach. I arrived early and wandered around the huge boulders which made up the viewing point. A couple of local lads asked me to take their picture on one of the highest peaks. It turned out they were a couple and went into smouldering kissing poses. I loved it, they were so sweet together. With minutes to spare before darkness descended, Charlie and crew rocked up and we sat watching the burning sun disappear over the horizon with whoops and cheers from the gathered crowd.

Next day I was up early and it was finally time to visit Rio's most famous landmark, Christ the Redeemer. It has to be a clear day to visit the big man or else you'll just be looking at a load of clouds. I met a couple from the UK, Jonno and Harriet, en route, and we shared a taxi bus up. But what do you know, by the time we reached the top the very clear day turned cloudy, shrouding the monument and making Christ invisible. What else to do but get the beers in and wait for it to blow over. An hour later it did, and we skedaddled upward, as did hundreds of other visitors. The monument is pretty impressive, and the views of the city below from the peak were panoramic, but honestly once you've taken your pictures there really isn't much else to do, so it was back down and adios to one of the most spectacularly placed statues on the planet.

Next it was back to Lapa to see the famous beautifully tiled Selaron Stairs created by a local man named Jorge Selaron. People from all over the world heard of his mission to beautify these once plain steps outside his home and sent ceramics from countries far and wide. Unfortunately the artist, who dedicated over twenty years to decorating the two hundred steps, was killed in 2013 in what was rumoured to be a revenge attack after a dispute with a gang member who he stood up to, but his memory lives on forever on these colourful footholds. That night, myself and Fraser took in the light show and street markets of the area and a samba club, where there was more free caipirinhas on offer. We danced the night away with locals, tourists and some scantily clad samba girls. Before myself, the Welsh boys and big crowd of fellow travelling buddies met up in Shenanigans Irish pub to watch the legend Conor McGregor in a much hyped UFC fight, and although the 4am fight lasted only thirteen seconds the atmosphere created was electric and full of Irish pride.

Last thing to scratch of my list in Rio, and the one thing I'd been looking forward to most, was visiting a favela. Myself and Fraser opted for a local guide called Eric, who lives in Rocinha, the biggest favela of them all. Rocinha has an armed police presence but is still very much under the influence of the drug lords. Eric started by showing us some government funded projects including a sports centre, just across the road from the entrance. He told us how after much campaigning and protests the government had promised a list of improvements, but so far had only provided ones like the sports centre which are visible to any visitors. He told us that prior to the Olympics being held in the city in 2016, the government provided various favelas with paint to spruce up their dwellings and to make them more pleasing on the eye for all the incoming international visitors.

We took a harrowing motorbike taxi ride to the top of the favela, the driver insisted I held onto the bars at the back of the bike not to him. So with the tightest of grips and gritted teeth, we sped up the winding hills in and out of oncoming traffic with the driver trying to chat to me about the Conor McGregor fight. The views from the top over the city and the surrounding affluent neighbourhoods were incredible, and it was from this high vantage point that we made our way on foot down through the rickety alleyways and main streets of Rocinha. The armed police presence causes tensions and there's regular gunfire. We didn't encounter any gun-toting gangsters on our visit but we did get to meet and interact with the community. They all greeted us with nothing but smiles and a welcoming manner, especially one of Eric's friends who invited us into his home on what happened to be his wife's birthday. The man, named Caesar, is an artist and quite a character. He was always smiling and excited to have us there. The whole family welcomed us with open arms, sharing their food and drink on their amazing balcony overlooking the tightly packed colourful abodes below. We bought some of Caesar's homemade personalised postcards before thanking our hosts and heading down deeper into the complex and feared favela. We made our way through some stinking alleyways with garbage-filled dilapidated sewage systems, and through passages where hundreds of live electric cables hung within arm's reach. All of the locals said hello and they seemed to make the best of what they had, although they could help themselves and find better ways to dispose of their rubbish.

We met a group of youths hanging out as they would do in any council estate back home. Eric translated back and forth for us. A young dad sat opposite on his door step playing with his daughter and their pet snake which he said he found in the surrounding jungle growth. We also met a young lad who was suffering from some deforming condition that meant half of his head was caved in affecting him both physically and mentally. He was a happy and loving little guy who gave me a huge hug and joked to Eric that he was much stronger than this gringo.

As we reached the busiest part of the favela, I noticed that life here wasn't too dissimilar to regular life anywhere else on the planet. Local people zipped about doing their shopping or having some drinks while the much-loved funky music played in the background. No masked papis or thugs approached or tried to intimidate us, although down a side street one guy decided to projectile vomit right in front of us, causing me to wretch a little too.

Favela life is poor and raw sure enough, at the bottom of the food chain as it were. Yes there are drugs and gangs, but there's also normal life with a massive sense of community and resilience which you don't get in the Chelseas or Beverly Hills of this world. The people living here vary in poverty, some, like Caesar, higher up the in the hills have quite a nice life, and for others their whole world is in one room. But they all deserve respect and should never be looked down upon just because of their starting point in life. I hope the new generation with more access to education and the world outside those streets get the chance to flourish. I was proud to have seen the favela up close and through the eyes of the people living there, and wished I had more time to visit the other neighbourhoods too, because this was definitely my favourite experience in Rio.

Being around the families and seeing them all so happy with not very much inevitably brought thoughts of my dad. After I left Wexford, he moved into a new flat, away from the last one we lived in together. On visits home, he would clean up as best he could before I got there, and would fill the fridge with the foods he thought I liked. As the years rolled on he would get my aunt to help clean. I would plead with him not to drink on the day I arrived, I know he wanted to make a good impression when I went home and he probably felt the pressure too, but nevertheless he generally did still drink on the day which overshadowed everything. I would arrive from the boat with whoever picked me up and sit for a minute in the car feeling anxious about whether or not he would be drunk, and it would immediately get my back up. If being around each other sober was awkward at times, being around him when he was drunk was even worse.

We were always together at Christmas. We generally spent it in Ireland, but sometimes we would go to my aunts in London. I loved the whole feeling of Christmas. It had always felt like an escape into a sort of Charles Dickens' cosy imagination. Me da loved it too and would always have the flat kitted out like Santa's grotto for when I got home with lights, tinsel, and balloons all around – we both loved the shiny things. He kept cards from all the previous years and displayed them about the place. He would get so excited that I was coming home and tell all his mates. He would always give up his bed for me too. He wanted to make me happy, and at times he really did.

We made the best of Christmas days, but I would hope someone else would be with us too, so that there wouldn't be any silences and me da had someone his own age there. My uncle Murty was usually with us in Ireland. I would cook the dinner and serve it up to them along with a Guinness. We would watch Only Fools and Horses or Home Alone or an old film together on the telly. Even though things were awkward or strained at times, he loved me being home, and I relished these moments. He just wanted it to be normal too but I felt so damaged from the past and always on edge knowing too much drink could ruin it at any moment.

Me da had no idea how my life in London was really. All he wanted to know was if I was ok, or if I could get myself a council flat, or if I was courting – a term that always made me feel like some old maid! I wished so bad we could talk about other things. I wished I could express to him the loss and loneliness I was feeling inside. How I was plagued with anxiety and experienced waves of depression. I wished I could tell him how things really were, but through those dark and lost years, it eluded us. I was reaching for a different kind of relationship with him, a more open one, but it always seemed just beyond my grasp. I resigned myself to the fact that the relationship I dreamed of might never happen, and I don't think he ever understood the enormity of us not being able to talk properly had on me.

He sometimes visited London, but as usual I urged him to stay with my aunts and I would go see him there. He came to see the places I lived but it felt easier if he stayed with people of a similar age. What was I going to do with me dad for a week with the way things were? I felt guilty thinking like this, but having other people around made his visits more enjoyable for him and for me, and we could talk a little more freely. The only time he actually stayed with me was in an apartment I shared in Putney with James, which was just down the hill from my aunt Kathleen. His first sight of the building didn't go to plan. After eating a dodgy pie in the Wetherspoons pub down the road, he projectile vomited on the lawn outside! But he stayed the night and he loved it, and if I had my own place in London he could have stayed all the time and come and gone as he pleased.

Me da could handle most situations. He had his head kicked in and was dumped in a river in Belfast for singing Republican songs when he was younger and wilder and survived, so I knew he could handle himself. It didn't stop me worrying though, so I felt better knowing he was with his family. As he got older, I urged him to give trips a miss, which he mistook for me not wanting to be around him. I worried about him too much, London wasn't the same place he spent all those years in.

It was in these years that he received his payout from his testimony at the abuse tribunal. I was so proud of him for going through with it. He got a big sum, more money than he had ever had in his life, and I don't think he knew what to do with it. He told me everything when it came to his money, but always told me to keep it to myself, which I did. He asked me what I wanted out of the payout. I had stupidly got a loan out from the bank, which had somehow spiralled from £1000 to £7000. I asked if he would pay that off for me and he did.

He had just opened his first ever Irish bank account. My aunt helped him as she always did after she moved back to Ireland from London. She was there to talk to him if he needed it or to help him understand things. He transferred almost €10,000 so I could pay the loan off and I did. That was the first and last time I ever got a loan.

With the payout, he bought himself new furniture for the flat. Me da was never really bothered with what furniture we had or if it even matched. We often had mismatched carpet and lino cuttings off the gypsies who sold door to door. But my aunt helped him pick the nice new stuff and he was delighted.

He was always generous with his money, buying drinks or slipping people money if they needed it. He used to walk around with €50 notes in his hand ready to buy his mates or nieces and nephews a drink, and never saw those close to him go without. He went on his first airplane journey after the payout too, off to Spain with my aunt, uncle and their other halves. He loved it more than anything. In the days they would go off on tours, me da with his sandals and socks combo. At night they would visit cabaret and drag shows, me da would almost piss himself laughing at the drag queen comedy. In any bar they visited, the whole place would be in stitches by the time they left. They say money can't buy you happiness but it sure helps buy you experiences that you will always remember.

He never saw me go without either and I was always grateful. On visits home he threw me €50 here and there. When I couldn't afford to be at home, he would give me the money to see me through and to go out with my mates. At Christmas or birthdays, he loved buying me gold, be it chains, bracelets or rings. At one point I had six gold rings and looked like Mr T! I had to put a stop to the jewellery after a while though. I never meant to upset him but he just wouldn't listen when he was asked not to do something, he was such a hard man to get through to, but always with good intentions. From there on in he would get me a laptop or a camera, or something I needed. He never said no if I needed help financially. That payout money was never an issue for us, he would always say to me 'fuck it, if it's gone it's gone'. He wanted the people around him to be happy, and that was a way he could effect that. I thought he should have appealed and thought he deserved more, but he just wanted it all to be over. The whole thing still angered me, the Catholic Church, their blood money, what they got away with, the devastating effect it had on my dad's life and the knock on effect it had on mine.

.

When we drank together, it always made me feel conflicted as I felt like I was giving him the green light to get drunk. But before he did, we would talk, and I felt like I could ask more questions then too. He told me about me mam, the old days, his childhood, and the women before my mam. It was in those moments when the ingrained awkwardness was gone, if only for a second.

Drinking would also cause our rows. I didn't like it when he rang me drunk and he would get angry. I'd retaliate and hang up, then call back five minutes later with overwhelming guilt and we'd both say sorry and that it's alright. But it all got too much for me, fighting with myself in my London world, I needed him to listen, to understand. So after a heavy night on a weekend away on the south coast with a mate, I let it all out. A blazing row ensued, and we spent half an hour arguing on the phone, a record time for me da to even stay on the phone. In an alleyway outside a pub as my breakfast went cold inside, I cried and shouted down the phone, getting years off my chest. He shouted back but he didn't hang up, and neither did I. Me da could be very scary when he lost his temper but I stood my ground. Maybe this would be a turning point, but as good as it felt to talk, things remained the same.

We had a breakthrough in openness a couple of times. Once when I was in the band, and he was on a visit to London. He met me on my lunch from work and we sat in a cafe. I told him that if the band took off we might become famous, and that when you're famous people say things about you in the papers. He turned and said 'as long as I know the truth Larry it doesn't matter, I'm proud of you'. That sentence meant more to me than he would ever know.

The other time was when I found the courage to tell him I needed him to understand a part of my life better, that it was important to let him in and know more, his reply of 'can you not go see the doctor or the priest about that' cracked me up laughing, even if I didn't want it to.

He could always make anyone laugh, his one liners and hilarity, especially in the pub with his mates made me smile. But none of them were his son, and that was always what I had to battle against

I went home as often as I could, and felt a massive pressure to visit everyone when I did. I always felt pulled, I made an effort to see various aunts, uncles, cousins and planned as much as I could with my friends. The trips home were never what you'd call relaxing though, and that was my fault for letting it all get to me, but that's how it was then. Me da was the same. He'd go out of his way to make an effort to see people.

He would wake up at the crack of dawn every day, and be out the door to meet my uncle and his mates in the pub in the morning, sometimes even before it opened. He would always leave me breakfast, even when I asked him not to. Eventually we agreed boiled eggs were a safe bet for us both – he used to boil them in the kettle with the tea water – and leave them out for me, as well as potatoes which he would peel for that evening. Sometimes he would have already cremated a chop on the pan too, ready for when he got home.

I usually met him down in the pub later in the morning, and I did enjoy sitting with him. It was an old sailor pub looking out at the sea. We didn't say much most of the time, but I loved listening to him and his mates and their stories. As the years went by he couldn't manage the drink as much, so he would be home by one or two in the afternoon to settle down and watch some sports or a film. I'd make his dinner, and sometimes stick a wrestling DVD on for a bit. He loved the vintage wrestling which we used to watch together when I was younger, from Giant Haystacks to The Undertaker. I was more into the Ultimate Warrior and Bret Hart. I'd then go out with my mates, calling him in the evening to check if he was ok. Again I felt guilt, like I shouldn't be out having fun, or like I was preferring to spend time with my friends over my own dad. But without the films or drink or other people around, we just didn't know how to be with each other. He was just happy to have me there sitting with him, and he loved I had such great friends. It was wrong to feel such guilt, but I did.

After a few days at home I needed to get out of the small town mentality, but leaving Wexford was always hard. It was my home and it broke my heart saying goodbye to him. He would stand there in tears telling me to look after myself. We would awkwardly hug and he'd wave me off every time from the window or door until I was out of sight. I'd be consumed with guilt and my mind raced with memories.

Looking at me da broke my heart at the best and the worst of times. I wanted him to be ok and have peace, we had been through so much together. He always looked after me, maybe it was in his own way but I knew that he did. I just wished things could be different. I wished we could talk to each other properly and that he could be there for me emotionally, to guide me.

Above it all, I knew me da was proud of me, and he did tell me he loved me at times, as I did him. Even if we didn't understand each other, even if we were worlds apart, he was my dad and I loved him and he did me. As the years passed and with his health fading, I had to settle that our relationship wouldn't ever be what I wanted and needed, a stark reality which left me in a manic ball of thoughts and sadness, which he would never understand.

My last couple of days in South America came, and I wasn't just saying goodbye to Rio but to the lovely and funny people I'd met along the way, and my first ever backpacking adventure. A nerve-racking and scary journey but so rewarding. Most importantly it gave me the time to step away from the chaos of London, to breathe and to start sorting through what had been the toughest few years of my life. I knew that travelling the world would be an untouchable experience, but now realised that the mind is the location we are always in, the permanent one, the one place we travel and explore the most. I have to be strong enough to fight on through any storms and turn my mind into my own little paradise. I know there will be times ahead when I might drift far from shore or get a little lost at sea, but hopefully I can continue to reach inside and find that bravery and strength to sail in the right direction again.

Chapter 15

Next up was Australia. I spent a night in a Santiago airport hotel before my connecting flight to Sydney. I took care of some much needed manscaping and splashed out on some chips and a bottle of wine, and watched Adele perform songs from her new album on YouTube. Although a huge fan I should've known by now that Adele and the likes should be avoided when trying to mend a broken heart!

It was now mid-December and I would normally be arranging an annual boy's Christmas drinks. As I wasn't there to organise it, I didn't expect it to happen this year, but then I received a picture message. It was all the boys along with some new faces out and about in frosty London Town in all their Christmas jumper glory, and wearing masks with my face on them. It was the most heart warming moment, all my besties, knowing I'd be missing them, made the effort to make sure I was there too and it made me feel amazing. Any thoughts of missing out or being forgotten evaporated and I loved them more than ever. Lord knows what the rest of the festive punters must have thought seeing those frightening masks with my mug on.

Finally, after a five hour delay, my flight was boarding. I felt a little anxious on the plane, South America had become familiar and I had met the best people along the way. What if Australia was a let down? I hadn't done much research at all, so it was only the unknown ahead. The fact I was going to actually be in the Land Down Under after all the years of imagining it felt strange. I told myself it was another new chapter, another step forward, and I was getting to see family and friends too.

I expected customs to be like Border Patrol on TV, with cameras and cavity searches, but I sailed on through to Arrivals without any hassle. I felt so excited to be there, and seeing families standing with balloons and banners waiting for their loved ones coming home for Christmas only added to the emotion.

I planned to spend three weeks in Sydney taking in Christmas and New Year, firstly staying with one of my old friends from London, Luke. We've known each other since I was 18 and he was just 16. We have similar backgrounds, although Luke's estate in North London was much more ghetto than my Wexford one. Sydney is his home now and he has a great career in TV. After going the wrong way on the tube, I finally reached the city centre, passing the Harbour Bridge all lit up on the way. Luke was waiting for me at the station with a smile and a hug.

I'd heard so much about Sydney, some good, some bad, but I reserved judgment for myself, and it didn't disappoint. In the morning, the view from Luke's balcony was of a clean, pleasant and unique skyline. Straight away I got a good feeling about this far away land and so it was time to explore.

In the next few days leading up to Christmas, I caught up with a whole host of Aussie, Welsh and British mates. Including Tom, Joe and Sarah who had all relocated here, and Rhydian and Chris on their global travels too. Then there was the natives, my old flat mate Ari, a talented aerial artist and yoga teacher, Jason a friend I'd made when he was backpacking Europe, and Angela whom I worked with in the corporate world of The City in London.

While exploring Sydney, I discovered that Jorn Utzon, the architect behind The Sydney Opera House, never got to see his design masterpiece completed. I had my first encounter with a harmless Australian spider the size of my hand – but I still stayed well back, envisioning it launching onto my face like a scene from Arachnophobia. I marvelled at the majesty of Sydney Harbour from Mrs Macquarie Point, and fell a little bit in love with Sydney right there and then. I found out that Mrs Macquarie was one time Governor Macquarie's wife, called Elizabeth. I also fell in love with Bondi Beach and learned that you can't drink alcohol on its sands, so have to sip discreetly and be on the look out for police patrolling in their little beach cars. I learned that the city has a thriving breakdance scene which Luke was shooting for a documentary. Also that you shouldn't sneak up to the closed top bar at Shangri La Hotel to take in views of the harbour without expecting to be turfed out by security. I discovered that chai latte is my new favourite drink, and I had my first ever experience with jet lag, and boy did it hit me hard – I almost conked out right in the middle of a conversation. Oh, and that depression and anxiety can still wash over me at any given point without explanation.

Maybe it was the aftermath of boozing and the jetlag, or maybe it was the fact that I was surrounded by normal life again and it was in the run up to Christmas. The reality that I didn't have a clue where I would go or what I would do once I left Sydney was playing on my mind too. But rather than wallow, I picked myself up and asked Chris and Rhydian for recommendations. They had already been to most of Australia so could help me make a plan. Within an hour, I had a route of the East Coast marked out and I immediately felt better. I was determined not to let these bouts of depression and darkness last too long and was slowly learning how to view them now. Instead of them creeping up on me, I was now more aware when they were coming and maybe even one step ahead. The months away were helping me to see the road ahead with a little more clarity.

Before I landed at my cousin Debbie's door for Christmas, I spent a couple of days with Angela and her family. Her little girl, Molly, handed me a Christmas card and one of her little toys as I walked through the door which put me on cloud nine. We visited a local koala park housing all sorts of Australian wildlife like dingoes, koalas, galahs and a sheep sheering display from an outback farmer. The unmanned enclosure where you could wander in and get up close and personal with the kangaroos, all laying there in the heat or hopping around hoping you would feed them, was a rough and ready Aussie experience. I expected them to be in a fenced area but there they were eye to eye with me. I hoped I wouldn't be knocked out with a kick when I got close for some pictures. The barrage of flies and the whiff of Skippy and his mates got a bit much after a while, so we headed home. Thankfully there was hand sanitizer on the way out.

I hadn't seen my cousin Debbie in years, and I was looking forward immensely to spending Christmas with her and the kids. I felt nervous on arrival and hoped we would still get on, we hadn't spent that much time together back in Ireland as Debbie also left home when she was young. I needn't have worried one bit, as I walked through the door I was met by a familiar accent and a big hug from Debbie and her now not so little kids, two of which I hadn't even met before.

It was a madhouse just like I thought it would be, and I felt right at home. What followed was one of the nicest Christmases I've had, meeting all of Debbie's brilliant friends, or the Real Housewives of Sydney as I named them, and their hilarious husbands. Debbie has made a cracking group of friends and a lovely life out on the other side of the world and I was chuffed to be part of it. They all welcomed me with open arms, a truly marvellous bunch of people who I'm glad I got to become friends with too. There I was meant to be backpacking the world but there wasn't a hostel in sight, instead I was drinking champagne in beautiful houses with Debbie and her crew. If we weren't visiting her mates, we were running around the casinos and pubs of Sydney or having fun on the beaches. Unfortunately I didn't get to experience Bondi on Christmas Day as it was cloudy for the first time in years, but being around Debbie's table and with her family and friends was priceless.

I lay there in my little cousin's bunk bed which he had given up for me, I never imagined this is how my 30s would unfold. I thought back to my laughter filled 30th birthday in Ibiza with all my friends and remembered I had a determined 'right lets make this decade better' attitude. How I'd hoped to find lasting love. Now here I was at 36, only a few months previously suffering so bad on the inside that I couldn't even function, but now on a life-altering journey to change it all once and for all, absorbing and appreciating every part of it.

And then it was time for the big one, New Year's Eve in Sydney Australia. The iconic harbour fireworks attract visitors from all over the globe, so the place was buzzing. I had moved around the city a bit by New Year's Eve, staying with mates and Debbie, and now crashed at Sarah's city pad for a couple of days to be in the thick of it all. I met up with Tom and we decided on a spot at Mrs Macquarie's Point. We hoped to bag a decent patch of grass with views of the harbour bridge. It seemed half of the city had the same idea. After two hours of queuing in the blistering heat in a snaking line which felt like it wasn't going anywhere, and with no sign of the end, we took matters into our own hands and finally jumped the rest of the queue. Mission number two was getting past the security check with our booze. A group of loud tipsy Scottish lasses were ahead of us and I suspected they might cause a bit of commotion at the check. They did, and while the guard was preoccupied with this Rab C Nesbitt ball of energy we took our chance, and quickly walked in and up the road before the confused looking security man could raise the alarm. Our bottles of spirits were intact and boy did we need them with almost twelve hours to wait until the rockets and illuminations started to welcome in the New Year.

Every patch of grass was covered with picnic blankets or sleeping bags stretched out to almost tearing point to mark territory. We eventually found an oddly shaped spot big enough for the two of us and amidst eye rolls and 'don't you dare step on our patch; looks from the surrounding party goers, we took our place. Some people had been there all night or from the early hours. One guy opposite was vomiting his guts up from over indulging since sunrise on the vodka. The lad eventually conked out as his mates rubbed his head. The people around us finally let their territorial guard down, so we got chatting to two couples, one on their honeymoon in Sydney and the other backpacking around the globe. By the time darkness descended, the rum and Tom's vodka had well and truly run out, so we were on the wine, a drink I really shouldn't drink in public as it turns me into a drunken fool.

Myself, Tom, and the backpacking couple, Jacob and Siobhan, stayed until midnight and the atmosphere was electric. Blazing red fireworks cascaded from the harbour bridge and twinkling yachts and barges out in the harbour set off explosions of colour. It was a New Year's celebration like no other, and we drunkenly hugged strangers and raised our plastic glasses to the sky above. I hoped along with the rest of the planet that this new year would bring with it only happiness, but I knew in my heart I had to make that reality for myself. The sparkling skies above wouldn't be providing any heavenly miracles, but the fact I was still here and moving forward was a small miracle. My firework still had life in it yet.

I landed in Cairns in tropical Northern Queensland a few days later with not much but a cartoon map, advice and tips from Debbie and the boys, and a thirst for adventure. Admittedly I didn't even know Australia had a 'tropical' region until a mate Arron back in London told me he stayed in a rainforest here. By the first evening I was so laden down with brochures and glossy pamphlets from the various tour operators I felt overwhelmed. I threw the bulging plastic wallet of information onto my bunk and headed to the bar instead. If I heard the word 'reef' one more time I might have screamed. I was most definitely all reefed out and I hadn't even been near a sprig of coral yet. I was so knackered that night that not even the bombsite of a dorm which I was sharing with four young German lads, or the oldest hippie in the hostel taking to the open mic and spitting out Eminem lyrics with all the flow of a dumpster truck right outside the window didn't bother me.

I moved onto Port Douglas, a pretty and much more laid back town and popular nautical portal to the reefs. I checked into Dougies, a hostel set with a natural backdrop, and with its own pool. I was also welcomed with news that a brown and highly venomous snake was caught and bagged around said pool that very morning – lovely. My dorm had some long stay backpackers housed up there. A quiet lad called Paul who worked and spent a lot of time playing video games in his bunk, and Michael a Geordie who had just started his backpacking adventure a few weeks earlier and was waiting for his friend Gareth to save up enough money so they could start their Aussie road trip together.

I clicked with Michael straight away, I liked his laid back, let the world go by attitude, and his determination to strengthen his body and become as bendy as possible through daily yoga poses, exercises and handstand techniques. He loved the alternative natural diet too and always carried seeds or powders with him. We chatted around the pool that afternoon in the sweltering heat, and were careful to avoid any snakes while another resident, an old outback biker with a long grey ponytail and mouth like a sewer when he spoke about pulling women, interjected with his conquest stories.

Michael and a sassy American girl called Sal, a lesbian who lived in a tent at the back of the property, took me out for beers in the local Irish pub that night and a quick friendship was formed before I headed off on a tour around Cape Tribulation the following day.

I saw more wildlife in the area doing my own thing rather than on the walking tour. I was starting to have my fill of organised tours already, but with only a month to travel back down to Sydney I had to roll with it and hoped any future pre-paid packages would be more rewarding.

That night brought a stay at a large rainforest cabin right next to Cape Tribulation beach, where the rainforest meets the reef, plush greenery meets the aqua blue glistening seas, with the brightness of the sands the only partition. It also brought a very large orb spider who hung right outside the window for the duration. But I was taking the spider folk in my stride. On a walk along the beach, I jumped from rock to rock in the shallows in my flip flops, being careful to avoid any of the box jellyfish which I was warned about, and keeping an eye on the mangroves after seeing signs warning of crocodiles in the area. It was there that I met Grace, a girl from the UK on her global getaway too. It turned out we were both sharing our huts with rampant and quite annoying teenagers. After a word with the camp's chief, he gave us a new hut and we ended doing a flit during the night when our roomies were out, laughing as we ran along the rain forest path to our new peaceful abode.

A few backpackers had a bonfire on the beach that night too, so we grabbed a couple of bottles of wine and joined them. It was here I met Bridget and Reese, a true Aussie tornado of a couple. Bridget was in her forties with lips and breasts that would rival Dolly Patron's and her beau, a blonde laid back and fun loving surfer dude, was quite a bit younger. Together they were just hilarious and very much in love. She shared stories with us of her childhood hunting crocodiles and rodeo riding with her dad in the northern territories, surfing amongst great white sharks and her current life as a stunt woman and model.

As the fire died down, Reese disappeared into the thick tangled forest to collect some wood and Bridget joined him. Yelps in thick Australian accents followed and then out of the total darkness they appeared like Tarzan and Jane with mounds of sticks and dead trees ready to get the sparks flying again. The roaring fire was nothing compared to the spark they had between them and I hoped one day soon I would find that kind of crazy adventure and laughs with someone.

The surprises this part of Australia kept on bringing made my lack of research seem like a good thing. On the banks of the Daintree river in the afternoon sun, I got to see a big daddy crocodile basking in the sun, toothless and scarred from fighting and staking his claim as the don of his territory. Little archerfish appeared and spat water up at the boat with ridiculous precision. In the rainforest enormously long monitor lizards suddenly shuffle across your path like something out of a Sinbad adventure. At Mossman Gorge, with its indigenous history, I jumped into the gushing rapids, being careful not to slice my head and float off down stream.

If I thought the crocs on the Daintree were big, I was in for a shock when visiting Hartley's crocodile farm on the way back to Port Douglas. It was like a rough and ready Disneyland, and also a working breeding farm, with a huge man-made lake full of reptiles. They lunged right out of the water to snap at their lunch of chicken heads on sticks held by the boat's guides. My lunch was a meal deal in the cafe beside the lake, not your usual cheese sandwich and crisps combo but crocodile kebabs with a glass of wine. I avoided eye contact with any of the beasts swimming beside me, feeling guilty for eating their kin.

The place is packed with adventure and any kid's dream place to visit. I got up close with snakes, kangaroos, koalas and even had a chance to feed the elusive cassowary, a prehistoric and terrifying looking bird, think of an emu mixed with a turkey and velociraptor! They communicate with each other through strange, almost outer worldly vibrations, summoned by bending their heads into their chests. I fed them some fruit, hoping to keep my fingers attached to my hand, and fed a few of the snappy fresh water crocs too with my own pole and chicken heads. Then came the big show, and when I say big, think monstrous. Hagrid, yep named after the Harry Potter character due to his size, the biggest crocodile I've ever seen lunged metres out of the water as the Steve Irwin-esque feeder swung his dinner above him and then Hagrid smashed back down into the murky water. The beast's head was the size of a small car and the snap of his jaws echoed around the enclosure.

When in Australia, it would be a crime not to visit The Great Barrier Reef. After an evening back at Dougies sharing beers and stories with my new pal Michael – I was really starting to like the cut of this boy's jib – it was off again to cruise to the outer reef. Our boat, Silver Sonic, looked like a super yacht and it brought us out to the iconic seas with their fragile gardens of living wonderment beneath.

In the dive class, I again kept quiet about my asthma. The group consisted mainly of American Jewish kids on a break from finishing law school. Loud and brash as you would expect, but also welcoming and fun. They were on a trip to embrace this world of adventure before their corporate lives began and the money became too tantalising to escape the lives expected of them.

Thankfully anchored away from any other boats, the first of the dives was pretty tame and safe, with our group all annoyingly linked for the entire time. I'd already dived in the seas of Brazil so felt like a pro now, hello! I even avoided snot bubbles on this dip, but never the less we were submerged in a natural wonder of the world surrounded by all its unreal beauty. You can't help but smile being part of this famous, fearsome but delicate eco system. Thirsty for more and wanting to do my ow thing, I opted for a second dive where we swam nearer to the advanced divers and were allowed to go solo. I swam around huge underwater mountains of coral, with lion fish nestled in between and all sorts of brightly coloured tropical life bobbing about. I was careful to avoid the trigger fish though as they have a bad boy attitude and will attack if you get too near. I also missed a reef shark by seconds, a few months previous and I would have been off like a torpedo at the yell of shark, but now I was looking for them.

Note to self: to avoid being made a holy show of by the instructor don't accidentally stand on the coral with your flipper, even if you feel like you're lungs might explode and arms fall off from snorkelling doggy style.

Back on the boat I met a Brisbane guy called Rob and his girlfriend, a chatty couple who love life and wanted to explore the big wide world too. We had some beers to celebrate the day. Rob even offered me a couch and said he would show me around his home city if I decided to visit on the way down the coast.

As we made our way back across the Coral Sea all I wanted to do was tell me da what I had just done, I knew he would have smiled and been so proud. I wished more than ever he was still with us. He had been to Australia with the merchant navy and I would've given anything to share this with him.

Back in Cairns, I marked onward locations from a Greyhound bus map with a pink highlighter pen and was ready to go. I messaged Michael and told him of my plans. I kind of hoped he would join me. I knew we would have a laugh and by the sounds of it his mate Gareth was going to be a while getting some dosh together, so why sit in a baking hot hostel dorm wasting time? And then what do you know a message back saying he had decided he would meet his friend at a later date and was coming to join me on the next leg of my travels. He was on his way to Cairns to meet me and sort his ticket. I was very happy to have a pal to head off with me.

With it being my last day, I thought I would spruce up me old Bruce, I don't know what that means but it sounds Aussie enough so I'm running with it. I visited the local barber, one that looked pretty decent and traditional but by now I knew not to take a barber shop at face value. My first mistake here was arriving fifteen minutes before they closed, as I sat in the chair I realised I'd found the world's angriest barber. Think Jack Nicholson in The Shining but with clippers. He called all backpackers cunts and when he asked what I wanted he barked at me 'not to tell him how to do his fucking job'. The other barber on duty was happily laughing and chatting with his client, why did I have to get this nut job? After ten minutes of insults I was starting to get angry and was about to lose it and stick his head in the sink. But instead I tried to remember all I had learned thus far and I took a different approach. I asked him about his hometown, family, obvious barber talent and basically tried to kill him with kindness. It worked and he finished by apologising and shaking my hand. I wished him well and wondered if he would make it to forty with his blood pressure that high, but at least he did a decent fade and that's all I wanted.

After we talked through my plans and where he would hop on and off, myself and Mickey boy were ready to go and left Cairns behind, waving goodbye to its grid system of streets with fruit bat-filled trees, party thirsty strip and endless stream of backpackers. We travelled down to Townsville and hopped over to Magnetic Island, where we thumbed lifts off girls driving around in the islands famous pink Barbie cars, and hiked over sweltering ridges (me again in flip flops!) to the nudist beach which was totally deserted, bar one fella with his willy out soaking up the rays. We lounged in the hostel pool on inflatable swans and fed the wild possums by the bar. I held the lizards, parrots, snakes and a koala bear in the adjoining nature park. Next, we headed for Airlie Beach, yet another gateway, this time to the Whitsunday Islands, seventy-four majestic islands speckled around the coral reef.

To tour around the islands only one vessel stood out for me from the tidal wave of brochures, as if it was a Siren sat upon on a rock, beckoning me with her sparkling breasts and heavenly voice. I didn't care about the cost as it couldn't have felt more right. A vintage tall ship and not just any tall ship, this one looked like a freaking pirate ship. The Solway Lass, a ship built over one hundred and fourteen years ago that has since gone through numerous reincarnations. It now sailed the Whitsundays on a weekly basis. I was so excited, even though Michael was sitting this one out and off to his next stop before I got back. So before I set sail on my three day and three night nautical adventure, what else to do but have a blinder of a night out with my Geordie pal. We danced around the clubs and bars of Airlie Beach like two big tools.

This was swiftly followed by a hangover cure of a fry-up and veg smoothies the next day, while trying to rap battle each other around the man-made lagoon, where travellers congregated and tanned with conviction as if their lives depended on it.

I said adios to my compadre, we would meet up again soon, and although I wanted to do the sailing adventure solo, I felt sad parting ways. Spending time with Michael had made me look at myself differently, and like all the great buddies I had met so far I took something from the experience. He helped bring a calmness to me, helped me somewhat understand and dissect myself a little more, made me alter my outlook slightly. Hopefully another step in the right direction, and maybe some more of the weight lifted. I didn't want to get too excited, I know that my mind can be a little trickster, but I felt meeting all these people was helping steer me out of the manic and tormenting lane and helping me shift down a gear, reminding me to keep my eyes on the road in front, rather than the rear view mirror.

I thanked Michael for being part of that, and I looked forward to seeing him again soon, and hopefully beating him in a battle. They don't call me the Eminem of Wexford for nothing – nah seriously, no one calls me that.

As I walked down the jetty at Abell Point marina towards the tall sails of the Lass, I was full of hope, excitement and wonder. Visions of her history and the stories its walls must hold ran through my mind. I couldn't wait to get below decks and see my cabin. We were welcomed by the surprising young and fun crew and my shipmates all seemed like a good bunch from all over the globe. I was bunking up with a French family, slightly awkward in a cabin the size of a bathroom, especially when the mademoiselles were of ample proportions. I didn't care though and we all sat together that evening listening to the crew's tales of the ship and themselves, Captain Lyndsey at the helm.

Four dolphins swam beside the ship as we cruised into the sunset towards our first anchoring point for the night. The rains came the next morning but it didn't matter and made it a different experience. We snorkelled with shoals of fish off the blinding white fine sands of White Haven beach as the warm rains broke through the watery surface above. We had to wear skin-tight and oh so flattering stinger suits anytime we got in the sea as it was jellyfish season. We sailed on to Tongue Bay to take in the view of the swirling sands and sea from a lookout point. Scotty the head deckhand introduced us to edible green ants along the trek which taste like bitter lime and you have to be careful as they bite back.

At a stop called Lucheon Bay, a boyhood dream came true. I got to help hoist the ships sails. In the spitting rain, myself, Scotty and first mate Chris heaved with all our might and as the sailcloth glided upward, scenes from Mutiny on the Bounty, Moby Dick and all the other sea films I had watched with my dad flooded my head. I saw him in my mind, through all the stages we knew each other, but most recently in his chair, hands clasped and content watching his sea pictures. I wanted to cry, I wanted him to be here, I wanted him to have all his Tommy Meyler strength and might back, and to be on this adventure with me. As the sails flapped and the rains fell, I took some time by myself at the bow of the ship, legs dangling over the side above the old rope net now used as a hammock. The sea sliced into white waves breaking below. I looked out and felt some peace, my ocean rehab, and I remembered, remembered the day things changed forever.

Chapter 16

It was November 13th 2010, me da's 77th birthday. I called as usual early that morning before he went out, but he seemed disoriented, like he didn't get what I was saying. I presumed it was a hangover or he had just woken up, so I said I would call him back once he got to the pub. I had arranged to put some money behind the bar so he could have a drink for his birthday with my uncle and his mates, but when I called the pub the landlady, Stephanie, who my dad loved and always looked out for him, told me that he was already there but seemed very confused. She said he wasn't making much sense so she called my aunt and they took him up to her house and called his doctor.

Me da's health wasn't the best. He had a heart scare and a bypass was recommended, but he turned it down fearing he was too old to get through it. He also suffered with his breathing which as he got older had gotten worse. His feet were a constant blight, mainly due to a heavy hammer which had fallen on his big toe on a building site years previously. But he never had the operation to correct it as he hated the sight of needles and the thought of being cut open. He wore these fake leather zip up boots which didn't help his feet but he wouldn't change them. No matter how many pairs of shoes and trainers we bought him he would revert back to his favourite boots, much to my dismay.

When it came to his doctor, there was no point in trying to get him to change either, me da got on well and respected the one he had. I had conversations with the doctor, asking him to try and get me da to cut down on booze and eat better, which he said he would, but overall I found him blasé, with a tendency to cut you off mid-sentence. The fact that he prescribed me da Viagra, a man on medication for his heart, on a regular basis summed up his ethics. But I knew me da used to sell them in the pubs for a tenner a pop, so I didn't broach the subject.

When this same doctor arrived at my aunt's to carry out an examination on the day he was taken ill, the results were a little unexpected. He walked in and asked me da a couple of questions as he sat there confused and disoriented out of his mind. He proceeded to give him an injection and pronounced that he had fluid on the brain, that the injection would sort him out, and he would be fine in twenty-four to forty-eight hours. My relatives didn't know anything about a condition like this, so we all thought it must be a common condition with the elderly, given the quick visual diagnosis. The doctor left me dad at my aunt's house and we hoped he would come round and be back to his normal self the next day. Hearing this all over the phone left me confused and worried.

But by the next day he had gotten worse, he didn't even know what day it was, so they called another doctor for a second opinion. An immediate diagnosis came that he had already had or was on the verge of a major stroke, and an ambulance was called straight away. All that time sat in the chair on his doctor's orders and without real medical intervention was crucial time lost, and because we listened to that fool of a man thinking he knew what he was talking about, the situation became a whole lot worse for me da.

I finally got back to Wexford and I cried my eyes out seeing me da in the hospital bed. I hoped to God he would come back from this, thankfully it hadn't physically affected him, but mentally he was totally confused and his speech messed up. He knew what he wanted to say but his brain wouldn't connect to let him voice it, so he became increasingly worried and frustrated. They also found he had suffered two previous mini-strokes as well. He didn't understand the seriousness and enormity of what was happening. The hospital moved him to a rehab facility in the next town about half an hours drive away, which he stayed in for well over a month.

This period was a nightmare for all concerned, with my dad at the centre of it not really understanding what was wrong with him and just wanting to get home. Relatives and friends went up and down to see him to try and encourage familiarity and normality. My aunt was there every day with him hoping he would come round. He would be up and dressed and he really tried and did all he was told to do by the doctors and nurses. As the time rolled on and enough progress hadn't been made, the facility said they couldn't keep him there any longer, and that he needed twenty-four hour care. Doctors and consultants told me that unless a relative could dedicate the time the only place for him to be safe would be a care home, where he would have medical assistance and support twenty-four seven.

Inevitably all decisions lay with me, a pressure I have never experienced before. I always kept my distance and not been involved too much with extended family, but now all eyes were on me and the pressure was immense. Everyone had an opinion, but all just wanted to see me da get better. Ultimately I had to make all the major decisions and deal with the consequences.

I didn't want to send him to a care home at all. My aunts would do anything for my dad and they did as much as they could. But looking after and dealing with him full time needed specialist training and experience. My aunt Winnie suggested he go live with her in the west of Ireland for a while. She had no hesitation about it but I knew it would've been just too much for her after a while and too far away from all he knew.

But I decided to let the decision come from my dad, it was his life so he should decide. It was so frustrating as he had made some progress in rehab, some days on the phone he would string full sentences together and understand what I was saying. I would hang up and pray that it was a turning point and that he just needed a little more time. But with pressure mounting and the facility unable to keep him there, what nobody said, but was becoming more obvious, was that I should move back to Wexford and be his carer. This wasn't straightforward. We hadn't lived together in fifteen years and I felt it would do more harm than good in the long run, for us both. I was panic-stricken at the thought and I hated that I was, even thinking about myself at this time added to the building pressure and anxiety. I wished things were different but they weren't and this was reality. If I moved back to Wexford to live with me da it would have been the end of me, and I knew it.

From London I pleaded with the rehab to keep him there as it was doing him good, everyone loved him. He even helped the older patients too. He had the nurses in stitches, even through the stroke he had his eye on a blonde one who he called Shirley, as in Shirley from Eastenders, not much of a compliment for the poor girl. But nothing could be done. They couldn't keep him as the places were needed. In this new and sudden whirlwind of emotionally draining responsibility, I spoke extensively with the professionals, they gave me lots of reassurances and so I decided I would consider the care home for some respite. There he could continue on the road to a full recovery in the next couple of months. I returned to Wexford once again, this time to talk to my dad.

I sat with him alone in the TV room of the rehab centre. I held back tears as I tried to simplify my words, firstly telling him about the home and showing him the pictures. He knew where it was and what it was, and he didn't like it. I explained it would just be for a while. I knew he understood, he was my dad and no matter what had happened over the years I knew him. I asked him if he wanted to go live with my aunt Winnie in the west for a while, and he said as best he could, 'no too far, too far', and that was that option done.

I asked him if he wanted me to move home, he had often said to me in drink to come back, saying I could get a flat and decent dole money. But he knew I couldn't and he didn't want that life for me either, as much as he didn't know about my mental state he knew at least I had made a life for myself in London. He would always say afterwards, 'you stay over there, there's nothing here for you in this town', and now his opinion hadn't changed. I asked him 'will I come back and live with you?', and he repeated it back to me, 'you come home?', 'yes dad,' I said. He sat back and looked away while he tried to process it all, he then leaned forward and said 'no, no you stay over there, you stay son ok'. My heart broke in pieces. Me da was there in front of me, and even though he didn't look at all like the man I grew up with, in that moment I forgot everything, all the bad and all the hurt. I wished more than ever that we could have a normal father and son relationship and that I could come back and make it all better. I wished that we didn't fight or that I didn't get into moods around him. I was doing everything I could, everything I thought best, but there in that room I felt angry at myself that I'd failed him. We sat there together and we bonded without fear, but it was too late, through a cruel turn of events I had watch my dad drift away even more.

He asked me 'what's wrong with me' and again I tried to explain. He could see the tears in my eyes, and the conversation turned back to the home. I knew he didn't want to go but he did want to get better and so he agreed.

I promised him that no matter what anyone said it would be temporary. That conversation was one of the hardest things I ever had to do in my life. Sat there looking at each other, just a father and son. The thought of putting him in a home, somewhere he said he would rather be dead than end up in, then having to make it a reality brought on waves of guilt that I had never experienced before.

What followed was hell.

During my dad's stay in rehab, myself and my aunt ran around the place trying to get his affairs in order. I was back and forth from London as much as I could, consumed with worry, guilt, nervousness and heartbreak at the whole situation. I tried to keep a positive outlook and just get things done. My dad's brother Jimmy and sister Winnie did what they could too. His face lit up when his siblings visited him in rehab. They both reassured me things would be ok and not to take on too much, but I couldn't help it. He was my dad and I just wanted him to get better. I felt bad enough not moving home.

None of us wanted this kind of life for him, he always said himself he wanted to live out his days and go quick without even knowing about it. Not live in a limbo. I wanted to get him back to what he knew and his routine, his familiar life.

I used the opportunity while he was in the rehab's facility to sort out his living conditions. He lived on the first floor in a small one bedroom flat which was built for the elderly. I didn't like the place, with its morbid and dark entrance and a hallway like something out of the Green Mile, but he liked it, it was cosy and it did him. I went through everything, all the unnecessary clutter, his paper work, his clothes. I scrubbed the grease off the walls in the kitchen from his ventures into cooking. One big overhaul so it was a better environment for him when he eventually got back there.

While sorting through everything, I found numerous pairs of reading glasses, some never even used, and boxes of Viagra in his drawer too. His little enterprise to add a few quid on to his pension. Also proving what a moronic medical decision the doctor had made. Finally we met with dad's doctor and confronted him about his poor diagnosis and care. The doctor admitted he was in the wrong and he knew then I had him by the balls.

With time being of the essence, the rehab days dwindling and still so much needed to be sorted out, pressure mounted from all angles and I was at breaking point. As always my friends, Michelle and my other cousin Sarah were there without question. Michelle had moved back to Wexford from Essex with her two kids. They could all see I was physically and mentally drained. I cried at the drop of a hat and felt a constant pain in my head from the whole situation, but they were always there, always ready to drop everything and help me out and I loved them more than ever.

The day my dad moved to the care home was just horrendous. My friend Paula drove us down, trying to keep him upbeat and laughing on the way. He was meant to have his own room but they said they had to place him in with another man until one became free. I knew this meant until someone died, which made me feel even worse about the decision. We tried to make the place homely for him with pictures of my mam, and he had his little radio beside the bed and got Michelle to come cut his hair in the room, jokingly telling him it was in case he met a rich widow in there. Part of the new arrival protocol was having to stick stickers with his name on every single item of clothing including socks and underwear. I understood it but it made the home feel like an institution and that was the worst kind of place for me da to feel he was in. I prayed his time there and being looked after by the professionals would aid his recovery quickly.

To say it didn't was an understatement. He didn't understand why he was there and just wanted to go home. To make things worse his roommate would sometimes wake up in the night and walk around the room, the poor man not knowing where he was, which frightened the life out of me dad. It brought him right back to feeling institutionalised in the Artane. He started getting angry. He didn't want to do the folder of daily mind exercises the rehab had given him and he wasn't getting any of the physio like he had in rehab. I had to go back to work in London. All I could do was hope he would settle in and the support and love he had around him from his family and the good intentions of the home would help. I cried my eyes out in the toilet just before leaving him on the first day, not wanting him to know there was anything wrong. The upset continued back in London. I would break down with the stress and worry of it all. I felt guilty when friends would take me out for drinks, and knock the drinks back to numb it all. Even if I laughed or slipped back into normality for too long the thoughts of my dad would hit me again like a juggernaut.

It was obvious almost immediately that the home wasn't for me da. He hated it and had gone down hill since being there. He was constantly restless and memories of his sister who had unfortunately died in care flooded his mind.

Other patients were mostly older, apart from one young girl who had been in a horrific car accident. The poor girl unintentionally wailing for most of the day, every day. Me da didn't fit in there at all. I knew he shouldn't be there too but I wanted to give it a chance, to see if it could help bring him back.

My aim was to give it a go for about two months, but after two weeks and a talk with my aunt I arranged time off work, went back to Ireland and took him out of the home. The staff had done their best, but, for me da, being in there became completely counterproductive. The respite that I'd hoped for had failed miserably. The guilt and stress had become too much so I scrapped the plan which I hoped would help.

I told the managers of the care home I was taking him out for a break, so that he wouldn't lose his place there, but in truth it was to see if he could manage on his own. Even though all the medical opinions were that he couldn't, we had to try. He couldn't carry on in there. I took him home to his now revamped flat to live with him for the following ten days. He was delighted, but this was no holiday and I needed him to understand that, reiterating that if he wanted life to return to normal again he really had to listen and try hard.

And he really did try. He was frustrated as he didn't think there was anything wrong and he just wanted to get back to normal and head down to the pub with his mates. Getting through to him was more stressful than ever. We butted heads at times and living with me da again raised my blood pressure beyond, but I tried to focus on the task in hand. I taught him how to use the telephone again, make a cup of tea, how the cooker worked. I tried to get him used to washing up, and how to answer the door and work the TV. He had a simple daily routine so it was these basics he needed to understand and master again. It was paramount to see if he could be safe on his own, if he could manage, and most importantly if he could remember his daily medications. I tested him relentlessly over and over, to a point where I could see he wanted to lash out at me and he did a couple of times. He hated being told what to do and my patience was gone, but he stuck at it, and I didn't let up. This would determine his future and by the end of it we were both drained.

I also had to see if he could function outside, with lots of people around. I decided to let him collect his pension and see if he could make it to the pub on his own. We ventured out together to the post office. He received encouraging hand shakes and welcome back smiles from people who hadn't seen his familiar face around in a while. I stood back while he went to the counter, even though he couldn't get his words out properly, which I knew he felt very embarrassed about, he got his money and off we went. Then it was a walk up the quay to his second home, The White Horse pub. I let him lead the way and when he saw all his mates he had the biggest smile on his face. I warned him, as did the doctors, that he was only to have half a Guinness from now on. He didn't really want to drink anyway, he was scared and nervous that he would have to go back to the home or rehab.

By the end of the ten days I believed he could manage and I signed him out of the care home for good. He was doing things as normal and with help and support from relatives he got through each day. My aunt who lived close by was always there for her brother in a flash and we both would have been lost without her.

I was nervous about going back to London, but I called him every day. I felt a shell of myself but tried to remain upbeat for me da. Even though friends constantly reassured me I was doing the best I could and that a lot of lads my age wouldn't be able to handle this situation, I felt low and trapped I suppose. I had to come to terms with the fact that as time went on and he got older his health would deteriorate further, and the realisation that there was no hope of us having that open relationship I so longed for. He had to try hard just to say basic sentences, so any chance of father and son talks was gone. I mainly kept these feelings to myself through this time, it wasn't about me and feeling bad for myself. I mourned these further losses inside, mourned what could have been. I didn't want to be 'woe is me', I was so glad he was still here and getting to live his daily life at home again. The future was about making sure he was ok and that he got by. He just wanted his life back and as frustrating as the next few years would be, we had given it to him.

I started putting the wheels in motion to get him out of the flat he was in and into something more suitable. The clean out while he was in rehab had highlighted that he needed somewhere safer and a better environment. I wanted to get him somewhere bright and by the sea, so he could look out at the water and the boats and end his days there instead of a poky run down flat. The council played ball for a bit and assessed my dad's situation as urgent. He needed a flat within easier walking distance to the town, instead of up almost vertical hills, and one with better facilities and an extra room for me or anyone else to stay in and keep an eye on him. Myself and my aunt saw a couple of places but they wouldn't do, until we noticed a modern apartment right on the quay was empty and enquired about it straight away.

It looked directly out at the sea but the only problem was it had stairs and needed a shower with a seat installed. But the location was perfect and that was a huge factor too. They kindly offered him the flat and he accepted, I was so happy for him. My mate Liam helped me move everything while me da stayed with my aunt for a few days. Over the following weeks we kitted the place out for him with lovely new furnishings, including a huge sofa and arm chair in his favourite colour, mauve. But he couldn't settle for a long time. He loved the location but he felt it was too big. At times

I felt maybe I should've let him just stay where he was, but I knew this new environment was better for him and hoped eventually he would see that too. When he got frustrated or angry he told he hated it but most of the time he would say what I wanted to hear, and then moan about it to my aunts and uncles. My aunt brought him everywhere and did anything he needed. As he went about his daily business again, me da never realised all that went on behind the scenes for him to be in this position. I never knew if it was the stroke or him being himself, but when he was ungrateful it made me angry since everyone was trying to help him. But me da had always done his own thing, so having other people involved so much was hard for him to take.

Almost as soon as he moved in, a battle with the council started. I was at loggerheads with them and the Health Board, trying to get basic stair lifts installed in the apartment. A battle which was truly ridiculous in the first place, but I was used to fighting by now so I added it to the ever growing list. How a government department could offer a man who had suffered a major stroke a place with two sets of stairs, then refuse to install stair lifts was beyond me. My work was being affected by all the time I was taking off, and when I was there I felt like all I did was write emails. I refused to back down on the stair lifts, and as much as the council had helped by offering the flat I knew that they must have hated it every time an email or call came from me thereafter. It got to the point when I even had to take it to a political level, involving local ministers and got anyone and everyone I could onside to help. And still they refused to budge.

My back and forth with the council and Health Board did eventually pay off. They agreed to the bathroom renovation, and I had managed to get my dad a part time carer too. A lovely women named Joan, who would come up daily to make sure he was okay, her main role to help him shower and get dressed. At the start, through gritted teeth, he allowed her to carry out the tasks, but he hated waiting for her because me da being me da he was up at 6 or 7 every morning. He stopped letting her shower him after a while, but if he was in a good mood he would let her look at his feet and help ease the pain he felt from various calluses and bunions and the old injury. Visits to a speech and language therapist continued, sometimes he would get it and sometimes not at all, depending on what form he was in on the day. My aunt was constantly on hand, which took its toll on her. Being in London made me feel even more guilty. She was the only one, bar me, that he would let help, which made Joan's job even harder. He had a soft spot for Joan, he would have tea and cakes ready for when she arrived, but he resented her being there and was rude at times. He just wanted to get up and out and didn't want to be waiting around.

I tried to have patience but this really got my back up as Joan was always so lovely to us, so I would sometimes lose it with him. I'd tell him to be grateful for what everyone was doing for him, but then immediately feel horrible as I knew he couldn't really understand me or the seriousness of the situation. But I refused to let him think he could do what he liked. He had suffered a major stroke and he was lucky just to be alive, not to mention all the work everyone had done so that he could get his old life back.

The council and the health service both still refused to provide the stair lifts, and it had become a game of ping pong between us. With both of them always asking for more proof of this and that, eventually the council said that if I could find and pay for an occupational therapist to assess the situation myself and confirm that the stair lifts were an instrumental part of my dad's needs then they would reassess. After much ringing around, I came across a seasoned professional occupational therapist and an incredible woman, who practised in another part of the county. I spoke to her from London and told her the story and explained the situation. I think she could hear in my voice that I was at my wit's end with it all. Within twenty-four hours she had the assessment done, had the letter written and gave the council a bollocking on the phone for the way they handled the situation. The stair lifts were installed, and a massive sigh of relief all round.

From London I would call dad every day, giving him a break on Saturdays to have a day off to himself. The conversations were always the same, which upset me, but as long as he was ok that was the main thing. I was constantly in contact with my aunt. I felt for her as I knew how difficult me da could be and as time went on this only worsened.

My relationship with him had now plateaued, repetitive phone conversations when he told me everything was fine, when I knew it wasn't, and asking me if I was ok. He still worried about me all the time. We tried to talk about other things but he couldn't comprehend what I was saying and would get confused, so we always ended on 'go get yourself a cup of tea and I'll ring ya tomorrow'.

On visits home, we still sat in the pub together and with my uncle Jimmy. Ironically, after a childhood ruined by drink, the pub was a little haven for us to be together. After a few hours he would get a taxi or Jimmy would take him home, unable to walk at times because of the pains in his feet. We went out on drives with my aunts and uncle, down to the harbour or the seaside. At his flat I would be in the kitchen cleaning up or making his dinner while he watched the racing on telly or a film. Even when I was hungover from a much-needed night with my mates, I tried to wake up early and get him to have breakfast before he went out. He did at times but mainly he'd rush out to walk slowly down the quay and wait for the pub to open, back to his old routine. The difficulty of getting him to do what he was told worsened. Some days he would be so confused and might stay in and watch the telly, which I was glad of as at least he was safe.

We tried every way to make things easy for him. His pill boxes were a nightmare, especially when he started thinking they weren't important, but he promised he was taking them. His sight wasn't the best either so we would sometimes find a pill on the floor. My aunt brought him to the doctors weekly to have his bloods taken and dosage amended. He absolutely hated the needles and his arms were always bruised.

The running of the flat wasn't easy. I had to hide bills as he hated them and they caused him to worry, so I had some of them paid directly from his pension instead. He didn't understand the heating system so didn't want the radiators running at all. He worried about the cost and favoured wearing his coat inside and a foot heater over turning them on. He was so stuck in his ways it was sometimes impossible. I knew old men were difficult, but at times me da was on another level. The forty-six year age gap between us continued to be a glaring reality. It's funny, he would happily hand someone a 50 euro note or buy them drinks, and even though he always did pay them, he detested paying bills. Again highlighting there was only one Tommy Meyler. His rebellious streak never waned, but unfortunately now hurting and confused it was the people trying to help him who he rebelled against.

It became so difficult for all involved. I would stand in the kitchen making him tea and burst into tears, feeling so sorry for him and looking at him sat in his armchair, deep in thought, knowing he was hurting inside and feeling trapped and lost with a condition he didn't really understand. I knew his past haunted him and the present was now a daily struggle. He was trying to be the man he was, but old age and frail health were stopping him, he felt embarrassed and frustrated.

I tried to have a normal life, but I couldn't. Being in London and the stress from back home made me miserable. I was determined not to let my positivity flounder but eventually I was exhausted. I told myself all the time that there was people in much worse positions, but the emotional strain of both my own battles and now this mammoth scenario were becoming too much to bare. The old circle of getting drunk just for a break, then feeling even worse after continued. I was constantly frustrated and guilt ridden, having to say goodbye to my dad in many ways but at the same time trying to make his life as happy as I could. But no glamorous parties could put any sparkle on how I was feeling inside.

I went home when I could to take the pressure off my aunt, but also needing someone to tell me it was going to be ok. I felt like a lost little boy again in yet another nightmare, dealing with my own mind and trying to find some happiness in my daily life. I would sit with my dad and I appreciated it, just the two of us, still annoyed at him when he was drinking but now trying to have more patience, something he lacked entirely and I guess I also inherited.

As he was getting older, I was also more aware that with all his health concerns he needed to drink less and that he was no longer sticking to half pints. Although he still went home early, he was drinking more like four or five pints while he was out, which wasn't helping the situation. He wouldn't listen, but any shouting matches had stopped between us, I was broken from it all. He just wanted to have a laugh with his mates and smile, a release for him from his own inner struggles, it was his life at the end of the day. He didn't understand when we tried to talk to him about important subjects and it was pointless now to try to explain, the stroke had done its damage. The main priority was that he was safe and taking the pills daily.

He was such an unbelievably kind and warm man, chronically hard working, endlessly funny, he would have you in fits of laughter one minute and your heart broken the next, and he worried about those close to him so much. At times I would catch him staring out the window or wiping a tear away. There was one weight on his shoulders he thought about a lot. I wanted to try and do something about it. I wanted to help him lay to rest some of the ghosts from his past and have some peace. I knew then and there what I needed to do.

The dinner bell on the Solway Lass brought me out of my nautical trance and I joined the rest of the crew for an evening under the stars, as the calm sea lapped gently against the ship.

The next morning the clouds took a break and we took off snorkelling around the bay. I met Wally along the way, a famous and massive hump head wrasse who swam around me and was almost as big as me, as were the giant clams underneath. Now it wouldn't be a pirate adventure without a swashbuckling rope to swing from and what do you know the ship came complete with one. Myself and my shipmates who I'd bonded with the most, George, Sam and Will, a group of rugby playing farmer lads from Hereford in the UK, cousins David and Javitt from the Netherlands and the most awesome and adventuresome American couple from Colorado, Stephanie and Andy, took turns climbing up on the wet rails to get swinging. After a few false starts, one where I slipped and fell into the net below, we swung around the boat like Tarzan on the high seas. The waters at this depth were quite dark but I still bombed right in, facing my deep dark water fear in the deep dark face.

We had been promised that we would get a chance to swim with some sea turtles. We sailed on to Black Island on the final day, a tiny jellyfish-laden feeding ground for the turtles. From a dinghy we spotted a shell popping out of the water, and with a backwards flip I was submerged in the deep waters. The bubbles cleared and I could see I was surrounded by tiny jellyfish, I didn't ask what type they were, I just hoped my stinger suit would keep me sting-free. As they bobbed and pulsated past my mask, the turtle came over for his lunch and munched on the little creatures like he was in an all you can eat buffet. I swam along beside him, and gave him a little pat on the back, this was a serene experience until a group of Japanese tourists were dumped in the water close by. They splashed about with their safety noodles and screamed loudly, my little turtle buddy swam off as I rolled my eyes in my now foggy mask.

Stephanie and Andy called me over. I swam towards them and left the mayhem of Japanese excitement behind. They had spotted another bigger turtle munching on some sort of grass on the ocean floor. We swam down to say hello and have some pictures, me with all the majestic poise of a pig rolling in shit. We had been in the water quite a while and with the excitement of turtle swimming I didn't notice how utterly knackered I was until my arms started to ache and my breathing started to become heavy, damn you asthma. I was still quite a way from the shore so I started to doggy paddle like my life depended on it before I sank to the bottom like a brick. By the time I reached the closest rock I thought my chest would explode and my arms would fall off, the fact the rock surface was razor sharp and I straight away cut my hands and feet didn't matter. I just needed to stop. I started having visions of sharks swarming round after sniffing some Irish blood in the water, and swam the rest of the way to the shore faster than Michael Phelps on speed.

Our seafaring adventure had come to an end, the sails were lowered and we glided back to Abell Point. Scotty and first mate Chris climbed high up the mast to secure the sails with the ease of two nautical monkeys. A wonderfully memorable time on the high seas of Australia and I very much hoped me da had been there in spirit with me.

Chapter 17

I wanted to get involved in real Australian life, so I went to live on a farm in the outback for a few days.

Rockhampton, beef capital of Australia, was next. I arrived late and a cabbie who used the word cunt in every second sentence dropped me off at a YHA hostel. The morning light brought with it a wall of mega-heat and a butch female receptionist informed me that Wednesday nights are rodeo night in Rockhampton. My eyes lit up with this news, as I love me some rodeo and that cowboy lifestyle. After an afternoon walk taking in the modern art gallery followed by a few schooners with the locals, I was first back for the free transfer to the rodeo.

The Great Western Hotel was a traditional looking Australian outback pub, wooden framed and oozing with cowboy charm. Once inside it unveiled a huge rodeo arena, with TV screens ready for channel 7 live broadcasts, seats for hundreds of people and lots of local cowfolk mooching about, drinking beers and eating steaks with their families. A few of us from the hostel grabbed a table together and I got chatting with a ballsy and fun 19 year old girl called Megan from Kent, as well Harry and his missus Katie from Bournemouth. The cowboy hosting proceedings, a local bloke with a thick and no nonsense outback accent, threw it out to the audience if there were any gringos brave enough to take on one of steers and compete to see if they could stay on and buck as long as the Australian rodeo wizards.

All of a sudden my mind was filled with all the old Western films I used to watch with me da, bucking cowboys, Indian chases, rodeo champions, and a worrying fire grew in my belly. This was a once in a lifetime chance to ride in a rodeo and no matter what my head said, it was overtaken by the chance to live out that fantasy. I looked at Megan, an accomplished horse rider, and could tell she was up for it too. Before I could say yee-haa she beckoned the host over and told him we were in. A Geordie boy from the hostel put his hand up too, and just as our dinner and drinks arrived we were escorted across the arena and backstage. I thought at one point the joke would be on us, and a mechanical bull would be wheeled out for these greenest of gringos who thought they might actually ride a real animal. But as we signed a waiver stating that the venue wasn't liable for any death or broken limbs, the reality set in.

A redneck teenager plonked a helmet on my head and told me through gappy black teeth to just get on and do it – how motivational. I wondered if this was actually happening and if I had left my wits on the Whitsundays. He then took off, barking incomprehensible instructions at me as he went, the others looked just as perplexed. I was first up, confused, sweating and feeling about as prepared as a donkey taking a driving test I was led up onto a platform above my chosen bull. This wasn't a movie and I wasn't in Kansas anymore. This animal was right there below me, real and uncensored. No PG certifications, this was the raw XXX edition. Finally a real cowboy appeared to tell me what not to do. I couldn't hear a word he said as I stood with my legs spread on the bars above a bull. It went into a spasm of bucking underneath with deafening noise from the pen as he frantically bumped and kicked. I shouted to the cowboy to tell me what to do, not what not to fucking do!

The cowboy said, 'lower yourself down mate'.

My legs were shaking, and I gulped and lowered myself down on to the black and white bull below.

'Now get yer balls right up here, Larry,' he said pointing to a rope by the animal's bulky neck.

I yanked my balls up and then he tied a rope around my hand and wrist numerous times, as I pictured being dragged around the arena like a rag doll.

'Keep your hand up Larry mate and hold on with all your grit...ready?'

I thought, what the fuck am I actually doing and what a stupid Irish fuck I am, but suddenly I became filled with a rush of adrenaline and shouted 'READY!'

The gates opened and we were off. The crowd cheered and like a bull out of hell he bucks, twists and throws me around as we dart across the arena. My legs stayed firm to his ribs and with dirt flying I held on one handed with all my might, 1, 2, 3, 4, almost 5 seconds before I lost my grip and walloped to the dirt. My head, wrist and ribs took the brunt of the fall, and my initial reaction was to run towards the gate like in the films before I get a horn through my arse cheeks. Dazed and with adrenaline pumping, the host put his arm on my shoulder and says to the arena 'Whatcha reckon all, that wasn't too bad for an Irish – welcome to Australia'. I felt unbelievably proud at what I'd just done, also unbelievably stupid and dizzy.

The Geordie lad seemed to fall off before he'd even left the pen. Then Megan was up. I was wearing Converse, not the most practical of footwear when riding a moody bull. Megan only had flip flops on, and that definitely didn't seem right. The cowboy told her to go barefoot. She was guided to her animal, a much less frantic brown beauty who let Megan mount him like a teacup at the fairground. Mounted and ready she raised her arm as I stood on the platform like an encouraging but worried big brother, and off she went. She was like a pro out in the arena staying on her now wildly bucking beast for the same length as me, maybe even longer, amid cheers from the crowd until she hit the ground. I could see she was sat in a weird position, as she tried to get up I could also see the pain in her face and thought please no. Again she tried, but couldn't stand as her leg kept giving way, so the cowboys carried her off and lay her on a counter backstage. I ran back and she just said 'it's gone, it's gone'. You didn't have to be a doctor to see her ankle and foot weren't looking how they should.

The staff called an ambulance. I grabbed her drink for her to sip on and mine to steady my nerves. The paramedics arrived and dosed her up with methoxyflurane, a pain relief which comes in a little green whistle device to suck. Even though she was in a lot of pain, she still managed to stay upbeat and with the whistle high she laughed, joked and took selfies and Snapchats with the paramedics and myself en route to hospital – one crazy and brave girl.

The laughter subsided though. After four hours and numerous x-rays, the doctor delivered the news that she had broken her foot in five places. One month into a year trip, there she was having to call her mum back in the UK to explain and let her know she was alright, as the doctor with me as his new nurse plastered up the bottom half of her leg. But Megan was determined to carry on with all her pre-booked trips and hobbled on crutches some way down the coast over the next couple of weeks until her insurance company made her fly home when her follow-up exam showed her injury wasn't healing as it should be and she needed an operation. Although disappointed, she took it all in her stride and was back on her adventures once her foot healed. What a crazy night in the rodeo arena we got to share, and I would have said yes over and over again. It's safe to say I didn't get a whole lot of shut-eye that night before my 5am wake up call, and the realisation that I might have fucked up my own trip set in too. My wrist and ribs throbbed in pain.

But with the morning came a positive outlook, so ignoring my now swollen hand and aching ribs, I packed my stuff and jumped in the car with Shane, the farm manager, for the two-hour drive to the farm near Baralaba. I tried to keep the conversation going and make a decent impression but it didn't last long as I conked out within twenty minutes. I woke up in a new open landscape environment as we drove up the country road to Myella.

I was greeted in the open kitchen area with its wooden beams, galvanised roof and old iron kettles strewn about the place, by Lyn. She and her steadfast parents, Peter and Olive, own and have kept the farm going for decades. She was ready and waiting with some fresh cow's milk and breakfast, before introducing me to the resident joey kangaroo and German farm hand, Michael. I was the only guest so got to do more that day than normal as Shane's new apprentice.

It was off with the Converse and on with an over-sized shirt, Levi jeans, ill-fitting boots and a proper Aussie cowboy hat. I made up the food and fed the horses including my own one named XXXX – a stallion, who according to Shane, was previously very highly strung and got angry at times. But he had found some calmness and was sorting himself out, something told me we would get on just fine!

We rode out into the bush, and apart from being spooked a couple of times by wild kangaroos, XXXX mainly did as he was told. The thick humid heat topped 36 degrees as we got out further into the expansive farm land, the wild bush and red dust backdrop fulfilled exactly what I thought Australia would look like, but with more beauty. It brought with it a calmness that made it feel like it could be everlasting. That was until XXXX fancied some grass and yanked me forward, reminding me I was on a huge horse and not a sun lounger.

Back to the farm with Hobo the dog in tow, it was time for some motorbike lessons. Apart from being a passenger I'd actually only handled a real motorbike once before.

I choose my bike from the shed and made sure to check the helmet for any spiders or scorpions. Although the actual riding part was cool, I couldn't understand the gears, when or how to change them. It reminded me of my driving test, when I rocked up to the car and set the window wipers and alarm off without even starting the engine. After an hour I could feel Shane's patience wearing thin. I felt frustrated and deflated that I couldn't grasp such a simple thing, so I said to Shane he could carry on with his work and leave me to it. I refused to give up. I wanted to ride with confidence, even if in the wrong gears.

After zooming around tracks for what seemed like hours, next I lubed up some cow titties for milking, where I tried not to leave the poor things red raw from my yanking. The sun was about to go down so I jumped back on the bike and headed up some dirt tracks to a vantage point with Michael driving behind in the battered 4X4, just in case my gears exploded. I couldn't have asked for a more wondrous way to end the day, as dusk approached the sky filled with burning red colours, sun on one side, moon on the other, cattle and wild kangaroos silhouettes far out on the bushy planes. We sat on the rusty bonnet looking out as the crimson sun lowered behind the horizon. An Irish council cowboy out in the Australian bush, feeling like I just might be on the way to winning a battle with myself and my mind. I realised having this hardcore thinking time was one of the greatest healing luxuries of travel. At that moment, a peace emerged.

The dinner triangle rang for some proper Aussie tucker and that night we all chatted about our different worlds, and the guys asked if I had any brothers and sisters. It brought to mind an unexpected turn of events and what I knew I had to do to make my dad's last few years happier.

Way before I was even a twinkle, or probably a sty, in me da's eye, and before he laid eyes on me ma, he got through life fighting. Fighting with the demons in his head from his torturous years in the Artane and fighting with drunken fists. The impact of the Artane played a key part in many areas of his existence. His inability to settle, his anger, his survival instinct and the decisions he made both with and without the crutch that was the drink.

Back in 1959, he met a woman named Agnes at a fair in England, she was 18 and he was 25. A whirlwind romance began and within the year they were married.

A baby girl named Hannah was born the following year, and in 1962 another daughter, Teresa, was born, prior to a third baby, which Agnes devastatingly miscarried after being involved in a bus crash. They never knew that babies sex as the accident was so severe.

Over the following few years, they had a volatile on and off relationship. With very little money they moved around the country living with relatives or in grotty rentals. Me da would disappear for days, weeks, months on end to find work either at sea or labouring to support them, sometimes taking Hannah with him to Ireland. Leaving Agnes on constant tenterhooks for fear she wouldn't see one of her daughters again. But he would always come back and she would take him back. Both as bad as each other caught up in some misguided love, burning each other emotionally but they were each all the other had.

When Tommy left, Agnes thought that was it and she had to start again. At such a young age herself, she foolishly fell for the advances of other men, even though still married to Tommy. On his first and the longest hiatus, Agnes met a man named John and a short relationship followed. It finished as soon as she realised Tommy hadn't gone for good, and so they carried on again. Teresa was then born shortly after. But trying to make it work as a family didn't last long, Tommy's drinking worsened, the fights became unbearable and once again he took off with Hannah. Why he left only he will ever understand, but in his heart he wanted both girls whom he loved dearly to have a better life.

It was on this last break when they probably both knew they couldn't carry on that Agnes met another Irish man, and another affair started. But once again Tommy returned and took Hannah back to her mum and he tried to piece together and fix an unfixable family unit. This time Agnes, fearing Tommy would take her daughter away again, agreed to try work things out one last time. She continued to see the other man as well, until one day Tommy came back from work early, and found the two of them together. All hell broke loose and Tommy left angry and heartbroken, this time for good, leaving the girls with their mum. Agnes was fearful he would take Hannah away again, so she kept her out of school for a while. They had one last talk after that but it was obvious there was no going back.

Tommy didn't get to say goodbye to Hannah this time, but he did call to the girls' school a few days later in a lorry bound for Ireland with his brother-in-law where he had hoped to say goodbye to both his girls. Hannah wasn't there but he met Teresa at the gates and told her he had to leave, he couldn't stay anymore and that he loved her and he was sorry, and with that he went. She stood at the school gates confused and wondering why. What had happened? Why did her daddy have to leave his little girls? He never got to explain it to Hannah himself.

And with that, contact stopped. Tommy, a wrecked man, had to leave behind a life he wanted so bad but didn't know how to handle. He did what he thought was best and left them to grow up with their mum and have some peace.

I never knew of my two half-sisters existence until I was a teenager. When I was 15 and about to go on a removal trip with me da and Mick to Birmingham, he told me about his daughters, not in great detail but that he had arranged to meet Teresa when we got there. I was so excited. I always wished for a family, for my mam to be there and to have siblings. Now I was told I had two ready-made sisters. They'd reconnected after Teresa came to Wexford with her husband in 1989. She had two kids of her own and she hoped she could find and build a relationship with the only man she knew as dad, and wanted her kids to meet their grandfather. She asked around in a few pubs and was given me da's address, so she went to his flat. Their emotional reunion led to contact again via letter with his other daughter too. Hannah now had a husband of her own too, and three young boys.

The few letters that were sent back and forth included pictures. I think my dad was a bit shocked to see the boys were mixed race, this was Ireland in the eighties and a lot of attitudes were generally a bit backwards when it came to race. He carried that picture around with him, and I remember seeing it too. But for whatever reason contact between Tommy and Hannah dissolved again, but at least he now knew that his daughters were fine and had families of their own.

Teresa and my dad did get in contact again, and this was when the meeting was arranged in Birmingham. Unfortunately, whether out of stubbornness or fear of more hurt, contact between me da and Hannah stopped and they never spoke again. They both lived with the pain, heartbreak, guilt and what ifs. I knew this weighed heavily on my dad's shoulders, but they were both too scared to make another move, thinking it easier to both let each other be.

But in the summer of 1993 he was ecstatic at the thought of seeing Teresa again. I remember Will Smith's 'Boom Shake the Room' was on the radio and I was also chuffed to bits. We all met in the car park of a lorry depot in Birmingham, not a quaint long lost families scene but good enough for us and the meeting went well.

From there we met Teresa's family and visited their home. I loved having a niece and nephew, Rebecca and Gareth, and met her husband David. They took me ice skating and showed me their rooms and games. Me da even asked Teresa if I could come live with her as I was unhappy in

Wexford and that he just didn't know what to do with me. Not surprisingly that was a bit much for Teresa and didn't happen.

Not long after the initial get together contact fizzled out again for a few years, and wasn't picked up again until I was 18, now living in London, and we visited Teresa for Christmas dinner. I don't know how this visit happened but I didn't care as it was nice to see them all again. I looked very different to the last time they had seen me. Platform trainers, skinny as a rake, eyebrows like rainbows thanks to Michelle's plucking marathon. There seemed to be a difference in the atmosphere on this trip, like everyone had too much else going on in their lives. After that all contact faded bar the odd Christmas card and me da didn't see Teresa again.

I did call Teresa once when I was 21. I tried to get across that no matter what had gone on in the past it wasn't anything to do with me, and that I would like a relationship, hopefully with both girls. But unbeknown to me there was too much going on, and Teresa explained to me that Hannah's husband had recently died and she was heartbroken, as were her sons, and it was just an extremely difficult time. With hope, I asked her to keep in contact but it never happened.

Now age 32 and with me da in the midst of his stroke limbo and getting older, I decided to try once again. Maybe I couldn't patch things up with Hannah, I wouldn't have even known where to start, but I was determined to find Teresa and bring some peace to them both at least.

I had no phone numbers now but I remembered the area where Teresa and David had a car garage. I eventually found their work address and an email address. With trepidation and many rewrites I sent off an email, explaining about my dad and his heath. If she felt up to it, I asked her to meet me for a chat, even that would bring so much happiness into me da's life.

Many weeks went by and nothing, I felt gutted. But then one day out of the blue I received a text saying it was Teresa. She had got the email and would call me the following day. My heart was pounding, I replied and we arranged a time to talk on the phone. We chatted with ease and arranged to meet up near a station. I was so excited and hoped she might agree to visit Ireland, and to find out if Hannah would consider contact too.

I waited at the train station coffee shop nervous and full of anxiety. The last time I saw Teresa was 1997, but when she arrived we hugged warmly and I knew it would be ok. We sat down to talk but what followed not only shocked me, but knocked me for six.

I asked how Hannah was, and through sad eyes Teresa told she was sorry but Hannah had passed away in October 2005 after a battle with cancer. My heart sank and I was shocked. I sat there stunned and saddened. I would never get to meet my sister and never get to reunite her with her dad. I asked if she had asked about me or my dad and Theresa said

Hannah never really spoke about any of it. When she was very sick, Teresa asked if she wanted dad to come and see her but she said no, there was no point and it would be too much for all concerned. She didn't want him to see her like that and she felt it wouldn't have been right. He had his memories of his little girl and it would stay like that. Teresa did say that if I had turned up at Hannah's door she would have welcomed me in, and that hit me like a brick. Questions ran through my mind, but how could I have? Maybe I should have after all. Maybe I should have tried. Maybe I should have been the one to break the circle.

I would never get to meet Hannah now, but by God I was going to get things fixed with Teresa. But before I could think any further she uttered her next sentence. She said she had to tell me something else. I could tell it wasn't easy for her to say, but she told me that she wasn't actually my biological sister after all. I sat there speechless, a double whammy of punches. No words could pass my lips. I didn't believe her. Me da had always referred to her as his daughter, as my sister, and he loved her so much. He always portrayed to me that he loved and saw both his daughters the same. Why was she saying this?

And then she explained. After returning home from school on the day that my dad left, she was distraught, she cried her little heart out and didn't understand why her dad had come to say goodbye and why he wouldn't ever see her again. Then her vicious aunt interjected with a bombshell that no 6 year-old little girl should have to hear, 'he wasn't your dad anyway' which shattered her world.

Her biological dad was actually the man named John, who Agnes had met when me da had taken Hannah off to Ireland the first time. He had returned wanting to make it work and was devastated by the news that she was pregnant. His love for Agnes and wanting to keep their family together took over. He said he would take Teresa on as his own, and they would be a family no matter what. This must have been a very hard decision for a man like my dad, but his heart took over and he did what he thought was right. It also makes sense as to why he didn't take Teresa along too when he kept going back and forth to Ireland when the relationship was on and off, he had no rights by law. But I know 100% that he loved her just the same. Even at times when his resentment of Agnes' infidelity was used against her, he never showed that towards Teresa.

I sat there with tears building as Teresa told me all this. I had just learned I'd lost one sister, now I had lost the other. But Teresa is such a kind and selfless woman, she told me nothing had to change, and that she still saw Tommy as the only real father figure she ever had in her life. She was unsure who within the family knew and she apologised for not keeping in contact with me when I last called her age 21. She didn't need to apologise to me at all, I understood how hard it must have been for her knowing these facts. My dad never broached the subject with her even in adulthood. He saw her as his own, and he never mentioned anything about it to me.

I found it hard to take all this in, I still half didn't believe it. I mean Teresa and my dad look very similar and she definitely had a Meyler look in general about her. My response to this news was that nothing would change, and that I would still see her the same too.

We continued to talk, and discussed Teresa coming back into my dad's life. She wanted to very much, but felt nervous and uneasy about not knowing if she would have to hide the truth. But I knew me da loved Teresa so much, and that was fact.

I said if she felt she needed to let extended family know about the biological reality then that was up to her, but I did ask her one thing. That me da must not find out about Hannah, it would kill him, he wouldn't be able to cope with that heartbreak. In his current state he couldn't ask any questions or take it all in so it would be nothing but cruel for him to know. She promised, and again I said if she wanted other relatives to know about Hannah then so be it. I would warn them all that me da must not find out.

I knew everybody would understood and knew concealing her death was for the best.

Teresa felt a massive weight off her chest telling me all of this. I knew how hard it was for her and how sad she felt for me. I had to go away and digest it all, and I did. I felt so sad as I boarded the train back to London. I thought of Hannah, what she was like, and tried to deal with the gut wrenching feeling that I would never get to meet her but have to mourn her instead, a person I never even knew, not only for me but for my dad too. My mind then swapped to the fact that the blood bond with Teresa had been snatched away within the same breath. But I knew she still saw me the same and as I did her. I called my mates and met them in London, I needed a drink.

I now had to try and explain to me dad that Teresa would be coming to see him. He eventually took it in. I could see the mixture of emotions in him: he was upset, happy, anxious and worried. Up until the day she arrived he thought about it. He never stopped thinking about those girls and his past was bubbling to the surface again now and he couldn't communicate how he felt. He asked me if Hannah would come too, he wasn't able to get her name out, just calling her the other girl, and I just said no, just Teresa.

The day she walked into his flat, he was all done up in his best clothes. He saw her and tears filled his eyes as they hugged. I knew this was the right thing, instantly I saw a weight lifted as they sat together. He hugged her constantly and had a beaming smile full of pride. He tried to get his words out but

Teresa didn't need him to say anything, she could see the love and happiness in his eyes. I knew he would ask her how Hannah was though, and when he did she replied, 'she's ok…she's happy'. I was grateful, not only for her kindness, but for her bravery too.

Teresa stuck to her word and stayed in his life regularly after that. He loved hearing from her on the phone and loved dialling her number when he could get it right. She visited him a few times right up until he died. He was always on his best behaviour when she was around, and he got to meet her daughter, Rebecca, again too, now grown up with her own daughter.

Teresa was there with me the last time I saw him alive. We took him to the seaside and a fishing village with my aunt Winnie and uncle Jimmy, and I knew how happy that made him. Although it hadn't been the full reunion I had wished for, having his daughter there and just knowing that his other one was ok was all he needed on this earth.

That last weekend sat together in the pub, I knew that whatever way things went, a haunting darkness and sadness had been lifted from my dad's shoulders, which let some light shine into his life. This kind hearted man who had it so hard in his life, who had to live with his mistakes and cursed demons which never let up, could now smile a little more and feel some peace.

Back on the farm, I thankfully woke up without any spiders on my face but with the cogs of my mind still on the gears of the bike. The only way to fix that was to get back on and practice. Gears mastered, sort of, I went about collecting some eggs. Putting my hand under a hen's fanny was another new experience, as was feeding Roxy the baby kangaroo from a bottle. Myself and Shane jumped on the bikes again and headed out to round up the horses for feeding. This was an adventure and a little boy's dream. We zoomed round the fields, I only stalled once or twice, and revved and rounded the stallions back into their enclosure. I felt very proud that Shane asked me to do this with him as not many visitors got to be part of it. The two of us sped off to see the entire farm, all 2650 acres, bulldust bellowing behind us as we jumped over mounds and crossed fields, and what do you know the gears finally seemed to click into place. Shane noticed and praised me for sticking with it, this unlikely and unexpected bond felt great.

We raced each other back to the house, to find a bus load of young backpackers on an East Coast package had arrived for an afternoon of farm life. They all seemed to think I was a working cowboy. I went with it and as I was introduced I masked my Irish accent by just tipping my hat instead, the girls in the group giggled at this.

It was time for me to head back to Rockie and my farm adventure to end. I said goodbye to this wonderful and hard working farm family, and thanked them so much for having me. Lyn took me aside and said Shane had heaped praise on my efforts and if I had a month spare they would love to have me there as a farm hand, food and board sorted. I wished I did have an extra month free, as the faith they had in me after being there only a couple of days was priceless.

This outback experience really did surpass my expectations. Like an overheated horse on a dusty plane, I was thirstier than ever for the adventure ahead to unfold. With a firm hand shake and man hug I said goodbye to my new mate Shane and thanked him for being such a bonza bloke. I felt privileged that he had taken me on as his protégé for those couple of days.

Over the next couple of weeks, I made my way down towards Byron Bay on the trusty Greyhound line. I met up with my main man Michael again in Rainbow Beach, where we stayed in the worst Australian hostel yet. It had rooms stinking of minging vomit and by the look of the rampant teenagers swimming in it, the pool was more chlamydia soup than water. The age difference here really was noticeable, mainly party seeking teens getting pissed on Goon and throwing up everywhere. What else to do than join them, minus the vomit and chlamydia. We knocked back the beers and I shrieked though a version of 'Wannabe' at the karaoke night, like Gangsta Spice wrecking the mic and everybody's ears.

Across the bumpy tracks and endless beaches of Fraser Island we saw dingos, funnel web spiders and submerged ourselves in the giant fresh water lake, Lake McKenzie. From a propeller plane we took in the magnitude of the world's largest sand island from above, its butterfly shaped lakes precisely carved into the forest below, and expansive sting rays glided through the blue waters just off shore in the Pacific Ocean.

Back on the mainland, we ran for the hills from our teenage party hostel and shacked up for the night in a much more dignified dwelling, Debbie's Guesthouse. Run by, you guessed it, Debbie, a divorcee who had taken back control of her life with an upbeat positivity and full of beans demeanour. She told us the 'best site in town' for sunset was Carlo Sand Blow, a carved valley where the sands drift through from the Pacific to the forest on the other side, the trees cut into the sand like waves on the shore. On the Pacific side, the eroded cliffs which looked over the ocean are full of spots for romantic picnics. The type of place you might get down on one knee and get ready to jump the broom with the one you love. It also reminded me how very single I am, but that was fine. I had my buddy with me and what better way to finish off the night than with some fish and chips and a DVD at Debbie's.

We carried on bussing and got to the upmarket costal town of Noosa for Australia Day. It was a wash out so there was no crowds to be seen, but our new hostel was the plushest yet with a free wine and cheese evening. Oh the fickle world of hostel life. We gathered a fun UK contingent made up of Jo, Kathryn, Stevie and Katie. Once the rain stopped we descended on the local surf club and got pissed with the locals on Aussie pride day. A couple of days of beach yoga, getting thrashed around like teddies in a washing machine in the two story waves and Goon-fuelled party games, and we were off again.

It was time for another Larry and Michael hiatus, but we planned to meet up again in Byron. I was off to Brisbane to meet Robert from the Great Barrier Reef trip and kip on his couch for the night. His snazzy white Ute pulled up at the station and I hopped in. I literally had to hop after hurting my foot in the waves and was worried an old injury was reoccurring. Australia Day was more rawkus in Brisbane and Rob had a huge hangover, but true to his word he still took me around his city and a hair of the dog sorted him out quick. Beer at his bowls club and an open-air cinema with his missus followed. Rob's hospitality and my first couch-surfing experience couldn't have gone any better. I left him my South American travel guide as a thank you, sharing as part of backpacking life is quite important.

By the time I got to Surfers Paradise for the night I couldn't deny the fact anymore, the dreaded condition plantar fasciitis had returned. It is a painful and halting condition which had left me on crutches for a month a few years earlier, and I'd worn insoles ever since. I guess my choice of flip flops in the previous few months for activities ranging from dancing to hiking had taken its toll. In my sweaty blue plastic hostel bunk, I desperately looked up online exercises to find something to fix it, hoping I'd caught it early. With a belt wrapped around my heel I yanked my toes backwards to try and stretch it out. I started having sleep hallucinations that my trip would be fucked, the thoughts danced around my head like little devil trolls. I had to catch a flight to New Zealand one week later to meet my friend Gareth there. The buses and planes were booked, and a tankard of beer awaited me at Frodo Baggins house at Hobbiton. I frantically called my cousin Debbie who calmed me down and said we would get it sorted when I got back to Sydney the day before the flight.

I arrived into Byron Bay, my foot throbbing, but the surfer feel of the place cheered me up. I met Michael for a twenty-four hour reunion before he was off again. Our hostel was just outside of town and right across from the beach, overlooked by a lighthouse in the distance. We took some free rusty bikes into town to explore. After a haircut by a friendly local barber whose unique tales of running the famous Gatecrasher clubs back in the UK and loyalty to the skinhead movement made my time in his chair fly by. We got pissed with two feisty Essex girls and ended up trawling the town for clubs that would let me in without my ID. The alcohol numbed the pain of my foot, but slut dropping with the girls probably wasn't the best idea. And with that and through a stinking hangover I had to say goodbye to my bro Michael, until we would meet again in Melbourne a few weeks later.

He left and I felt like shit, but had to board a packed bus where I was the oldest by far for a day trip to the hippy town of Nimbin. The journey on the rickety bus didn't help my hangover but the sight of the rolling green hills that looked like Tellytubby Land which unfolded on the way made me feel better. What can I tell you about this place? It's a tiny town, with one main street awash with cafes, and hippy and hemp shops. It attracts busloads of young backpackers in search of the famous Nimbin high from hash and weed cakes which are on offer here, although not blatantly.

The last time I had a hash cake was in London and I had to get off the tube on the way home to vomit. It took me hours to come round and for the spinning to stop. But when in Rome, or Nimbin! So I went three ways on a cake with a couple of lads and we sat by a river. Later that afternoon I felt a little tingle as I looked down over a huge 100 plus metre waterfall, but that was probably more vertigo than the hash. Hardly a Rolling Stone high but enough for me.

In desperate need of a kip I turned in early that night. Unfortunately one coughing and spluttering roommate had the same idea. The ceiling fan wafted her germs around the room. I finally fell asleep only to be woken by the sounds of the bird in the opposite bunk groaning gleefully with that night's conquest. Shame the sheet she had erected for privacy wasn't fucking soundproof.

I left Byron wishing I could have stayed longer, it was my kind of town. But with a gammy foot and time ticking on I thanked the hostel staff for giving me a pair of crutches and got my bus to my final stop before Sydney, Coffs Harbour, home town of Woody, one of my best mates. Hopalong Larry would be staying with Woody's lovely parents for a couple of days. Back on the solo trail, I made the time alone count, and used it to work through the mounting anxiety and worry. I realised I would probably have to spend the following couple of weeks on Debbie's sofa rather than taking in the breathtaking valleys and gorges of New Zealand. But I told myself it didn't matter and that as long as I got rid of this injury and could finish my trip that was the important thing. Whatever the outcome, I would take it in my stride.

The bus passed the famous big banana as I arrived into Coffs Harbour, one of the many massive and random icons on view as you travel down the east coast. So far I'd seen a big crab, a big cowboy, and a big prawn. Woody's parents, Norma and Grant, were there to meet me as I hobbled off the bus. My nose was dripping too thanks to my spluttering roommate back in Byron.

We explored the beautiful and eclectic landscape Coffs had to offer, with its banana plantations, scenic look-outs, vibrant valleys and coastlines, and the surrounding towns where old Australian charm worked side by side with hipster cafes. Above all that, the warm family feeling which came with being at Grant and Norma's warmed my cockles no end. I tried to go unnoticed while snapping a picture in front of the Woody's old high school sign, squinting like a gargoyle in the blazing sun, while a classroom of pupils looked out at me like some sort of clown. Just like my own school days, so I quickly jumped back in the car before I got expelled from a school property for a third time.

Chapter 18

Snoozing with my leg up in the front seat on an overnight bus to Sydney, I awoke to find an old guy had joined the bus and filled the seat beside me. He was a cowboy in his eighties with a walking stick, and looked like he lived one hell of a life. His white Stetson proudly in place, with glimmers of his silver hair poking out underneath. I listened as he told the driver about his rodeo days and how there wasn't much of him left after all the injuries and falls, and how he was on his way to visit his son. I helped him off as we stopped on a coffee break and watched him make his way across the forecourt, then back on board with his coffee and stick. He mumbled a joke about his broken body, then looked up at me and said 'thank you son'.

In his weary, now-greying blue eyes, I saw a life which had been lived to its fullest potential, and I saw my dad. I laid his stick on the empty seat beside him and watched him slowly drink his coffee, the cup seeming to swamp his battered fingers, shaking as he lifted it to his lips. He smiled after he sipped, and he was content. Images of my dad in his final days when I watched him drink a pint of Guinness flooded my mind, and I wished for a moment I could've been the son that cowboy was on his way to visit.

As the bus pulled away I stared out the window, the world outside being replaced with the final memories of me ol' da. The window was vivid like a cinema projector, and I closed my eyes.

I was a couple of months into my new job. I had sat back at my desk from our morning conference ready to dish out the day's tasks to my researcher and deputy, a position of authority I was still getting used to. I saw two missed calls and a voicemail from my aunt's number. Straight away I knew something was wrong as she never leaves voicemails, but it wasn't her voice on the message it was from his new doctor asking me to call her back ASAP.

As I stepped out into the backstairs area, a massive anxiety enveloped me as I called my aunt's number back, the next few minutes are a blur. Amidst the background noise the words 'Larry, your dad has died I'm so sorry' were delivered. It was as if time had stopped and I broke down in floods of tears, the words swirling over and over in my head. My mind raced as I was told my aunt had found him that morning in the downstairs bathroom. The doctor told me it was a combination of a massive stroke and heart attack which would have been so quick he wouldn't have felt any pain. All I could picture was my dad on his own in the bathroom slumped on the floor. I had only spoken to him the previous evening and he was ok. Through a haze of rushing thoughts and emotion I stood there desperately trying to piece the last conversation we had together. He had been trying to read Teresa's mobile number to me as he was getting confused dialling it. I asked, 'are you alright da?' and he sounded ok. He struggled with his sentences and comprehension as usual but he said he was about to have a cup of tea and watch the telly before going to bed.

'OK da I'll talk to you tomorrow then, don't forget to take your tablets ok?'

'Ok hun I won't, going in there now to take 'em.'

'Speak to you tomorrow da, love ya'

'Bye Larry bye son, loves ya hun'.

We hung up.

Questions from my cousin-in-law about a funeral home and a suit broke my thoughts. I tried to listen and be helpful, to take it all in. The call ended and I stood there in limbo feeling sick at the thought of having to go back into the office and speak to anyone. I just wanted to get home to Wexford.

I burst open the editor's door and asked could I speak to her. I hid by a cupboard as I told her the news, she hugged me and brought me into her office. She rallied around with colleagues and tried to calm me down, asked what I needed and I said I needed to get home. They booked me the next available flight and a car to take me back to the house I had just moved into to pack my bag. They said to just go, and not to worry about things there, they would sort it all. They never asked for the money for that flight and gave me almost three weeks off to deal with everything. I was so grateful. James was nearby my office. He stayed with me and took me to the airport. I called Michelle, she was in tears. I was in tears. I got James to text everybody else as I let the news sink in, but it didn't.

I couldn't stop thinking about me poor da, even though I knew this moment would come one day, I felt so unprepared and couldn't absorb it.

I sat on the plane and tried not to make eye contact with anyone. Instead I looked up to the bright blue sky above the clouds, and asked me mam to make sure he was ok, to hold his hand so he didn't feel alone. I stared out the window hoping to see a sign that she would. On the other side in Dublin, James Doyle drove me straight to Wexford. On the way I dreaded that I would have opinions barked at me, or someone would have something to say about this or that, but they didn't and everyone left me alone to do everything the way I saw fit for me da.

My day had started out as normal, I never imagined that by 6.30 on that Tuesday evening I would be sat in an undertaker's picking out a coffin for me da. I refused to see his body that evening, it was all too much, I couldn't face that, only twenty-four hours ago he was talking to me and now he was laid in the next room without life. I thought, should I have noticed something?, I had only seen him just over a week before.

I thought of the trip to the coast with Teresa, Jimmy and Winnie. His feet were in a dire state in recent months. My aunt would constantly take him to the foot specialist but no matter how many he saw, he would still go back to wearing his faithful boots. His feet combined with his breathing meant he had to sit down after walking just a few metres. Getting a lift or taxi the couple of hundred yards home after the pub had become more frequent as he couldn't manage the walk. He would sit in his stairlift to take him up to have his cup of tea. We got him a wheelchair, he didn't want it at all but agreed to use in it on trips or drives out of town where no one could see him in it.

We took it for a test run that last weekend. It turned out to be too small for him. When I pushed him up a ramp he shouted 'fuck, fuck' thinking he would fall out, before it rolled back on my toe. It was like a Lou and Andy sketch from Little Britain. He loved that weekend, I did too. It was nice to be by the sea with me da, sitting on the beach with an ice cream and looking out at the harbour boats with a pint.

But it was also where for the first time he looked really frail. I watched him as he lifted his Guinness to his lips shaking as he did. I knew there and then that me da, this once strong, life-worn and not to be messed with character, had become an old man.

After the stroke when I was at home I would lay his clothes out for him the night before knowing he would be up at the crack of dawn. I'd have to get up early to check his washing routine and spray him with deodorant. He'd jump and curse when the cold spray landed which always made me laugh. He would hate me fussing around him. But even without anyone's intervention he was always turned out well. He wore his 'DAD' ring as well as his gold anchor and cross chain with pride.

Prior to that weekend visit, I spoke to his doctor. She suggested respite in a different care home to get him back on track and to try and sort his feet out. On the weekend visit I assured him it was for two weeks only and they would be able to look after his feet and make sure his medication was in order. He listened to doctors and nurses so I hoped it would do him good. Again I had to decide to put him in the hands of professionals. I hoped he would calm down and see it as a break. After I left for London again, he worried about going to the care home, which once again racked me with guilt, but I had to stand strong on this one to see if it would get him back on track to some degree.

The evening I arrived my friends and relatives were waiting with love and support, I sat with my aunt and my cousin in the understakers and I chose a solid coffin with purple and gold handles and trim. The colours of Wexford and me da's favourite. From then I went into robotic mode to get everything in place and right for him. I didn't care about the cost. I knew what ever he had left was for me and with the agreement he had with his credit union to pay a lump sum towards the funeral, I ploughed on. I didn't care if I was left with just a euro, I wanted him to have the best.

Irish funerals are traditionally held very quickly after a death. It was proposed the funeral would be on Thursday, barely two days after he died. I categorically said no, how the fuck could I sort all that in two days and deal with the reality of the situation? It was agreed that the funeral would be on the Friday.

He had been getting used to the flat by the sea after moving in over two years before. My cousin David, and his missus Kim helped him settle and did odd jobs for him, he loved them being around. He constantly struggled with the TV remote buttons, something he had initially been able to get but it had been lost through the cruelty of the strokes progressive aftermath. My aunt and uncle were constantly down to help reteach him, and to fix the TV or DVD player when he knocked them off. He had all the TV channels written on scraps of papers beside his chair to help him remember.

When I arrived at the flat after being at the undertakers, I noticed the little calendar in the kitchen. He changed the date every day and any appointments were marked on it by my aunt. He had marked that day's date himself with no explanation. No other dates around it, just that date, 29th July. It was marked in the corner with a star and his betting shop pen lay beside it. It freaked me out, for some reason he had marked the day he died.

I stood outside the bathroom and stared at the floor, the tears fell as I pictured him lying there. I felt cold and any outside noises struck me rigid. I couldn't stay there ever again, it was too much so I rang my friends to come back and pick me up.

The calendar date stuck in my mind and I thought how crazily things can change in just a few months. The previous November, I threw him a surprise 80th birthday party in his local. For the invite, I superimposed his face on to a picture of Del Boy, complete with Rodney, Grandad and the three-wheeler van from Only Fools and Horses. I had a cake made up in the shape of a pair of boobs, to get him back for the huge breast shaped cake he had presented me with at my 21st!

The night of his birthday, he was in his element, stroke or no stroke. He was up dancing and laughing with everyone he loved and who loved him. He was so proud to have his daughter and me by his side. I had just turned 34 years old. He sat there, having defied all the odds with the life he had led. There was a poster on the wall above his head, which I had blown up from a picture of him as a young man. He was handsome with his hair slicked back and smiling, and he was still handsome at 80 years old, with smooth skin, and a glint in his eye even after cataract surgery.

I pushed on with the funeral arrangements for the next couple of days. I rang one of his best mates, Mick, his travelling buddy on the lorries. He was on his way to a European job. I asked him to help me carry the coffin along with my uncle and cousins, and he turned right around and came back for his friend.

I was hesitant about meeting with the priest, the Catholic foot soldiers not being my favourite people. But this guy was younger and approachable, if a little rushed, and I told him in no uncertain terms that I would be mentioning the Artane nightmare me da went through at the funeral whether he liked it or not. He didn't have a problem with it and said as long as I didn't swear I could say whatever I felt would do my dad proud. Thankfully the older priest who usually took funerals at the church was away. I was told he hated any alterations to his religious services and would kick up a fuss. I think the way I was feeling that day any objections would have been met with a counter tirade or a swift box in the jaw.

I couldn't put off seeing him laid out in the coffin any longer. I was dreading it. This would make it all the more real and I didn't want this to be real. I wasn't sure I could take another punch in the gut, another loss. Me da had always said he wanted to be buried in his wedding suit, a late seventies piece of tailoring which he still had in his wardrobe. In the midst of the phone call I hadn't thought to mention it, so I packed it up along with a purple tie and white shirt to see if he could be changed. Paula came with me. I felt sick walking into the funeral home. Although I had seen dead bodies before this was different. I was shaking while walking towards the open casket, afraid to look up. But I did and there he was laying under a harsh spot light, me ol' da, and I broke down in Paula's arms.

I composed myself and stood beside him. If I'm honest I didn't know what to do, how to feel, what to say. They had dressed him well and he looked smart in his outfit. He had a bruise on his head from falling in the bathroom and the life had gone from his cheeks. I asked the undertaker if changing his suit was a possibility. He went into graphic detail about what would happen to the 'body' if they were to change any of the clothing now. When he started chatting about 'rigor mortis' I'd heard enough and asked Paula what she thought. She said he looked lovely in blue so we left him be. I wasn't happy the bruise was still visible and that the spotlight was glaring down on him making him look like a corpse. I asked the undertaker if he could do something with make-up. I fixed me dad's hair to his usual style, his comb over to the side, not backwards like some old Westminster politician. The undertaker returned and I couldn't believe what happened next. He produced a brush and some make-up and started applying it to me da's face right in front of me. I was shocked, looking at me dead da being painted up like a mannequin in the shop window.

I had to turn away. I looked back when he was finished. To say he wouldn't land a job on a make-up counter is an understatement. I had to get him to reapply some more foundation and concealer. How the fuck did I end up standing at me da's coffin giving Maybelline direction to an undertaker? Me da, an 80 year old Irish sailor and man's man. He would have been mortified at the thought of me having him done up like a Girl's World doll. Later on I couldn't help burst out laughing, then crying, then laughing again at the thought of it.

With the funeral approaching way too fast, I moved from one task to the next. I opted for tropical and colourful flowers to represent his life, none of that granny carnation shit. He'd sailed the world with the navy and that should be represented. I created a memorial book with the printers and an order of service with fitting pictures for everyone to have. I tried to stay strong. With everything in place, I asked to be left alone in my aunt's the night before the funeral. I hadn't even started my eulogy and I was freaking out. I hadn't a clue where to start, there was so much to say, to be condensed. I sat alone on the bed, pen in hand, and it just poured out of me, as did the tears. Forty-five minutes later it was done, a natural flow of words hoping to encompass an adventurous life and unique man. Now I just had to stand there in front of a church full of people and deliver it.

I stood on the alter shaking, but I knew I had to do it right. Nerves could fuck off. I tried to speak calmly and followed my finger along the sentences, trying to breathe and look up at the packed church. Those couple of minutes felt like an eternity. For the rest of the service I stared at his coffin. His cap, ornamental ship, betting slips, a mini-Guinness and little radio laid on top beside his picture.

As we carried the coffin from the church, I tried to look straight ahead and not catch any faces. Once he was in the hearse, people poured up to me. First were the mams who had helped us growing up, who provided motherly figures for me. His friends and relatives had travelled from the UK and far and wide to pay their respects, including my friends to support me through it. I didn't think I had any tears left but still they flowed. Memories cascaded through my mind. All his mates, family, and people who knew me da and knew what a loss this was.

Irish funerals always seem never ending, and there was still more to go. We walked the streets behind the hearse up to our only real home, Maudlintown, then drove out to the graveyard. This was the part I dreaded the most, as we carried the coffin to the open grave where my mam was. I had visions of slipping or dropping the coffin and me da rolling out. The thoughts of seeing the open grave scared the life out of me. I was an anxious mess as we walked on the grass, but told myself to keep control. As we approached I tried not to look down. Then it was time, leaning back and taking the strain, we lowered him down. I looked blankly, like I was floating above myself rather than through my own eyes. But rather than the terror I anticipated of seeing my dad lowered in the cold mud and darkness, a surprisingly warm feeling came over. The feeling that it was right. He was going back to my mam. She was gonna hold him in her arms now like he had yearned for so long, and that gave me comfort.

I stood there on my own for a couple of minutes, saying goodbye, looking at the solid coffin below with the purple and gold, roses scattered on top and said goodbye to my dad. What a life we had had together: loss, anger, tears, fights, awkwardness, hurt, yearning, laughs, loyalty, understanding, fierce protection. I flashed back to being a little boy with my dad, through all the pain and haze of alcohol, remembering how much he loved me. Him holding my hand at my communion, putting me on the bar of his bike, or perching beside him on the sofa in the pub, legs dangling down and sipping on lemonade. Tommy Meyler and his little Larry, chalk and cheese, but in a lot of ways the same. Now it was the end, and no matter how much frustration I felt and how much I needed a father figure more than ever, standing there at the grave the unwavering father and son love we shared was enough.

I'd never needed a pint so much in my fucking life. So with the people who mean the world to me in tow, it was time to give Tommy Meyler the send off of all send offs, to put the pain aside and just get drunk. An Irish wake is a celebration, everyone having the craic and raising their glasses with pride, and boy did we do that. What a party it was, the whole place was packed, the band played and everyone danced and cheered for me da. There was no fights, and people who generally didn't even speak stood there in the same room with nothing but respect for this one off man. People came up to me and said it was better than any wedding or party they had been to, and I felt like we had done him proud.

That first week may have been over but there was still a daunting week ahead. I had a week to sort out all of me da's affairs before I went back to London. I felt overwhelmed, the fact that he had died just didn't seem real. How was I going to pack up his life in a week? I couldn't do much until the Monday and I was emotionally drained from the funeral week. I needed to get out of the town so went to stay with James Doyle in Dublin. I drank myself stupid through the pain that weekend, knowing it was only going to make it worse, but I didn't care and we drank Dublin's fair city dry. The place brought back memories of the day trips me da used to take me on. I remembered being evacuated after IRA bomb scares at Connolly Station. I'd use this as a chance to throw away the bag of hard sandwiches he had made as we ran up the platform. It was the city where we would sit listening to the ol' Dublin men in the pubs with their thick inner city accents and hear the women of Moore Street Market shouting above each other selling their goods. Where we would try to pick up Christmas bargains or nick the odd leather coat. Where me dad would say he was gonna take me for 'a meal' and we would end up in the post office headquarters canteen, eating cheap grub off a paper plate, the only ones not in uniform. The city where it was just me and me da together.

Travelling back to Wexford wasn't pretty. I was hungover and depressed out of my head. I sat in the front seat of the bus and looked out at the passing lush greenery of Ireland, trying not to vomit into my hands. I dreaded what lay ahead but had no choice but to get stuck in. I had to clear his home, I gave some of the furniture away and sold the rest. Going through his personal possessions was the worst part, trying to divide them up to give some memories to my aunts and uncle, a family of ten now down to just four. Eimear came with me one evening. I stood in the living room surrounded by a lifetime of memories. I picked up me da's glasses, the ones he would always take off for pictures but so desperately needed, the ones that had caused so many problems to get right since his stroke. I held them in my hand and burst into sobbing tears as Eimear held me up.

That week drew to a close, and I registered his death, cleared out the rest of the flat, and cut off the bills he hated so much. I stood there in an empty flat, looking out at the sea from the bedroom window. I felt numb, it still didn't feel real. But it was real and this was it, a life gone and tied up over two blurred weeks. There was no home to come back to now, no more tearful goodbyes, no more pints in the pub side by side. All I could see was uncertainty and loss, a void ahead, and I felt yet more cracks appear.

Chapter 19

I never expected to arrive back in Sydney in such a state, hauling my snotty, sweaty and limping body across the city to my cousin's house. A podiatrist appointment confirmed that there would be no Kiwi adventure ahead, just box sets, rest, physio and time to think on Debbie's sofa. I hoped the insurance would cover the lost dollars, and the specialist $250 trainers I had to buy. I was gutted having to let my mate Gareth know I wouldn't be meeting him and his parents in their native land. There would be no visit to Frodo Baggins house on this trip, but I was still in Australia, my amazing cousin was looking after me and I would still be able to carry on to the end of my travels once mended.

Following lots of rest and with so much stretching I'd surely added an inch to my height, I was back on my feet and wanted to make the most of my final few weeks down under. I zigzagged the city, catching up and staying with old mates whilst making new ones along the way.

I lost my opera virginity to The Barber of Seville at the stunning opera house. I strolled the beautiful costal walk from Bondi to Coogee with Lewis, a travelling wonder boy with a brave heart, a majestic setting running alongside the wild ocean swell. I bumped into a bewildered looking Freddie Flintoff in full drag in one of the many camp and hilarious bars on Oxford Street. I took in the Blue Mountains with my Scouse bro, Terry, and new Aussie mate, Brad, who quickly became a true friend, a one in a million man who went out of his way with hospitality to show me the nooks and crannies of Sydney. There's a few people you meet in your life who have no agenda, who are just decent and kind, and this guy, who had beaten off cancer and lives his life to the max each day, was nothing short of inspiring. I felt blessed to share my time with him.

I caught up with Plum (aka Paul) who was over from the UK and drank schooners in Manly, partied the nights away with my ace new Aussie pals, Aaron and Luke, and caught up for rooftop drinks and views of the harbour with Susan and Spencer, friends from back in Wexford.

I flew off for a whistle stop tour of Melbourne with Terry to meet up with his brother Antony and take in the shameless delights of a Neighbours set tour. It made it all the more enjoyable getting to experience the riverside cafes, graffiti art and chilled vibe of this Aussie metropolis with the diamond that is Tezza. And it culminated with one final catch up with the Geordie boy himself, my consistent Australian travel partner and firm friend, Michael, who had decided to settle in Melbourne and give working life a go to save some dosh for his onward travels.

Back In Sydney myself and Terry took in the lights of Darling Harbour and Chinatown with Joe and his fella Rod.

I had morning swims and peaceful walks with Ari at Marubra beach, and got pissed on so many varieties of wine I was sweating grapes with Tom up in the luscious green hills and vineyards of the Hunter Valley.

Myself and Debbie visited Palm Beach which doubles as Summer Bay in Home & Away. We got to watch some new cast filming but we're gutted to just miss an Alf Stewart scene by half an hour, flamin galahs! I remembered getting home from school and plonking myself down to catch up on the far away dramas of Bobbi, Sally, Fisher and Eireen.

As the days dwindled in Sydney, there was one stand out event I was asked to be part of, the world famous Mardi Gras. Luke asked me to join an annual float with him and his friends. I jumped at the chance, adding it to my say yes to everything backpacking ethos. The theme was, 'For the love of sequins'. Not wanting to end up looking like a cheap Argos Christmas tree, I decided less would be more and I tried to create some sort of bad boy ghetto version of glitzy. With the help of the float's costume maker extraordinaire, Stephen, we came up with gold sequinned running shorts, gold sequinned trainers, a baseball cap and not much else. If you can't bare your nipples at a Mardi Gras when can you, even if my backpacking body shape begged to differ!

What I didn't bank on was how huge this event is. It took quite a while to get from the prep hotel to the holding area with people wanting photographs and to say hello to our snowball of glitter and dazzling sequins, which headed towards them in the Sydney afternoon sun. The attention continued for the day, we felt like celebrities. Pose, flash, pose, flash, I lapped it up knowing I probably wouldn't get to do this again. Stephen showed me around all the other floats. We met an eclectic cast of participants dressed in everything from rubber dog suits to Mad Max cyborg drag queen outfits. Everyone was feeling the pride and spirit of the event and greeted us with smiles and friendliness. When we did eventuality take off into the parade run it was about 10pm, and after a gut full of Prosecco the dance routine went out the window. I ran along side the ten deep cheering crowds slapping their hands and cheering along. It was probably the closest I'd get to becoming that Fifth Element popstar, I even got my two seconds of fame on the live TV coverage as I drunkenly danced past the camera. Being part of that with Luke and his friends was unforgettable, the camp cherry on top of a sweet sweet Sydney pie.

Never far off, anxieties and thoughts of the previous couple of years decided to raise their heads and cloud mine for the final few days in Sydney. But I was able to face them in a fight, standing up in the ring now rather than broken and bloodied on the floor.

I spent time at the beach, using it as mindset training. I worked hard on swapping any anxiety-ridden or depressive thoughts for productive and positive thinking. It's not always easy, especially when these thoughts would start to whistle for the black dog, but I forced myself to focus on the here and now rather than dwelling on any negative. I tried with all my might to change the relentless feelings of doom as the days went on. I was determined to change the impact, not to let the depression become an engrossing and exhausting pattern anymore. Thoughts of my ex crept in. I could see us in front of the log fire at Christmas or sitting together looking out over Paris with a beer on the hill of the Basilica du Sacre-Coeur de Montmartre. I thought of the over excitement and how I had tried to cram so much in on that trip to Paris and make it 'perfect' that I almost ruined it. Negatives and positives would swirl but I fought to push any romanticising out, and continued reconstructing the relationship in my mind and stop playing the what if game. To let that scene of my life fade to black.

I tried my best to fill my remaining time with fun and laughter, and to end this part of my travels with a bang. I had a final weekend blow out with Debbie and her friends, the hilarious, fun, encouraging and loyal bunch of women with equally top notch husbands. The unexpected embrace from them all really did enhance my time. For the ones who couldn't make that night out it was a sophisticated goodbye over brunch, followed by a pub crawl with the rest. We laughed the weekend away across the city, dance offs on wet tiled dance floors and Irish jigs on beer stained carpets. In one pub Debbie sprawled out on the floor after tripping over her heels on the way back from the bar. She flew through the air in a cascade of blue chiffon and landed halfway across the pub, somehow managing to not spill a drop of her drink. Now that's an Irish pro right there.

I said my goodbyes to everyone. Saying goodbye to Luke at the Opera Bar with the sun going down over Sydney Harbour was especially hard. Tears filled my eyes, I felt so proud of this boy, he'd come through so much too and had carved a lovely life for himself. It felt great to be part of his life again for a while. My homeboy done good.

With my backpack zipped up, I said a fond goodbye to the kids, and Debbie drove me to the airport. I knew there would be more tears, especially with a few anxieties still bubbling away underneath. We were both temporarily distracted from the emotions by Hollywood actor Jack Black who arrived at the same time. But the inevitable happened and tears flowed as we hugged at the departures entrance. Getting to know this amazing woman, to be part of her life after all these years, was not only emotionally rewarding but instilled a sense of pride in me. I felt proud of her and the kids, of her life here and of the love and warmth she showed me. She made me feel part of a family again for a moment in time. As I waved goodbye and the car disappeared, a sadness struck. It was just me, myself and I again. But that was ok, and I decided there and then it was time to give myself a break and let the excitement of the final leg of my travels be the dominating emotion. I walked past Jack on the way in, gave him a wink and headed off to see what treats Malaysia would have in store for me.

I had forgotten to check what currency they use in Malaysia, and come to think of it what language they spoke. The laid-back backpacker electrodes in my brain must be on the up and over taking the more manic OCD bolts.

Thankfully I was staying with my friend Gavin's sister Lucy, and her fella Terry in Singapore. She text me detailed directions to her place for a whistle stop over before heading to the jungles of Borneo. It was drinks in Marina Bay that night, where the luxurious three-columned futuristic Marina Bay Sands hotel dominates the horizon. Cocktails, beers, street food and a late finish wasn't the usual Tuesday night activities for two Singapore professionals who had early starts the next day, so it felt even more special they were so nice and had gone to the trouble of showing me their adopted city. Before jetting off again I caught up with Rod and Joe from Sydney for a swig of a Singapore Sling at the famous Raffles hotel, where an old colonial vibe and history oozes from its walls.

My first night on the island of Borneo wasn't as expected, but I was taking all this in my stride now. In Kota Kinabalu, the capital of Malaysia's Sabah state, I ended up looking down a dark rat infested alley trying to find the door to my hostel. Eventually a man sat in his porch behind the bars of the security cage pointed me to the right one. I learned it is custom in Malaysia to take your shoes off before entering a building. I snuck back down the hostel stairs ten minutes later to grab my jazzy $250 trainers and hide them under my bed.

I had emailed Howard a month or so prior telling him of my plan to reach his place at the tip of Borneo on recommendation from a travel agent in London. His cheerful response told me I had made the right choice. I crammed into a shared taxi amongst boxes, luggage and big smiles from my fellow taxi goers to take me north to the town of Kudat. I would be met by one of Howard's colleagues at a central hotel ready for the onward transit to Tampat Do Aman, aka Howard's End. The sun blazed as we passed the beautiful scenery of endless thick rolling palm trees. Although stories of deforestation for palm oil production marred that a bit.

After a few hours, Moos, a small stocky guy with a friendly and excitable disposition, arrived to pick myself and another couple of Czech backpackers up. He chatted away in his best English, which he was proud to be mastering, and never lost his smile the whole way, like every day was a celebration. I liked Moos a lot. We arrived to find Howard, the man himself, building a compost toilet in the blistering early afternoon sun. With a firm handshake it was great to finally meet this very English gent. Howard had moved across the world to build up his dream from scratch along with his

Malaysian wife and their family, and now had an eco-dwelling carved out within the jungle at the tip of Borneo. His aim was to compliment the surrounding environment and wildlife, with an ideology to help and work alongside the local community, respecting their traditions and history. He brought his love of rugby with him, and had started tournaments and coaching all over the state.

Moos showed me to my home for the next few days and I couldn't have been happier. From under a twisted hanging jungle vine surrounded by little flowers was my own little Hobbit hut, Chilli Cottage. Stepping stones led up a tiny path to this triangular wooden structure, with its little white double doors. Inside it had a double mattress on the floor in a mosquito net cocoon, and a little shelf and light. It was the perfect cosy hideaway. A little boy's dream tree house, and I fell in love with it right there.

It was a special day to arrive, St. Patricks Day. The news that there was a sister beach cafe just a couple of kilometres down the road which had cold beer, views of the Tip and amazing sunsets made my Irish heart jig with delight. Shame I would be on my own though. But what do you know, I walked in and the first person I met was a Dublin fella called Alan, along with his girlfriend, Catherine from Chicago. We clicked straight away, so I sat and chatted with them and some other travellers, Mateos from Switzerland, and an Austrian couple, Lucas and Verena. As sunset approached myself, Alan and Catherine plonked ourselves on the sand for the rest of the evening and raised a can of Tiger beer (famous in Australia apparently, although I'd never come across it once on my visit) to all the fellow Irish around the world. A surreal but perfect setting for Paddy's Day, we talked about life and shared stories as the sun disappeared beneath the horizon and the moon and stars lit up the sky.

After a tepid at best, but refreshing outdoor shower the next morning, I made my first trip to the compost toilet where I gritted my teeth and hoped a huge centipede wouldn't latch on to my bare arse. I made my way to the point where I'd envisioned standing for so many months, the Tip of Borneo. I walked up along the near perfect sands, past a blue and white fishing boat pulled up on the beach covered over with palm leaves, its nets drying in the morning sun. Fully clothed fishermen and women cast their lines just off shore, apparently jelly-fish season was following me around the globe, and there was all sorts bobbing about in the waters here.

I approached the Tip sweating like a bitch in the sizzling heat, and a group of giggling Malaysian teenagers ran after me. They surrounded me and asked for pictures. I rolled with it as the sweat rolled off me, for a moment feeling like I was in One Direction and their smiles made me smile. I climbed down a bumpy cliff and there it was, the place I had aimed to reach all those months ago when feeling broken and lost. I walked out and stood on the furthest point, trying not to get washed away like Harold Bishop in Neighbours. I smiled out at the ocean as the waves swirled around my feet and let the air fill my lungs and clear my mind. I still had a couple of weeks travelling left but this was a momentous moment, I'd done it and reached this part of the world which I didn't know much about but for some reason had stuck in my head. I knew I needed to make it here, and I had, digging deep and trying to rebuild myself piece by piece along the way. I felt elated and proud and couldn't help but well up with happy tears.

I was on cloud nine, and that evening I met up with my new American and Irish friends to celebrate. Lucas, a lad with unlimited energy due to his strict vegetable and fruit diet, with the odd glass of water added in, had been busy collecting firewood all day. A group of us walked up the beach to where he had set up a bonfire ready to go. I came across an entire vintage phone box washed up from some part of the world on the way. The scorching sun disappeared once more and the flames of the burning wood drifted up high. These type of gatherings while travelling are very special, bonding with new people and freeing yourself a little bit more. Having dreadlocks and wafting armpits aren't necessary for a hippy outlook, but that's cool too, washed or unwashed I feel everyone can embrace their inner hippy. This night in particular, something extra special happened: a sober Lucas led the way to take a dip in the calm ocean, with the liquor flowing the rest of us joined him and threw caution to the jellyfish season winds.

We stood in the ocean and swirled the waters around us and a natural wonder occurred: the dark night sea started to glow with millions of little lights, bioluminescence. A mesmerising parade of twinkling plankton surrounded us. They stuck to our hands, and as we splashed the water up on our bodies we became like human fireflies. Torsos and speedos sparkled and glowed under the moonlight above in a magical rush and phenomenal moment I will never forget, and thankfully no stingers to ruin it.

I had no plan for after Howard's. I could've stayed there for weeks but opted to fly over to the other side of the island with Alan and Catherine a few days later. These two were so genuinely nice, decent and fun. Great people to be around, and I was very happy to be spending my Borneo days in their company. We laughed the days away and talked about the world and our places in it.

I sat against a rock looking out at the turquoise sea one afternoon, the fishermen and women again in line along the shore reeling in their daily catch, and I drifting away in my music. Each track provoked a thought or created a smile. A musical loop had been constant in my head for the last few years, one line of a song would stick in my mind on repeat. I'd go to sleep and wake up with it still going, sometimes I wished I could open my skull and wash them out for some peace.

I spotted a tiny almost translucent crab near my foot. Its brothers and sisters constantly darted around the beach scattering at the sight of any humans who approached. This little fella seemed fearless and inquisitive though. He playfully scurried away from my hands and feet and then back again, like a ten legged ninja ready to fight, looking up at me to see what my next move would be. Finally he braved it and side stepped cautiously up my fingers, like he trusted me, and I liked this little dude. We mucked about for ages. His bravery and openness echoed what I had tried to keep prominent on my journey so far. I might sound like I've downed a bag of magic mushrooms here, but this little creature has the right idea and reminded me that it's ok to be me, to not follow the crowd. That we don't have to worry about what people think, just be true to you and go your own way – trippy! I wrapped up with my ninja crab buddy and headed off along the beach, feeling like I was making my way on a much clearer path.

My time here had been so rewarding, and so much fun with this new troop of travellers. I would miss my little Chilli Cottage hut, the resident cockerels roaming around, the cold showers, my early mornings sat with Catherine as she worked on her writing and we looked out at the men and women working tirelessly in the rice fields. I'd even miss the compost toilets a bit. I thanked Howard for this special place, and for bringing his dream to life for others to share.

Chapter 20

The local airport was a new experience: they weighed our bags and then us, and the local police thought Alan was a ringer for Bono from U2 so excitedly huddled around for pictures. We boarded a tiny propeller plane where the pilot was within touching distance and glided across the country with another American, Laney from San Francisco. Paganakan Dii, in the Sepilok area, is reached through a miniature park with an eerie zoo attached. Hungry looking deer hung around their muddy pen and four massive crocodiles were kept in a far too small concrete enclosure with only a rickety walkway above to view them. It all seemed quite cruel.

Our jungle huts were plush, one hundred times bigger than Chilli Cottage, with sliding doors opening up to unveil the multiple shades of green of the forest below, the same back drop for the open air hot showers. I was right next door to Alan and Catherine, unbeknownst to them their balcony would become the unofficial moonlight bar.

The days here were spent exploring the various natures reserves, from the orangutan rehabilitation centre, where one little minx came down to lap up the attention. She walked along beside the gathering crowd and stood calmly at my side eyeballing me. In a flash, she grabbed my new Dior copy sunglasses off my vest before swinging off into the trees. My pleas fell on deaf monkey ears, as she snapped them in half and proceeded to chew on the lens. The laughter of the crowd made it worth it – fuck this trip really must be changing me. We moved on to see the sun bears, seriously cute but seriously deadly with claws like Wolverine. The mischievous orangutan had somehow followed us in. We turned around and there she was on the rail of the stairs, taking a piss for more applause.

We bussed and hitchhiked over to Labuk Bay. The locals laughed as we tried to get directions from the bus driver to the proboscis monkeys sanctuary, waving our arms around as if any of it would translate. As soon as I laid eyes on these peculiar primates I was in awe, with their weirdly human like body and floppy noses. They hung out in the sun with constant erections and communicated with each other with some sort of honking noise. Silver leaf monkeys came and sat around us, picking the fleas off each other's back like they were having a girly sleepover and doing each other's hair.

After a goodbye group meal, it was time to head off on my own again the next morning to the Kota Kinabatangan river in hope of catching sight of the elusive pygmy elephants. Saying goodbye to Catherine and Alan was such a shame, meeting these two was meant to be, their friendship and constant encouragement over our short time together not only helped me regain belief in myself but strengthened my positivity. I felt honoured to have them as part of my memories and now as my friends going forward.

The river is a beautiful and peaceful place, its fine mist rising in the mornings with only the birds and call to prayer from the mosque in the next village filling the air. I ditched my first choice of accommodation though, it turned out to be a river tour conveyor belt, everyone desperate to find the elephants but only catching occasional glimpses of any exciting wildlife. I wanted to see this place up close and wild. I had researched home stays, and found one with a guy called Osman who seemed to be an aficionado on all things wild on this vast river. Many famous explorers and nature experts had tapped him up for his knowledge of the local wildlife and jungle expertise. If it was good enough for Attenborough, it would do me. The reception girls from the first place kindly gave me a lift to the closest jetty in a little purple car that resembled a Quality Street. I hitched a boat ride upriver to Osman's place and was greeted by his wife Yanti, their six kids, numerous cats and a happy looking chappie sitting on their jetty, Mikal from Germany. He was on a motorbike tour of Borneo with his Italian mate, Andrea, and a sidecar full of luggage. But there was no Osman, his asthma was playing up and he had to rest before going to see the doctor. After a chat with the lads they agreed to share the trip with me, I haggled the price with Yanti, and their eldest son Tom stepped in to be our river guide. We packed up the boat and headed up river with a positive outlook.

Tom signed to passing fisherman if they had heard of any elephant sightings that day, but their responses could be read universally as a resounding no. I believed in my heart we would find them. As we chugged along, Tom pointed out the other wildlife like the rhinoceros hornbill, various species of leaping monkeys and a croc. Thankfully no packed group tours were up this far, just the odd private tour and local river men. Two hours in and Tom spotted a friend of his. After an exchange of gestures we sped up, myself and the boys looked at each other with anticipation.

Tom turned the engine off and we edged around a bend and there in front of us was a whole family of pygmy elephants, the rare creatures quenching their thirst and within touching distance on the riverbank. It was an emotional sight to see these micro-mammals in the wild. They lifted their trunks to show us their gnashers before making their way back into the jungle. We quietly let the engine go again and worked our way along beside them. We turned a corner to find another herd plunged in the river under some vines. Splashing about, some with only their trunks breaking out of the water. I couldn't believe we had gotten to witness this so close up. The people back on the tourist trail would have given anything for this. It shows if you go off the beaten path and with your gut, wonderful discoveries are there to be made.

It was time to head back to the home stay for some grub, but not before Tom took us right inside a bat cave where tiny birds darted in and out of their nests amongst the hanging bats. Then down through an eerie side river, where metallic coloured humming birds zipped in and out of the water – tres cool. Myself and the boys fancied a beer to celebrate, unfortunately Tom couldn't drink alcohol so he got an ice cream from the local shop, which was actually a neighbour's house where a lady sold beer from her porch. There was little muddy puppies roaming around as well as prize fighting cocks in cages. They stood there silently ready to be armoured up with blades and go into battle. The only toilet was an outhouse with a hole in the floor hovering above the water, so when Andrea went for a piss it flowed straight into the Kinabatangan. It made me feel slightly sick thinking of the catfish caught from it that morning and which we had earlier for lunch.

We sat on the jetty back at the home stay, and Tom got a proud pat on the back from his mum for a successful river outing, especially after both he and his mum hadn't looked too confident about finding any mini-elephants that day. As the sun went down and the dinner was prepared, I felt very happy inside. What an adventure, and to top it off Osman made an appearance, much younger than I expected but larger than life and quite a character. He told us about the surrounding jungle, his famous visitors and how he had once prized a kidney stone out of his penis with a cotton bud. He washed the blood off and now keeps it proudly in a display jar.

I didn't really know where to go next, so made a loose plan to head towards the Crocker Range national park and possibly jump on a train back up to Kota Kinabalu. I thought I might catch a glimpse of Mount Kinabalu on route. At the main bus station I drank the sweetest cup of tea I've ever had, got a few inquisitive looks from the locals and made use of the public toilet, aka a hole in the ground with a hose and no toilet paper. A young fella sat outside selling packets of tissue – smart kid. As I mooched around the place, a little boy and his grandfather came up to me. The lad had a big smile and wanted to say hello so his grandad brought him over. He then gabbed my hand and kissed it before giving me a big hug, and the grandad patted me on the shoulder. I felt very embarrassed with the little guy kissing my hand so told him he didn't have to do that and gave him a big hug back. They waved me goodbye and off they went. As they walked away I saw myself and my dad walking along the quay back in Wexford. I felt bad I had nothing to give the little fella so quickly ran to the shop and bought a load of sweets. I ran after them and the boys eyes lit up and his smile got even wider as I handed over the treats. His grandad couldn't thank me enough, they obviously meant so much to each other. It was heart warming to see and I had to wipe my eyes as I walked off.

Mount Kinabalu is a major attraction in Borneo, booked up for weeks in advance with climbers wanting to reach its peak, but I wasn't that bothered. A couple of Swiss girls on the bus said they were on their way to visit the Mount Kinabalu national park but weren't climbing the mountain. Then a French couple recommended I should at least see the park. With my mind constantly changing over the eight hour journey, I thought fuck it, I would jump off with the girls and see what all the fuss was about, then move on to somewhere else the next day.

After one fruitless hostel viewing, we walked along the main road to find the next lodging, when a motorbike pulled up driven by a young Belgian guy with a hipster beard called Tibot. He asked if we needed somewhere and told us there was room at Jungle Jack's just down the road, where he and his Canadian girlfriend Naomi had been staying and working for a couple of weeks. We agreed to have a look and off he rode, arriving back a few minutes later with a van to take us to Jack's. This place was a treat, it had graffitied freight containers turned into cosy dorms, with free breakfasts of bread, eggs, cheese and as much tea as you like. It had a stellar view of the mountain in the background, when the mist wasn't blanketing it like it was that day. Jungle Jack arrived, a hilarious, friendly and very welcoming man who had set up the place. When not with his family in Kota Kinabalu, he spent his time looking after his guests and the climbers there, sorting out all the particulars. To top things off, every night Jack takes all his guests out for dinner, in an actual restaurant and it's all paid for. Now that was a hostel first.

When I woke up the next morning the only thing on my mind was eggs on toast. That was until I opened the freight dorm door to clear skies and Mount Kinabalu residing above in all it mountainous splendour. Far off and above the clouds, its peaky gloriousness was a pretty dazzling sight. I tucked into my cheesy eggs as the day's climbers prepared their necessities, but something niggled at me inside. This was after all a trip to change my life, to say yes to everything, to push myself, and the sight of that mountain wouldn't leave my mind.

With an hour to go before the others set off to join their guide at the base of the mountain, I pulled Jack aside and asked him if there was any way he could get me on the climb. I liked Jack and I think he liked me. He had swag, like he could get anything sorted, fingers in many pies and all that. He made a call and he didn't fail me. 'Larry get me your passport, my friend can make one more space for you and you pay this price, but don't tell the others.'

And with that I was off to climb a mountain, scrambling around the container trying to pack mountain-y things. Jimmy, a guy from the UK who was ready to go, guided me through. With a bag packed of I'm not sure what, some borrowed tracksuit bottoms and a head light from Jack, I was ready to go. Although I'm not sure my attire of trainers, white t-shirt, skinny denim shorts and a baseball cap would be approved by the mountain climbers' association, if there is such a thing.

We met Margaret our guide at the base, a smiley Malaysian lady, all of 5ft 2', 46 years old and mother of six kids. She guided climbers up to the peak of this mountain on a weekly basis and had taught herself basic English, I warmed to her straight away. We had a quick glance at the map, a short rules and pep talk and off we went. Our ascent began at 09.30 on that Easter Sunday, upwards through the jungle paths we went, our aim was to reach the mountain lodge at six kilometres high. There we would get some food and rest before the second and hardest part of the climb would begin at 02.30 the following morning, I began to think hadn't thought this through, and it excited me even more.

Myself and Jimmy buddied up. Half an hour in and we were both drenched in sweat, the humidity was thick and didn't let up. Not even a couple of kilometres up, my shorts gave way in monumental fashion. I looked down to see not only the shorts flapping around me, but my junk hanging out. Thankfully I was wearing undies, unfortunately they were bright yellow. Giggles came from people on their way down the mountain from the previous day's climb. I whipped my cap off and hung it strategically from my belt, until we reached a rest point and I swapped the shredded skinny denim for some very warm tracksuit bottoms. It was the bin for my tattered shorts, they had fallen just short of the end of my trip.

The climb up was insane. The relived and slightly broken looking people on the way down cheered us on and gave words of encouragement. Myself and Jimmy tried to take a snap at each kilometre sign and stopped for short breaks when we could, at times my legs felt like they were on fire, so it was easier not to stop and just carry on. We passed porters, mainly Malaysian men and women, on the way. They may have been short but by God they had strength and resilience in abundance. They carry everything from gas bottles to water tanks and food supplies to maintenance materials and tools on their backs six kilometres up a bloody mountain without any whimpering or moaning. The amount of respect I had for them was immeasurable, and spurred us on. We reached the lodge after four hours and forty minutes at 14.10, finishing the first hurdle was just joyous.

All I wanted was to sit down with a beer, and what do you know, half way up a mountain in Borneo they were serving cans of Guinness, fizzy weird tasting Guinness, but who cares? I raised a toast with my fellow sweaty aching mountain compadres. We took a seat on what could have been the edge of the world, on a ledge above the thick clouds as far as the eye could see. It was if we were in a fantasy film and the lodge was the floating castle in the clouds surrounded by pink, purple and indigo skies. With the sun about to set, I cracked open a mini-bottle of rum I'd brought and we all sat in a line pondering the vast beyond.

There was a buzz about the lodge for the 2am wake up call and the smell of cooked breakfast from the canteen area filled the place. I met Jimmy and the others for a hearty fry up to send us on our way. With head torches attached, mine to my Oakland Raiders cap like some ghetto miner, and iPods at the ready, we set off. Starting our trek to the summit at 02.39, hoping to catch the sunrise from the peak.

The steps were already congested with people. I wasn't feeling the snail's pace at all so told Jimmy I was going ahead, weaving in and out and overtaking the climbers in front. Half an hour later I found myself near the front of the pack. A little later again I found myself ahead of everyone with only one guide in front. I don't have a clue where this pace came from but it kept up until just the two of us reached a small hut. The guide went inside and plonked himself down ready to check everyone into a log before the next leg leading onto the mountain face, which was much rockier and steeper.

I found myself on my own, on my own on Mount fucking Kinabalu, with a fading head light and nothing but the moon, stars and a white rope to guide my way. I looked back to see twinkling headlamps in the far distance and a sudden fear came over me. Should I wait for the others? Was I going the wrong way? Would I topple off at any moment never to be found again? But determination started gathering in my belly and I couldn't stop, I carried on alone, my breathing becoming heavy with the thin cold night air. I had to stop every twenty metres and catch my breath, breathing like I had run a hundred metres rather than climbed twenty. After short rests, I stuck two fingers up to my asthma and onward I went. I reached a huge open space. I sat and looked around, surrounded by a barren but beautiful black and charcoal landscape high above the clouds, the mountain peaks silhouetted against the sky. I thought to myself, I could actually do this, I could reach the summit first – what the fuck! I looked up at the bright moon in the night sky and a sudden rush of emotion flooded every fibre of my being. I thought of my mam and dad, the last month, year, all of the years, all of the loss, all of the pain inside of me, still fighting but now fighting my only real opponent, myself. The ghost of the person I once thought I was vanished. In that moment I visualised a new future, one where I would go forward and I would be ok, here on a mountain face in Borneo something changed. With a huge adrenaline rush, tears in my eyes, I stood up, I stood up and shouted at the top of my breathless lungs 'C'MONNNNN!'

Onward I went, a weathered sign read 750 metres to the summit, lights still twinkling behind me even further in the distance. The landscape became jagged, rockier, but I didn't look back anymore. I scaled those rocks unsure if I was even going the right way, the pictures on the wall at the lodge of people celebrating at the top looked very different to what was around me. The image of the infamous naked backpackers didn't match what I was looking at, but I carried on, I was actually doing this. Then at an almost 90 degree terrain, I pulled myself up over rocks and jumped over gaps, sweating and breathless. I kept climbing until I saw a sign illuminated by the moonlight. I reached a very small clearing and with no where else to go, I read the misworded sign:

'You are standing at the highest peak of Mt.Kinabalu (Lows peak 4095.2m). The highest mountain between Himalaya and New Guinea. The mountain remain strong after rocked by a 6.0 magnitude earthquake at 7.15am on June 5th, 2015'

It was 04.39, exactly two hours after I had set off and I was elated. It made sense why it didn't look like the pictures, the horrendous earthquake the previous year had changed the landscape. Now I had thoughts of an earthquake in my head. There was no one else in sight and I was only a few feet from a sheer drop in the abyss.

I sat in the freezing cold, dressed in layers of Topman instead of NorthFace, there was nothing but silence, thinking time. I still didn't believe what I had just achieved, making it to the summit of Mount Kinabalu and somehow first, ahead of all those experienced climbers and even the guides. I repeated to myself 'this can't be real, I must have taken a wrong turn'. Just me sat on top of a mountain with my thoughts, so very far away from everything.

I thought of the dangerous and final paths in life I could have chosen but didn't choose. I knew I had always tried to make the best of situations and extract the positive from events, but it was here that I decided I was going to focus on and remember the good instead of always allowing the hardship to rear its evil head and torture me, affecting my life and behaviour. This was another positive step, no, make that a leap forward. Not literally though, or I'd be impaled on a rock. It felt like a triumph, I felt freer than I had in a very long time, if ever. That moment, just the mountain and me, the pain bowed down to elation and within me I found a new strength.

Twenty minutes passed, and there was still no sign of anyone. I started thinking that I might be in the wrong bit, that all the rest of them were on the other side of the mountain having a party celebrating their achievement. My sweat drenched body was now shivering, so I decided to climb down for a better view of the upward trail, and finally caught sight of a head torch. Mine was dead at this stage. A few minutes later a guy approached, exhausted and determined. We said hello and I told him he was almost there, so I left him to his stride, and sat myself on a rock so he could have his moment on the top. Then the third person arrived with her guide, an older Australian lady. I encouraged her onward and told her she was just metres away. After a few minutes, I climbed back up to join them. They were Radhwan, a young guy from Malaysia, and the very spunky Aussie, Jenny, both seasoned climbers.

We took snaps and congratulated each other, the three of us from all corners of the earth unified in this achievement.

The rest of the climbers started to trickle up then, everyone looking for a spot to take in the sunrise. Finally I saw Jimmy and the others and it was hugs all round. They couldn't believe I was first up, and the sunrise was crazy. It suddenly yet slowly embraced all and the mountain with its glow, and cast colourful shapes and shadows all around.

Everyone sat in awe, thinking of their own personal achievements and reasons for being there. A shared priceless wonder which will always overshadow any possessions or status. I felt calm in those moments as the sun rose. I had taken myself out of the darkest and almost final hour of my life. Consumed by grief and loss, I'd desperately dug deeper than ever before to get here, to hold the hand of a lost little boy and help him up, to give him, to give me, a chance. Situations are so important with depression. Finding that bravery to take myself out of a situation where it manifested and thrived was key. Having the honour to have this time, for the first time in my life, to dissect and understand myself. It has strengthened me in every possible way. I can't change the past or retrieve the losses, but what I realise now is that I can change, and don't have to be a prisoner of circumstance and of my own mind. A shattered heart can be put back together, piece by piece, and it doesn't matter if the cracks still show. I've finally learned how to be kind to myself, and to shift the weight of worthless guilt. I'd spent time with people in parts of the world who have nothing and still don't pity themselves, who carry on no matter how bad. I've experienced camaraderie which you don't get in day to day western city life, and I've made a travelling family. The people who shared and took me into their lives wholeheartedly, strangers but now life long friends. Bonded by a moment in time, each of us changed in some way. It's impossible to answer the question 'which was your favourite part', to condense it all into a five minute conversation. The answer that will always come first though is that it was the people I met, and the chance I gave myself.

The dark days will still come, I'll still have things thrown at me, and even if it gets blurry I now have these memories and cultivated feelings of strength and determination instilled in my soul to guide me through.

I'll always have a naughty little Artful Dodger in me, but this bad boy will make sure the good intentions shine through with kindness and love.

I never expected or knew what would come from this trip, but I know now how to lift my head up from the ground and look up to the sky. There's more mountains ahead and still a way to go, but I know I can do anything and do that by just being me. Because here at the end of the untouchable journey, I know I have saved myself, in every way a lad could be saved.

Be brave.

Acknowledgements

Firstly I would like to thank each one of my friends who have let me sleep on their sofas, in their spare rooms, and put up with me invading their space (and rearranging their fridges) so that I could dedicate the time to writing this book:

James Ingham, Antony Rush, Luke Thomas, Gareth Martin, Dennis Opara, Kerri Carty, Lia Nicholls, Jaime Smith, Dave Smith, Gary Willis, Robert Hogg, Gavin Sandilands, Martin Ruddy, Ryan Hatrick, Andrew Owen, Billy Kehoe, Emer Frayne, Valerie Martin, Liam Martin, Kris Pace, Adam Perkins, C.J Dunn, David Goldman. Darren Louis, Gareth Breeze, Shona Zaccaria, Jimmy McCauley. Thank you.

And to everyone who's helped and continues to help me. The genuine belief you have in me without any expectation, just through friendship, kindness and love, shows what a very lucky lad I am indeed.

To all my travelling compadres, thank you for helping me shape a new future and for creating memories and adventures that will always make me smile.

Thanks to Owain Moss-Proctor and Jordan Moore's abundant creativity in bringing my cover vision to life. To Philip Connor for his skilful and unique editing talent, and the patience of a saint! To the bleedin rapid Conor MacCabe for his straight talking and legal eagle eye.

To Nathan Charles Smith, thank you for for taking the time to champion my story, and for your kindness and positivity.

A very special thanks to Mr David Lazenby, you didn't have to, but you believed in me with this. Your advice, honesty and humour always helped stoke the fire back up again. May there be many more wine soaked meetings ahead, me and the swans will always be thankful you wonderful and funny lad.

To my mentor, the extraordinary Catherine Toops.

St Patrick's Day on a beach in Borneo helped change the course of my life. Meeting you and the gent that is Alan Rea helped me believe in myself again. From day one, your constant encouragement, talent, advice, guidance and mentoring have made this once imaginary scenario become a reality. When I've been sat in floods of tears trying to write on, when I felt like I was going out of my mind and around in circles, you've always known exactly what to say to get me back on track. I'm so very proud to have had you on this journey with me.

Thank you to my relatives on both sides who have supported and understood why I needed to write my story. Your positivity towards this project means the world. To Teresa, thank you for being so very brave, for trusting me and for showing such kindness and love as always.

And lastly, to the people in my life who are there for me without fail, the closest to me through it all, who make my life better each day and who I would be lost without. We laugh, we cry and we'll always have each other. You lot rock my world, you're my family and my best friends and it's because of you that I'm still here to share my story with the world. There's no need for a list of names, you know who you are and I couldn't be more proud of you all. Until the end besties, until the end.

Thank you, from my now mending heart.

This book is also dedicated to the family and friends whose lives ended before their time, and to the ones for whom this world became too much.

Soar high and free in eternal peace.

23309299R00217

Printed in Poland
by Amazon Fulfillment
Poland Sp. z o.o., Wrocław